Visual perception

Vision is our dominant sense. We derive most of our information about the world – about where things are, how they move, and what they are – from the light that enters the eye and the processing in the brain that follows. These functions are achieved by all sighted animals, including ourselves, yet despite the fact that we know more about vision than any other sense we still do not understand how these functions are performed.

Nicholas Wade and Michael Swanston take a refreshingly different approach to perception that gets away from the traditional textbook treatment of presenting vision as a catalogue of phenomena. Rather their starting point is the function that vision serves for an active observer in the three-dimensional environment. Thus the perception of location, motion and object recognition form the core of the book. The machinery of vision is also described. The book places the study of vision in its historical context since our ideas have been shaped by art, optics, biology and philosophy as well as psychology. The result is a readable, accessible and truly relevant introduction to perception that will be welcomed by anyone with an interest in the mysteries of vision.

Nicholas Wade is Reader in Psychology at the University of Dundee. His research is concerned with experimental work in visual perception, with the history of research in binocular vision, and with the relationship between visual science and visual art.

Michael Swanston is Senior Lecturer in Psychology at the Dundee Institute of Technology. His research has been primarily concerned with spatial perception, and with the design of the visual interface for human–computer interaction.

Introductions to modern psychology

Visual perception

An introduction

Nicholas J. Wade
University of Dundee

and

Michael Swanston
Dundee Institute of Technology

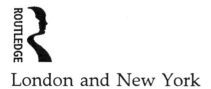

London and New York

First published in 1991
by Routledge
11 New Fetter Lane, London EC4P 4EE

Simultaneously published in the USA and Canada
by Routledge
a division of Routledge, Chapman and Hall, Inc.
29 West 35th Street, New York, NY 10001

Typeset from the authors' word-processor disks by
NWL Editorial Services, Langport, Somerset

Printed and bound in Great Britain by
Biddles Ltd, Guildford and King's Lynn

British Library Cataloguing in Publication Data
Wade, Nicholas
    Visual perception: an introduction
    1. Visual perception
    I. Title   II. Swanston, Michael, *1947–*
    152.14

Library of Congress Cataloging in Publication Data
Wade, Nicholas.
    Visual perception: an introduction/Nicholas J. Wade & Michael
    Swanston.
        p.   cm.
    Includes bibliographical references and index.
    1. Visual perception.   2. Visual discrimination.   3. Motion
    perception (Vision).   4. Vision – History.   I. Swanston, Michael,
    1947– . II. Title.
    BF241.W32 1991   90–47530
    152.14 – dc20   CIP

ISBN 0–415–01042–X
       0–415–01043–8 (pbk)

To
our families

Contents

Preface

Vision is our dominant sense. We derive most of our information about the world – about where things are, how they move, and what they are – from the light that enters the eyes and the processing in the brain that follows. These functions are performed by all sighted animals, including ourselves, and yet we still do not understand how. Vision is also the sense about which we know the most, because of the vast amount of empirical research that has been undertaken over the years. This large body of knowledge is celebrated in most of the textbooks that have been written on visual perception; indeed, it can act as a shroud that obscures the purpose of vision from many of those who study it. We feel that textbooks tend to focus too closely on the plethora of phenomena of vision rather than on its function: they frequently reduce vision to a series of headings such as brightness, colour, shape, movement, depth, illusions and so forth, while remaining blind to the uses to which it is put. We have tried to redress the balance a little in this book. The principal focus is the function that vision serves for an active observer in a three-dimensional environment – we must be able to see where objects are if we are going to behave with respect to them. Thus the perception of location, motion and object recognition provide the core to the book, and our intention is to make the ideas involved in their study accessible to the reader with no background in psychology. With this in mind we decided deliberately to avoid citing references in the text. This strategy might prove trying for the instructor, but it is hoped that it has the effect of making the book more readable. If it is necessary to qualify every minor point regarding the experimental base of a scientific discipline then it can not be very securely founded. We have provided reference notes at the end of each chapter, and these can be used to pursue the topics raised in greater detail. Another feature we have tried to stress is the historical context in which our present studies are conducted. The history of the study of vision is as long as that of science itself, and many forces have fashioned the conceptual framework in which it operates today – our ideas have been shaped by art, optics, biology and philosophy as well as by psychology. We need to appreciate these influences if we are to learn from, and avoid repeating, errors from the past.

The other framework that has structured this book is that of three-dimensional space: all our behaviour takes place with respect to it, and since behaviour is guided by perception it is logical that they share the same coordinate systems. In the course of our joint research on space and motion perception we have developed a scheme for examining the logical stages through which we believe perception passes. This scheme, which involves specifying the frames of reference for extracting visual inform-ation, has guided the description of vision presented here. It has involved the introduction of some novel terms in the text, but we believe that this is a small price to pay for maintaining a degree of coherence when dealing with widely disparate topics in vision. It has also resulted in some selectivity of subject matter, but this can be remedied by referring to the general references cited at the end of each chapter.

Science is a social endeavour, and we have benefited from collaboration with many colleagues, most particularly with Ross Day, Walter Gogel, Ian Howard, Hiroshi Ono and Charles de Weert. We also wish to express our thanks to Mark Georgeson who read the manuscript with great care; we have profited from the many insightful comments he made on it. The errors that remain are, of course, our own.

Vision is a subject of enquiry that has fascinated students for centuries and continues to hold our attention. We hope that some of those who read this book will be encouraged to join in the endeavour of broadening our understanding of it.

Nicholas J. Wade and Michael Swanston
Dundee

Chapter 1

Understanding visual perception

The world around us seems concrete and immediate, and our ability to perceive it is easily taken for granted. Objects have positions, shapes and colours that seem to be perceived instantly, and we can reach for them or move to where they are, without any apparent effort. Clearly, there must be some process that gives rise to visual experience, and it is not surprising that throughout history people have found it fascinating. If what we perceive is what we take to be true or factual about the world, are everyone's experiences the same? What is the perceptual world of animals, or infants, like? What sorts of errors do we make in perceiving? Can perceptual experience be communicated to others? Philosophers, artists and, more recently, psychologists have tried to find ways to answer such questions, which are among the most fundamental that can be posed about the human mind.

While we perceive the world around us, we have no direct knowledge of how this experience comes about. In fact, it can often be hard to believe that there is any mechanism involved in perception at all; for most people, most of the time, perceptions are simply 'given' as facts about the world that are obviously correct. Perception is indeed a fundamental psychological process, and a very remarkable one. Its success in providing us with accurate information about the characteristics of the world around us is an index of its power, because there are relatively few situations in which it is seriously in error. A perceptual process that gave rise to subjective experiences grossly different from physical reality would make survival virtually impossible.

This chapter provides an overview of central issues in the study of visual perception, many of which will be discussed in more detail in later chapters. It is important to understand both the functions that any visual system must perform if there is to be coordinated, effective action, and the problems of devising explanations for how this comes about. If perception is to be explained, appropriate measurements of its characteristics must be obtained, and related to the information potentially available from the physical environment. Each of these issues contributes to the general framework of ideas that guides the investigation of vision.

FUNCTIONS OF VISUAL PERCEPTION

Imagine an everyday task like crossing the road. We walk up to the kerbside, look in both directions and cross the road if it looks safe to do so. But what does this seemingly simple sequence entail, and how can it be explained? Crossing the road itself requires coordinated activities in many muscle groups that control balance and locomotion. However, before the walking is initiated a whole series of decisions have to be made on the basis of perceptual information. How far away is the kerb and in what direction is it? How wide is the road and how much time will be required to cross it? Is there a vehicle approaching? What size is it? How far away is it? How fast is it travelling? How long will it take to reach here? What type of vehicle is it? Each of these questions is directed to some aspect of the three-dimensional environment and our relation to it.

How far away is the kerb and in what direction is it? To answer these questions it is necessary to determine where the pavement stops and where the road starts. It could be on the basis of some markings (e. g., white lines) which we have learned to associate with roads, or on a difference in the perceived level of the two surfaces. Some theorists consider that we can derive information regarding the orientations of surfaces in the environment without recourse to knowledge about the nature and purpose of objects. That is, the information available in the pattern of stimulation is sufficient to specify the layout of space with respect to the viewpoint of the observer, and assumptions about the nature of the world are not necessary. On the other hand, perception can be likened to thinking and other high level cognitive processes like reasoning and problem solving. Such cognitive theorists argue that we use our knowledge of roads and their features to recognise the kerbside, and that we make use of a 'knowledge-base' to find and identify objects in the visual scene. Thus what we see is a logical, rational interpretation of sensory information on the basis of stored knowledge, in terms of possible real events. It is certainly not necessary to have verbal labels like 'pavement' and 'road' to perceive the positions and sizes of the actual objects, as guide dogs for blind people carry out such discriminations with remarkable skill. In the discussion that follows, we will contrast the capabilities of a human and a guide dog in crossing a road, as this helps to indicate how far the perceptual processes involved depend on verbal knowledge.

How wide is the road and how much time will be required to cross it? When the edges of the road have been isolated, by whatever means, some estimate of the distances of both from the observer is required. Distance information can be with respect to the observer or between objects in the visual scene. For example, the near kerb could be perceived as two metres away and the far kerb twenty metres distant, then the width of the road could be determined from the difference between the two estimates.

Alternatively, the distance between the two kerbs could be perceived in some relative way, such as 'three cars wide'. The time required to cross the road could then be computed as long as there is some value of walking speed available.

Is there a vehicle approaching? Before this question can be addressed it is necessary to define what a vehicle is. An abstract definition in terms of, say, a metal body with windows supported by four wheels, would not suffice visually, as we rarely see all the wheels on a vehicle at the same time; often we do not see any wheels at all. Moreover, some vehicles have two wheels, others ten, and so on, making any definition either very abstract or very long-winded. It is more fruitful to pursue the aspect of motion, as the vehicles of importance will be moving rather than stationary. Is some moving object on the road? The perceptual problems involved here are those associated with the principles of grouping, for example the perceptual separation of an object from its background. Such perceptual segregation can be difficult for line drawings, and so it may be all the more difficult for a real scene in which the light intensity differences between an object and its background (which may be other objects) can be minimal or non-existent. Assuming an object is segregated from its background how is its movement perceived? This might be particularly difficult if the background (other objects) also moves.

How fast is the vehicle travelling? A decision as to whether to cross the road is critically dependent on accurate judgement of the velocity of an approaching vehicle. There are differences of interpretation by theorists depending on the extent to which perception is thought of as 'data driven' or 'hypothesis driven'. In the former case other perceptual information about the distance of landmarks and size of the vehicle might be used to obtain an estimate of velocity. In the latter, knowledge about the likely velocity and acceleration of familiar vehicles could be accessed. The American psychologist James J. Gibson (1904–1979) rejected the equation of the eye with a camera, and the consequent analysis of vision in terms of processing static images. He replaced the concept of a static projection to the eye in favour of the notion of transformations of the pattern of stimulation over time. He referred to the total pattern of light entering the eye as the optic array, and the transformations of it, often as a consequence of the observer's own movements, as the optic flow. That is, he incorporated the time dimension in perception, so that all perception becomes motion perception. Optic flows can be produced by motions of objects with respect to the background or by motions of the perceiver, the projective consequences of which will be different. If a vehicle is moving then there will be specific transformations in the optic array: it will occlude parts of the road in the direction it is pointing and disclose other parts behind it. This situation only occurs with object motion. Observer motion would result in simultaneous displacements of all parts of the optic array. An alternative approach would determine that the vehicle was moving by comparing the information available in successive time frames. Speed would then be estimated by computing distance divided by time, in the manner of a physicist. The problem with this is that the moving object needs to be identified in successive instants, before its movement can be obtained. This requirement for matching different sources of information about the same object is known as a correspondence problem, and it is a feature of many theoretical accounts that rely on analysis of a series of static images. The guide dog can respond appropriately to vehicles travelling at different speeds, so its perceptual system, like ours, can either solve the correspondence problem for movement, or, if Gibson is right, never has to face it.

How long will the vehicle take to reach here? This question is based on the assumption that we have determined how long we require to cross the road. The answer is dependent upon the information gathered from the earlier questions: if we have determined the location of the vehicle, as well as its direction and velocity, we can estimate the time available for crossing the road. Here the guide dog is far superior to humans, for it could cross the road far more quickly than the person it is guiding. However, it has been trained to estimate the parameters that apply to humans rather than to dogs. Moreover, guide dogs are more likely to use pedestrian crossings than are normally sighted humans! If the approaching vehicle is very close to the observer then the time before contact can be determined from the optic flow pattern. This changes in a characteristic way that provides information about the time before a collision takes place.

What type of vehicle is it? This is a question of object recognition. A vehicle can be specified as having a certain size, shape and motion at a given distance, but it might not be identified as belonging to a particular category. The categories can be general like 'motor car' or specific like 'red 1982 Ford Escort saloon'. Object recognition involves two aspects, discrimination and naming. The first is essential whereas the second is not: the guide dog will perform the first but not the second. We perform many discriminations for which we have no verbal categories. For example, many people can differentiate between species of fish without being able to name them, although some are able to do both. It is the naming aspect that is uniquely human, and so tends to be investigated at the expense of discrimination. It also creates the impression of some implicit discrimination – some comparison of the presently available instance with a mental model of other instances. Here we have entered the cognitive domain, and we are dealing with processes that need not directly influence behaviour. The guide dog can discriminate between a Ford Cortina and a Ford Escort, and its behaviour can be suitably influenced, for instance if the Cortina belonged to its former trainer. Discriminations can be made on the basis of the perceived surface characteristics (size, orientation and texture) of objects, and that can be sufficient to guide our actions.

The approaching vehicle could be a toy bus nearby or a normal bus at a distance. According to their sizes and distances from the observer it would be possible for them both to fill equivalent areas of the visual field, that is, to subtend the same angle at the eye. This comparison seems ludicrous in the context of buses on roads, and so it is, because of the vast amount of other information that would distinguish between the two in the real world. Normally we can see other objects too, and most particularly we can usually see the surfaces supporting the objects. Along with other sources of information, called cues to distance, this would allow the ambiguity to be resolved. Alternatively, knowledge about roads, and the likely objects to be seen on them, could bias the observer towards seeing full-sized vehicles; this would constitute a high-level cognitive explanation. Gibson argued that there is no problem of ambiguity in the real world; rather the pattern of stimulation specifies the sizes and distances of objects. For example the amount of surface texture obscured by an object in contact with it remains constant at differing distances, and this invariant feature could determine the perception of constant size despite variations in optical projection. The guide dog can respond appropriately to vehicles of different sizes and at different distances, but this does not rule out any particular explanation. The dog would be capable of using either size and distance information, or optical expansion, and would have extensive experience of vehicles on roads.

MODELS OF VISUAL PERCEPTION

Our understanding of perceptual processes like those outlined in the previous section has very often been shaped by concepts and models drawn from other fields of scientific enquiry. These have provided ways of describing and explaining the processes that give rise to perceptual experience. At the present time, many of the terms that are used to describe perception, as well as other psychological processes, are drawn from the vocabulary of computer science. This has been a feature of psychology since the 1940s, and it has resulted in new approaches to long-standing problems. Perhaps the most significant concept is that of information processing, which refers to the logical operations performed by a machine like a computer. Such operations can be described and analysed independently of the particular physical device that carries them out. This was made clear by David Marr (1945–1980) whose contributions to visual science have been amongst the most important of recent years. His work brought together knowledge in computer science, psychology and physiology, and his ideas have had a great influence on the development of the new field of machine vision. Marr defined three levels at which any information processing system, including the visual system, can be understood. At the top, broadest level, is the description of computational theory. This involves stating the purpose and goal of the process, why it is appropriate in the context of other functions, and the general logic of the strategy needed to carry it out. Below this is the algorithmic level of representation. This level requires statements about the actual sequence of processes that take place, so that the computation is achieved. As an example, consider the process of multiplication. If you wish to multiply two numbers, then the goal of your computation is to generate a third number which is the product of the two. To achieve this, various logical procedures, called algorithms, could be employed. You could repetitively add one number to itself, as often as specified by the second number. Alternatively, you could make use of remembered information about the results of such additions, in the form of multiplication tables. Either procedure would in principle produce the correct answer. There will generally be a number of algorithms for any given computation. That is, the computational theory doesn't specify a particular means of achieving a goal, which must be determined independently. Marr referred to the first level as the 'what' and 'why' of the computation, and to the second as the 'how' of it. Independent of both computational theory and representation is the level of hardware implementation. Just as a given computational function can be carried out by a number of algorithms, so a given algorithm can be instantiated by various alternative physical devices. An algorithm for multiplication can be implemented in an electronic computer, a mechanical calculator, a brain or even an abacus. In terms of visual perception, Marr's analysis suggests that we should be careful not to confuse the different levels of explanation. In addition, the starting point must be a proper description at the level of computational theory, because only this can provide a framework for understanding the operations at lower levels. If we lack a good general description of the purpose of a perceptual process, we are unlikely to understand its underlying logic, or the physiological hardware in which it takes place.

The computer provides a useful metaphor for the brain, but we have to be careful not to take it too far. It has in fact proved very difficult to create anything resembling perception in a machine, despite the advances of recent years. Computer-based machine vision is a goal of many research groups, not least because of the considerable practical and economic advantages that it would give in industry, commerce and administration. However, it has proved exceptionally difficult to achieve, despite a world-wide effort. There are probably several reasons for this, one of which may be the unsuitability of current computer architectures for the simulation of biological information processing. Human vision relies on an extremely large number of relatively simple computations occurring in parallel. Many of the computing elements are interconnected in a complex manner, which can alter as the result of experience. Since nerve impulses travel slowly compared to electronic signals, and nerve cells take time to recover from activity, biological computation is also slow. A typical electronic computer uses serial processing, in which only one computation at a time can be performed, but at very high speed. There are beginning to be developments both in parallel computing and in the organisation of processes in the form of connected networks, but the scale of these is at present very far from that of even quite simple organisms. In addition, it is possible that we simply do not have a clear enough idea about the way in which perceptual processes operate to be able to recreate them in a computer. In terms of crossing a road, the output of a video camera would have to be used to find out, amongst other things, how wide the road is, if there are vehicles and how long they will take to arrive. While solutions to some aspects of these problems can be achieved, an effective machine vision system would have to solve them all, with a very high probability of success. It is certainly true that neither we, nor many animals, are wholly expert at road-crossing, as accident statistics sadly demonstrate. However, we do not know to what extent this reflects a failure of perception, rather than cognition; that is, the individual may see the environment correctly, but may make an inappropriate decision about the riskiness of an action due to memory failure or errors of judgement. Nevertheless most people would be happier to trust their safety to a trained guide dog rather than to the most advanced of machine vision systems.

The lesson from history is that our understanding of the brain has been very dependent on the use of analogies drawn from the current state of physical science. At the time these analogies may have been widely believed, but their inadequacy has become apparent before long. Clockwork automata of great ingenuity were built in the seventeenth and eighteenth centuries, and these seemed to indicate that living organisms might be thought of in terms of similar types of device, although of much greater complexity. Before the electro-chemical nature of the nerve impulse was understood, communication in the nervous system was explained by analogy with pneumatic or hydraulic devices, which were in common use. Later, in the nineteenth century, analogies with power and force were widely employed. More recently, the brain has been described in terms of the functions of a telephone exchange, switching messages from one point to another. No doubt all such metaphors are useful at the time they are proposed, but it is important to be aware that they are just metaphors, and that this applies as much to the computer as it does to clockwork. It is simply a measure of our ignorance that we do not know how to characterise the operation of the brain in terms that are independent of analogy with other sorts of mechanism. This situation is not uncommon in science, where an unknown process is described in terms of others that are understood. A good example is the controversy over whether light consists of waves or of discrete particles. Evidence can be produced to support either point of view, depending on the type of experiment carried out. In fact light consists neither of waves nor of particles, since these are metaphors drawn from everyday experience, and both are inadequate characterisations.

MEASURING VISUAL PERCEPTION

While each of us experiences perception of the world, obtaining useful measurements of this experience can be very difficult. The attempt to communicate subjective experience to other people has fascinated and frustrated writers, painters and other artists for centuries. The simplest approach is to ask someone to describe their experience, and to draw conclusions from their reports. Descriptions of the same scene or event can be compared across observers, and it may be possible to classify the verbal reports to give some degree of quantification. In principle, free description of experience offers potentially the richest source of information, since language is the most flexible means of communication we have. For many centuries, philosophers and others interested in perception, relied upon verbal description as the only means of obtaining data for analysis. Although perceptual experience is subjective, we are able to communicate quite effectively with other people regarding the nature of the world around us; disagreements about experience are much less likely than agreement. While language is a powerful means of communication, it is nevertheless restrictive; ultimately, only those experiences for which we have words can be described. Reliance on verbal descriptions has not always clarified our understanding of perception, and this can be illustrated in the context of colour vision. Suppose two people look at a piece of coloured paper: one says that it is red and the other that it is black. Can the same object have two different colours simultaneously? It does not seem likely for a piece of paper, so why are different colours reported? One possibility is that the two people are having the same visual experience, but they are describing it differently – the verbal labels attached to the same experience differ. This could be tested by asking them to describe two other coloured papers; suppose they agree in calling them green and blue. The problem becomes complicated by this because some colour names correspond and others do not. It would be odd to say that they were each having the same experience for all three colours while only one was described differently. Another possibility is that one of the two individuals is colour defective, that is, one does not have colour experiences like the majority of the population. If so, which one is colour defective? A straightforward way of determining this would be to ask a number of other people – a sample of the population – to describe the same coloured papers, and to note their descriptions. If most of the sample say that the initial paper is red, then it would indicate which of the two people is colour defective. It seems more reasonable to account for individual differences in perception in terms of variations in the mechanisms of perception rather than changes in the world.

One of the standard procedures developed for scientific enquiry into complex natural phenomena is to reduce them to simplified situations in which relevant features can be isolated and controlled. In the case of colour vision, we would want to ensure that a stimulus produced light of a known wavelength and intensity. We might wish to control the size of the stimulus, and perhaps its shape. Other sources of light would need to be eliminated, unless the effect of these was to be specifically studied. Such control over stimulation would generally require laboratory conditions, and usually special apparatus as well. Experiments carried out in this way can provide unambiguous and detailed measurements of visual performance. This approach has been very influential in studies of perception, which often involve visual environments so restricted as to be far removed from natural visual experience. Measurements of perception are obviously easier to obtain when the perceptual experience is itself very simple; for example, sitting in a dark room and pressing a button if and when a single faint light source is seen. The measurements obtained in an experiment are used to infer the nature of perceptual processes, since we can never measure perception directly. It might be thought that this makes the study of perception subjective and indirect, but the situation is not fundamentally different from, for example, an investigation of biochemical processes. Here too, measurements are used to infer the underlying chemical reactions, which cannot be directly observed. Probably the opportunity for error due to uncontrolled factors is greater with perception, since the system being studied is a good deal more complex and responsive to a wider range of influences.

Not surprisingly, it has been argued that we should be cautious about supposing that perception in the real world can be explained by the processes revealed in laboratory conditions. Gibson in particular argued that natural perception depends on complex patterns of stimulation, involving active exploration of the environment by the perceiver. He reacted strongly against the idea, drawn from the physical sciences, that any complex process can be understood by combining a number of simpler component processes. Under restricted laboratory conditions, perceptual processes are not reduced to their elementary components, but rather to an unrepresentative and impoverished form. Thus, Gibson claimed that visual illusions were simply the consequence of looking at scenes with very little information; under natural conditions in the environment we generally do not see illusions because there is plenty of information to tell us about the true sizes, shapes and colours of objects. In particular, if the observer is prevented from moving then his perceptions will be both unnatural and uninformative. In our view, an adequate account of perception should be able to explain what is seen under any circumstances, whether in a natural environment or in the laboratory.

Experiments on perception involve communicating the experimenter's requirements to an observer, and the discussion so far has been in terms of studying perception in someone who can communicate with language; but what about cases where this cannot be done? We may wish to investigate perception in infants, in animals, or perhaps in people whose linguistic abilities are impaired. For these, the requirements of the experimenter must be communicated by some other means, and the response cannot be verbal. Clearly, it must be some action which is within the behavioural repertoire of the observer. Thus, for example, it may be possible to use the methods of conditioned learning to study discrimination between stimuli. If one response, like turning the head or raising a paw, can be conditioned to a red stimulus, and another to a green one, then we may be justified in concluding something about the ability to perceive colour; provided of course that the discrimination is not based on some other characteristic like the shade of grey of the stimulus. If an infant spends more time looking at a picture of a face than at a random collection of lines, then this preference may demonstrate an ability to recognise faces as a special class of object. Clearly it would also be necessary to establish that these measurements did not simply reflect a preference for symmetrical patterns, or even for looking left rather than right. Such behavioural measures are not intrinsically different from verbal ones, and similar sorts of inference may be made from them. However they are less subject to biases, and the inferences are therefore likely to be more secure.

It is possible to be seriously misled by measurements of perception, due to their simplified and inferential character. We may suppose from observable behaviour that perception is limited or even non-existent, when in fact this is not the case. The traditional view of perception in early infancy was that human babies could see very little, and recognise essentially nothing. Only with the development of better methods of measurement, more closely related to the behavioural repertoire of infants, has it been shown that their perceptual abilities are in fact quite considerable. This finding has been important for the early diagnosis of sensory defects, and has given new significance to the potential effects of neonatal perceptual experience. Sometimes there may be no overt behavioural indication of perception, and more indirect physiological measures may need to be used. For example, a person may be present at a concert, but give no indication from their behaviour as to whether they are engrossed with the music, or bored to the point of sleep. For vision, we generally at least show by our eye movements that we are observing an event, but this is not invariably the case. However, it may be possible to measure a physiological response, such as a change in brain activity or in the electro-chemical state of the retina. These large scale changes, reflecting the activity of many cells, are known as evoked potentials. Studies of evoked potentials are of most interest when they can be correlated with verbal or behavioural indices of perception, but they may be of value even when the latter are not available.

Similarly, measures of the activity of single cells may be obtained, at various points in the visual system. More indirectly, physiological measures may be taken of functions which are partly determined by perception, such as heart rate or blood pressure. While the occurrence of a physiological response to a stimulus indicates that a corresponding perception may also take place, it is not a guarantee of this. On the other hand, we may have to be careful not to infer the existence of a perception without careful examination of the evidence. A well known example is that of the 'red rag to a bull'; bulls in fact cannot discriminate red rags from green or blue rags of the same brightness, and the effect, if any, is probably due to movement.

VISUAL PERCEPTION AND THE PHYSICAL ENVIRONMENT

The investigation of perception must include the definition of those characteristics of the physical environment that can be detected by a perceiver. We need to know at the least what sorts of physical event can act as an effective stimulus for perception. As the example of the bull demonstrates, we must know that a given event is capable of being perceived before engaging in discussion of its behavioural significance. The traditional approach in perception has been to define the qualities and quantities of physical energy that can be perceived, as for example in the measurement of the least intensity of light that can be reliably detected, or the difference in wavelength between patches of light needed to make them appear discriminably different in colour. These types of measurement define the limits of perception, so they can be used to find out if any perception is possible. They are therefore useful for identifying perceptual defects, as for instance when an individual's discrimination of certain wavelengths is systematically worse than other people's. Ultimately, the purpose of perception is to enable humans and other animals to guide their behaviour in a way that is appropriate to the real environment, whose most pertinent features are the location and nature of objects in three-dimensional space. Evolution has ensured that perceptual systems are adapted to the needs of organisms, whether for locomotion, foraging for food or finding a mate. In the most general terms, the environment can be thought of as a source of many varieties of potential stimulation; ranging from vibrations in the atmosphere to electromagnetic radiation of various wavelengths and molecules diffused from an evaporating source. Those aspects of the world that we can perceive depend in the first instance on the senses we possess. The senses which respond to external events play the major role in perception, and species of animals differ greatly in the types of physical energy that they can detect. For example, high-frequency sound waves are employed by bats and dolphins for recognising objects and for navigation. Certain species of snakes are responsive to the infra-red emissions of warm-blooded prey, and bees to ultra-violet, so that the appearance of flowers to them is very different from that which we experience. The world as it appears to us is therefore based on a selective sample of the many forms of energy which are available. One of the developments of modern technology has been the extension of our natural senses to a wider range of environmental events; we can convert x-rays, ultrasound and infra-red to forms that can be directly perceived. Whatever the sources of information, however, the outcome is perception of a physical environment which has spatial extent and in which objects can be located in space and time, with a particular size and shape. All perceptual systems must provide some such representation, even if it is based on a limited selection of available information, because they would otherwise be of little value for guiding behaviour.

It is not surprising that people have most difficulty in perceiving, and therefore in acting efficiently, when the information available to the senses is either greatly restricted, or provided by an environment with which we have no natural experience. Examples of the former are given by the gross errors of judgement that occur when attempting to drive a car at speed in fog or at night, and of the latter when people try to perceive correctly in outer space or underwater. In these cases we require special training and experience in order to perceive the 'where', 'when' and 'what' of objects, and without it we are liable to experience distortions of reality. In some situations what we perceive consistently differs from what we suppose to be correct, and this may be referred to as a visual illusion. There are many examples of these, and a long history of experimentation and theory designed to account for them. It is important to note that the idea of a visual illusion presupposes that the object or pattern concerned would be perceived differently under other conditions. For example, the apparent length of a line is altered by adding oblique lines, known as fins, to either end (Figure 1.1).

This is called the Müller-Lyer illusion, and it is an instance of the distortion of the perceived geometry of simple plane figures. That it is an illusion can only be shown by measuring the lines with a ruler (which assumes correct perception of the ruler itself), or by comparing the perceived lengths of the lines with and without fins. Essentially, illusions are defined by comparisons between perceptions, although we naturally assume that at least one of these is physically correct. One view of illusions is that they can be used as tools to probe the mechanisms of visual perception, because perceptual errors can give us clues about the way in which normal perception takes place. For example, the Müller-Lyer illusion has been explained in terms of depth due to perspective. If we interpret two-dimensional drawings as representing an object in depth, then there may be systematic distortions of apparent size. This would be due to the process which ensures that real objects appear to remain their actually constant size despite being at different distances, and projecting different

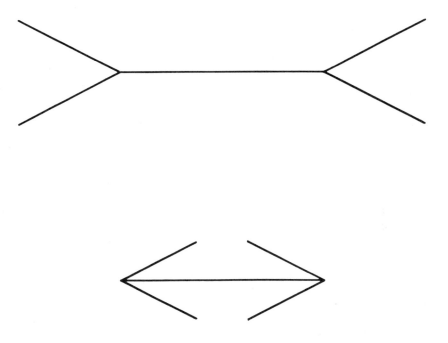

Figure 1.1 The Müller-Lyer illusion. The two parallel lines are equal in length, but may not look so.

sized images on the retina. A normal perceptual process would thus have been revealed by its inappropriate influence on a line drawing, and it could be studied by this means. One problem is that many visual illusions appear to be the result of several different perceptual processes, and it is hard to separate their respective effects. In any case, it is necessary to be cautious about assuming that an illusion figure really is illusory; a survey of illustrations of the Müller-Lyer figure in textbooks showed that in many cases the lines had actually been drawn with different lengths, presumably to ensure that the illusion was convincing!

Debate has continued for many centuries as to whether, and to what extent, we should trust the evidence of our senses; or more precisely, whether we can believe what we perceive. Attitudes towards this issue have ranged from a denial that there is any physical reality at all, to a straightforward acceptance that all perceptions constitute objective truth about the world. Such arguments about truth, knowledge and reality belong to the branch of philosophy called epistemology, and they remain as intractable as when they were first posed in Classical Greece. For humans and other animals, perception exists as one means of ensuring survival. If our actions are not guided by accurate information about the world, then we make errors and put ourselves and others at risk. The important questions for a psychologist concern how we come to gain information about the environment, the way in which such information is represented in perception, and the limits to our ability to perceive correctly.

REFERENCE NOTES

Textbooks on perception tend to concentrate on two-dimensional stimuli and the effects that they generate. Accordingly, they have chapters concerned with phenomena like contrast and colour, size and shape, constancies and illusions. The function that perception serves is often hidden amidst the plethora of experimental detail that has accumulated in these areas. This trend has been opposed by the two principals discussed in this chapter. James J. Gibson has written three monographs on perception, starting with *Perception of the Visual World* (1950), followed by *The Senses Considered as Perceptual Systems* (1966), and finally *The Ecological Approach to Visual Perception* (1979). In these books Gibson has stressed the importance of vision in guiding action, and also that vision cannot be divorced from the dimension of time. David Marr's book *Vision* was published post-humously in 1982. Marr emphasised that understanding vision can only be achieved by first appreciating the purpose that perception serves. He contended that this purpose will not be discovered by confining our enquiries to particular levels of functioning, like those of physiology or psychophysics or artificial intelligence, rather it should involve all three.

Despite this appreciation of a common goal, the paths proposed to reach it are radically different. Gibson analysed vision in terms of an information-ally rich stimulus – the optic flow – that rendered redundant any requirement for internal representations of the world. Marr's whole approach is based upon levels of internal representation, starting from distributions of light and ending in some description of the objects that would have generated the distributions. These contrasts can perhaps best be followed not in the writings of Gibson and Marr, but those of their students and supporters. Gibson's approach has been called *Direct Perception*, and a book with that title summarising his work has been written by Michaels and Carello (1981). The term direct perception refers to the perception of objects in three-dimensional space; indirect perception is concerned with pictures of objects rather than the objects themselves. Marr's computational theory and the stages of image representation are described very clearly in Roth and Frisby (1986). More detached and critical assessments of both Gibson's and Marr's theories can be found in Bruce and Green's (1990) *Visual Perception. Physiology, Psychology and Ecology* and in Gordon's (1989) *Theories of Visual Perception*. The latter is one of the few books concerned primarily with theory rather than data, and it provides an excellent introduction to the problems any theory must address. In addition, it includes a chapter on cognitive theories.

The cognitive approach to vision has been advocated in several very readable books. Rock's (1984) *Perception* is well-illustrated and also includes a book stereoscope for observing the stereograms presented. He commences by stating that 'Natural science begins with and depends upon perception', and vision is described as a process like intelligence. Gregory's (1977) *Eye and Brain* develops a theory of vision as an hypothesis testing process. He adopts an historical perspective, and addresses a range of topics like brightness, colour, motion and illusions. Favreau (1977) surveyed illustrations of the Müller-Lyer illusion presented in textbooks, and found that many of them assisted the perceptual inequality; she suggested renaming it the Müller-Liar! Examples of a wide variety of spatial illusions and other visual distortions can be found in Wade's (1982) *The Art and Science of Visual Illusions*.

Chapter 2

The heritage

The study of perception is essential in trying to understand how we derive knowledge about the world – an endeavour referred to as epistemology. All cultures have struggled to address this question, and their answers have often been radically different. In the following sections we will introduce some of the dominant influences that have shaped the ways in which we think about vision. The historical perspective is often overlooked or neglected in books on perception, which is a pity because it implies that we now have a priviledged viewpoint, superior to those of the past. In fact, the same theoretical issues often recur, disguised by the new jargon to appear different. Seeing through the shroud of the present can facilitate our understanding of such issues, and remaining ignorant of past attempts to grapple with them can inhibit progress. Vision is at the interface of many disciplines, such as art, medicine, physics and philosophy. Each has influenced the present state of our understanding. Hence it is instructive to look back at these diverse historical strands so that we are in a better position to appreciate the contemporary approaches to visual perception.

OPTICS

We now accept that light is emitted by incandescent sources, and reflected from objects to enter the eye, so initiating the process of seeing. However, for millennia it was thought that light was emitted from the eye to make contact with objects and returned to the eye with images of them; vision was then thought to occur in the lens. After all, is it not the case that we cease to see when we close our eyes, thus preventing the emission of light from the eye? Moreover, what we are aware of depends upon where we direct our eyes. The great Greek mathematician Euclid (around 300 BC) was of this opinion, although his contemporary Aristotle opposed it, preferring a reception theory (one involving light only entering the eyes rather than being emitted from them). Despite this misconception, Euclid appreciated that light travels in straight lines, and he was able to enunciate a range of laws that derive from this.

A later misunderstanding concerned the colours seen when light passes through a prism. These colours make up the visible spectrum, and a familiar example is a rainbow. Prior to Newton's discoveries at the end of the seventeenth century, the spectrum was considered to be a property of the glass prism rather than of light. Newton demonstrated experimentally that sunlight (white light) is made up of rays that can be bent or refracted by different amounts when passing through a prism, so forming the visible spectrum (see Figure 2.1). Newton was also able to demonstrate that the spectrum produced by passing light through a prism could be recombined into white light with the aid of a second prism in the opposite orientation. In the case of the rainbow, the sunlight is reflected inside each spherical raindrop, which acts like a prism, and the light is dispersed into its spectral components. Moreover, Newton realised that light itself is not coloured, because colour is a perceptual experience; we would now say that white light consists of electromagnetic radiation over a small range of wavelengths.

Thus, one traditional concern in the study of vision has focused on the definition of the stimulus. That is, what is the environmental energy that can excite the organ of vision, and how can it be measured physically? This

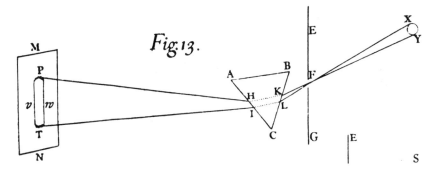

Figure 2.1 The spectrum produced by sunlight passing through a prism as illustrated in Newton's *Opticks*. 'For let EG represent the Windowshut, F the hole made therein through which a beam of the Sun's Light was transmitted into the darkned Chamber... let ABC represent the Prism.... And let XY be the Sun, MN the Paper upon which the Solar Image or Spectrum is cast, and PT the Image it self whose sides towards V and W are Rectilinear and Parallel and ends towards P and T semicircular. YKHP and XLJT are the two Rays, the first of which comes from the lower part of the Sun to the higher part of the Image, and is refracted in the Prism at K and H, and the latter comes from the higher part of the Sun to the lower part of the Image, and is refracted at L and J... This Image or Spectrum PT was coloured, being red at its least refracted end T, and violet at its most refracted end P, and yellow green and blew in the intermediate spaces. Which agrees with the first Proposition, that Lights which differ in Colour do also differ in Refrangibility.' (Newton, 1704)

reflects the influence of physics on the interpretation of vision: light is the stimulus for vision, and the laws of its transmission through different media – optics – will be important in determining the patterning of light at and in the eyes. The rules of propagation were known long before the nature of light itself was understood. Optics for Euclid was fundamentally concerned with vision, and he introduced many concepts that have shaped our understanding of vision. He proposed the idea of the visual cone – a broad cone, with its apex at the eye and enclosing all that could be seen at one moment. He also devised a way of representing the initial stages of the visual process that is still used in modern diagrams – the light rays are restricted to straight lines joining objects and the eyes (Figure 2.2). For Euclid these were visual lines, emitted from the eye. Now we know that light is reflected from objects to enter the eye, and yet the diagrams are still drawn as though the lines actually existed. We continue to do this despite

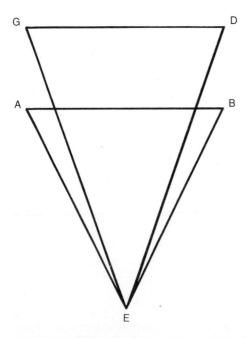

Figure 2.2 Euclidean diagram of lines of light from two objects to the eye. Euclid equated perceived dimensions to the angles subtended at the eye, as is evident from this description: 'Let there be two objects of equal size, *AB* and *GD* and let the eye be indicated by E, from which let the objects be unequally distant, and let *AB* be nearer. I say that *AB* will appear larger. Let the rays fall, *EA*, *EB*, *EG*, and *ED*. Now, since things seen within greater angles appear larger, and the angle *AEB* is greater than *GED*, *AB* will appear to be larger than *GD*.' (Burton, 1945)

the admonishments of Bishop Berkeley who said: 'those *Lines* and *Angles* have no real Existence in Nature, being only *Hypotheses* fram'd by *Mathematicians*, and by them introduced into *Optics*, that they might treat of that *Science* in a *Geometrical* way' (1709). Berkeley was drawing attention to the misconceptions that can arise from such diagrams, because they create the impression that the lines are seen, and that perception corresponds to the geometry of the retinal image.

The belief that light was emitted from the eye rather than transmitted to it was held for almost 2000 years until, in 1604, the astronomer Johannes Kepler described how light passed through the eye to form an image on the retina. The similarities between image formation in a simple camera obscura (literally a dark chamber, like a pinhole camera) and the eye were remarked upon in that period, and the emission theory of vision was replaced by a reception theory. Indeed, at that time it was considered that the problem of vision had been solved by the appreciation of the image-forming properties of the eye: the picture in the eye was like the scene imaged, and so it corresponded to perception. It was precisely this idea that was being attacked by Bishop Berkeley.

ART AND REPRESENTATION

Another historical strand facilitated this interpretation of vision, namely that of art or visual representation. In Kepler's time the art of linear perspective was commonplace, and many of the paintings and engravings he would have seen were constructed according to these principles. The rules of perspective were formalised in the intellectual cauldron of early fifteenth century Florence: linear perspective was demonstrated by architect and painter Brunelleschi and formalised by a contemporary mathematician called Alberti. Basically it was the application of Euclid's visual cone to a glass plane intersecting it (Figure 2.3). Thus the principles of reducing a three-dimensional scene to a two-dimensional picture were formulated before the image forming properties of the eye had been described. None the less, the differences between looking at a picture and looking at a scene were clearly appreciated by Leonardo da Vinci, at the end of the fifteenth century: he wrote 'a painting, though conducted with the greatest art and finished to the last perfection, both with regard to its contours, its lights, its shadows and its colours, can never show a relievo equal to that of the natural objects' (from a 1721 translation into English). That is, the allusion to relief or depth in a painting of a scene, no matter how well it is painted, will be different to the depth seen between the actual objects in the scene.

The influence of art was to prove significant because it framed a recurrent concern for theorists of vision: how can we perceive the world as three-dimensional when the image cast in the eye is two-dimensional? Isn't this precisely the problem that confronts the painter? Artists in the new perspective style seemed to answer this in practice if not in theory. An allusion to three-dimensionality could be induced if the rules of linear perspective were followed; this required a single, fixed viewing point and the depiction of objects in the scene in accordance with the angle they subtended at that viewing point. An object, say a person, will subtend decreasing angles at the eye as they walk away from us, even though they remain the same physical size (Figure 2.4). This change in projected size does not correspond to our perception; people appear to remain the same size as they walk away from us. Artists, in common with the rest of us, have a problem in depicting this state of affairs accurately because perception

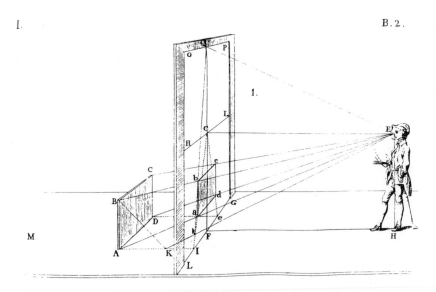

Figure 2.3 An illustration from Brook Taylor's classic treatise on perspective. '1. The *Point of Sight*, is that Point where the Spectator's Eye is placed to look at the Picture. Thus E is the Point of Sight. 2. If from the Point of Sight E, a Line EC is drawn from the Eye perpendicular to the Picture, the Point C, where the Line cuts the Picture, is called the *Center of the Picture*. 3. *The Distance of the Picture*, is the Length of the Line EC, which is drawn from the Eye perpendicular to the Picture. 4. If from the Point of Sight E, a Line EC be drawn perpendicular to any vanishing Line HL, or JF, then the Point C, where the Line cuts the vanishing Line, is called *the Center of that vanishing Line*. 5. *The Distance of a vanishing Line*, is the Length of the Line EC, which is drawn from the Eye perpendicular to the said Line: and if PO was a vanishing Line, then EJ will be the Distance of that Line. 6. *The Distance of the vanishing Point*, is the Length of a Line drawn from the Eye to that Point: Thus, EC is the Distance of the vanishing Point C, and EJ is the Distance of the vanishing Point J. 7. By *Original Object*, is meant the real Object whose representation is sought: and by *Original Plane*, is meant that Plane upon which the real Object is situated: Thus, the Ground HM is the Original Plane of ABCD.' (Kirby, 1755)

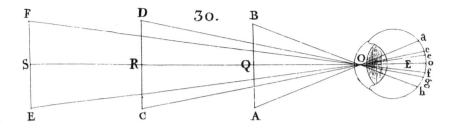

Figure 2.4 Objects of the same size, but at different distances from the eye, projecting differently sized images onto the retina, as was clearly described in Brook Taylor's treatise. 'The farther distant the Eye is from an Object, so much less will the Picture of the Object be upon the Retina: for let E be the Eye viewing the several Objects AB, CD, EF at the Distance OQ, OR, OS. Having drawn the several Rays Aa, Bb, Cc, Dd, Ee, Ff, through the Pupil O, it will be manifest, that the Picture of the nearest Object AB, will be painted at the Bottom of the Eye in the Space ab, the Object CD in the Space cd, and the farthest Object, EF, in the Space ef.' (Kirby, 1755)

does not correspond to the dimensions projected onto the retina; hence they must use all manner of artificial devices, like matching the angles with an outstretched thumb, in order to discount their perception and record visual angles.

LIFE SCIENCES

Following Kepler's description of the ways light is refracted or bent when passing through the eye, students of vision in the seventeenth century tended to reduce the analysis of vision to an analysis of the image formed in the eye. That is, vision became a problem for geometrical optics. They were also able to draw upon the then recent elucidation of the anatomy of the eye. Kepler's contemporaries had, for the first time, dissected human eyes with sufficient precision to make accurate diagrams of their structure. All the transparent surfaces were represented with their appropriate curvatures: for example, the differences in the curvature of the front and rear surfaces of the lens were correct. Experiments were carried out with an excised eye of a bull with the rear coats cut away leaving the dark retina intact; when it was placed in a small hole of a dark room an inverted image of the scene outside could be observed. A similar situation was depicted in Descartes's *Dioptrique* in 1637 (Figure 2.5).

What happened to the image in the eye itself was a matter of speculation, because little was known of the detailed anatomy of the retina or of the physiology of vision. Certain functional changes associated with vision were suggested. For example, Descartes proposed that we are able to see objects at different distances by changing the optical power of the eye, and he guessed (correctly) that this was achieved by variations in the curvature of the lens, a process we now call accommodation. Descartes realised that the processes of vision are not confined to the eyes because the messages from each eye need to be combined so that a single percept is achieved. He advanced a speculative physiology to account for this, by having the nerves from each eye meeting in a single location in the brain (Figure 2.6).

The significance of Descartes's theories does not lie so much in whether

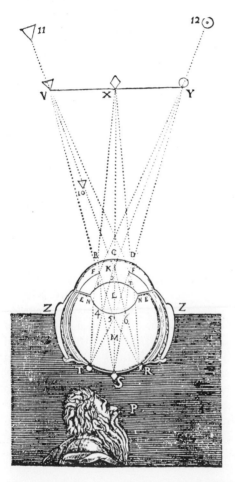

Figure 2.5 A figure from Descartes' *Dioptrique* (1637/1902) illustrating the optical image-forming properties of the eye. Rays of light from the object VXY are refracted at the cornea (BCD) and lens (L) to focus an image RST on the retina.

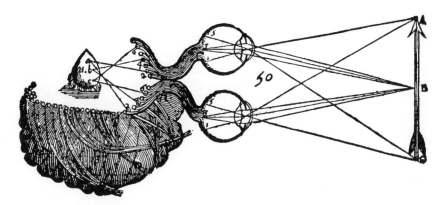

Figure 2.6 Binocular vision according to Descartes (1664/1909): 'the filaments 1–2, 3–4, 5–6, and the like compose the optic nerve and extend from the back of the eye (1, 3, 5) to the internal surface of the brain (2, 4, 6). Now assume that these threads are so arranged that if the rays that come, for example, from point A of the object happen to exert pressure on the back of the eye at point 1, they in this way would pull the whole thread 1–2 and enlarge the opening of the tubule marked 2. And similarly, the rays that come from point B enlarge the opening of tubule 4, and so on with the others. Whence, just as the different ways in which these rays exert pressure on points 1, 3, and 5 trace a figure at the back of the eye corresponding to that of object ABC, so, evidently, the different ways in which the tubules 2, 4, 6, and the like are opened by filaments 1–2, 3–4, and 5–6 must trace [a corresponding figure] on the internal surface of the brain.' (Descartes, 1972)

they were valid or not as in the emphasis they placed on physiological interpretations of vision. Increasingly, from that time onwards, texts that dealt with vision would have some diagram representing the pathways from the eyes to the brain, and some speculations regarding the site at which vision occurs. In the context of the visual pathways to the brain, it was believed that messages carried by the two optic nerves remained separate until they were united in the brain, as is indicated in Descartes's figure. Newton advanced our knowledge of the binocular pathways by describing the partial crossover of nerve fibres from one optic nerve to the other side of the brain. This discovery was used to support a mechanistic interpretation of vision, that is, one that did not make any appeal to non-material sources like the soul. The messages from each eye were thought to become one because the nerve fibres themselves were (wrongly) considered to unite (see Figure 2.7).

Physiological knowledge increased in the eighteenth and particularly in the nineteenth century – the power of the microscope was brought to bear on unravelling the detailed structure of the retina and the nerve pathways, and structure was in turn related to function. For example, in the 1860s the two different types of light-sensitive cells were found in the eye; they were called rods and cones because of their shapes when observed under the microscope. It was noted that the proportion of rods and cones varied over species. Indeed, some species only had one type or the other, and in all cases this could be related to the light conditions in which they were active. The retinae of nocturnal animals had rods but few or no cones, whereas those active only in daylight had cones but few or no rods: humans, who are active and can see under both natural light conditions, have a mixture of

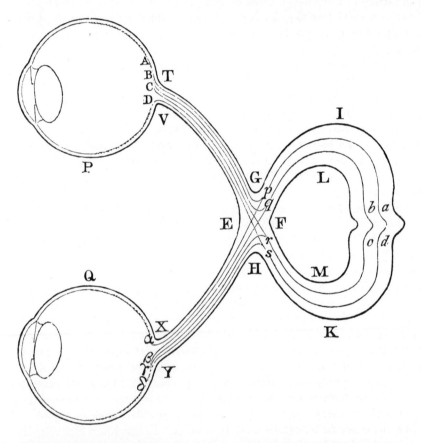

Figure 2.7 Binocular vision according to Newton. 'Now I conceive that every point in the retina of one eye, hath its corresponding point in the other; from which two very slender pipes filled with the most limpid liquor, do without either interruption, or any unevenness or irregularities in their process, go along the optic nerves to the juncture EFGH, where they meet either betwixt G, F, or F, H, and there unite into one pipe as big as both of them; and so continue in one, passing either betwixt I, L or M, K, into the brain, where they are terminated perhaps at the next meeting of the nerves betwixt the cerebrum and cerebellum, in the same order that their extremities were situated in the retina's.' (As described in Harris, 1775)

rods and cones. Accordingly, it was proposed that rods and cones had differing sensitivities and served different functions. Rods are able to detect light at lower intensities than cones, but cones are involved in colour vision and rods are not. Both rods and cones require appropriate pathways to the brain in order for us to experience light; however, in the nineteenth century relatively little was known about pathways in the brain, and so physiological analyses of vision tended to be restricted to the structures in the eye. The spirit of these exciting times was reflected in what is perhaps the greatest book written on vision, the *Treatise on Physiological Optics* by Hermann von Helmholtz; it was originally published in three separate volumes during the 1850s and 1860s, and the complete treatise was translated into English earlier this century. Helmholtz was both a physicist and a physiologist, and he amalgamated the strengths of these two disciplines in the analysis of vision. Amongst his many contributions to visual science were the elucidation of the mechanism of accommodation, the championing of a theory of colour vision based on three colour channels, and the invention of the ophthalmoscope for examining the inside of the eye. However, his most lasting impact on visual science was his theory of perception: he followed the empiricist philosophers in arguing that perception is like unconscious problem solving – making unconscious inferences about the nature of the external world based upon the inadequate information furnished by the senses. Helmholtz appreciated that the process of perception takes place in the brain, following transmission of the neural signals from the sensory receptors – the brain only had indirect access to the external world, via the senses, and it could only process messages in the language of nerve impulses. This realisation made any equation of the retinal image with perception unnecessary, and it removed a problem that had frequently been raised earlier, and was to return later: if the image on the retina is inverted and left-right reversed why is our perception not so? Helmholtz argued that this only created a problem if there was a picture in the retina that required further perception. If all that is available are nerve impulses then the brain can analyse them and make the appropriate inferences independently of the orientation of stimulation with respect to the retina.

A related problem had been tackled by Helmholtz's teacher, Johannes Müller (who wrote a textbook on physiology in the 1830s that was to remain a standard for decades). Since all nerve impulses are similar, how can the brain distinguish between impulses originating from the eyes and those from the ears? Müller's solution was to suggest that all sensory nerves have some specific energy or code that signals their particular origin. In this way, he argued, it would be possible for the brain to determine the sense from which the signals originated. According to this doctrine of specific nerve energies all the nerves from the eyes carry a specific signal that defines the quality of the sensation that will ensue; these visual qualities of brightness and colour occur no matter how the nerves are stimulated. For example, a blow to the head or pressure applied to the eye results in an experience of light rather than of pressure. The comic device of 'seeing stars' following a knockout punch fairly reflects Müller's doctrine. Later in the nineteenth century physiological recordings indicated that different regions of the brain act as receiving areas for specific senses (Figure 2.8).

Müller's textbook (written in the 1830s) contained a wealth of information on comparative anatomy. It reflected the widely held belief that all species were related, although the mechanism for such an evolutionary process remained unclear until the publication of Darwin's *On the Origin of Species by Means of Natural Selection* in 1859. In the latter part of the nineteenth century the relationship between structure and function was examined over a wide biological spectrum, due to the gradual acceptance of Darwin's theory of evolution. The relationships that were shown to exist between species also supported the extension of physiological discoveries derived from animal experiments to humans. For example, if the processes involved in nerve transmission in the frog could be elucidated then similar processes are probably operating in other species, too, including humans. Comparative anatomists were also able to chart the evolutionary paths of particular sensory organs, like eyes, and it was

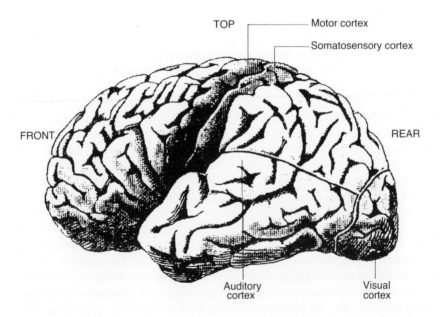

Figure 2.8 Sensory projection areas of the brain. (After Bloom and Lazerson, 1988)

evident that quite different aspects of information from light were useful to different animals – some can only discriminate differences in light intensity but not differences in wavelength, some can analyse plane polarised light, some can see into the infra-red region of the spectrum. Indeed, at an early stage two quite different designs for eyes evolved – one was a multi-faceted compound eye (as in insects) and the other a single-lensed image-forming eye (as in vertebrates).

Observations of animal behaviour were recorded with increasing skill in the eighteenth and nineteenth centuries. Darwin believed that behavioural patterns could evolve in a similar way to anatomical structures, and he wrote a book on *The Expression of Emotions in Man and Animals* (1872) charting the relationships between gestures and expressions in different species. Variations occur not only between species but also within them. Most particularly, changes in structure and function take place in the course of development to the mature state of the species. That is, within a given species there will be a developmental sequence for both structure and function. One of the features that seemed particularly perplexing was the ability of newborn animals to seek and find the source of sustenance (e.g. the mother's nipple for mammals) without any prior experience. This led some students, like Müller, to argue that this aspect of their behaviour was instinctive (i.e., innate or inborn) so that it occurred without any learning. Similar questions can be asked about whether human newborns also possess innate perceptual mechanisms. Paradoxically, the biologists' skills in analysing animal behaviours in the natural environment were not applied to newborn humans. Well into the twentieth century it was thought that the behaviour of very young babies was random and un-coordinated, and this presented problems for determining experimentally what they are able to see. Rather than refining the techniques for measuring behaviour in infants, it was usually considered that their visual world was as chaotic as their behaviour seemed to be. In the past this might have contributed to the view that the mind of the newborn is like a blank sheet upon which experience writes. In other words, humans were considered to learn the three-dimensional nature of their world, and this learning was dependent upon information delivered by the senses. These concepts of innate and learned behaviours have also been of central importance in philosophical approaches to perception.

PHILOSOPHY

Perceptual experience is subjective. Each one of us is able to reflect upon the nature of that experience, and to describe it to others. While the experience is subjective and inaccessible to others, the descriptions of what we perceive can be shared with others. Generally speaking, the descriptions given by different people of their perceptual experiences are in remarkably close correspondence; so close, in fact, that many people equate their perception of the world with the way it is described in traditional physics (or what we might loosely call reality). This has been the topic of much philosophical debate and the equation of perception with external reality is often referred to as naive realism. The close correspondence between perception of the world and other descriptions of it (e.g., as in terms of physical measurement) retarded the analysis of perception in general. The aspects that did demand scrutiny were those in which perceptual and physical descriptions did not match, or in which some disease, injury or intervention influenced perception; that is, when perception is no longer veridical or equated with physical measurements. We can cite two examples of departures from perceptual veridicality described by Aristotle – after-images and after-effects. In one set of observations he directed his eyes briefly at the sun and noticed a brief sequence of colours when he looked away, followed by a dark disc. It was obviously of interest to Aristotle because there was no visibly coloured object that corresponded to the briefly perceived colours. You should not try to repeat this observation, as it could damage the retina. There is an even more remarkable anecdotal account of such folly in the history of after-images: a friend of the seventeenth century chemist Robert Boyle looked at the sun through a telescope, and reported that he could see its after-image 11 years later! It seems more likely that he was not seeing at all with the part of the retina that had been exposed to the concentrated sunlight because the retinal cells would have been destroyed.

Another phenomenon described by Aristotle was the movement after-effect. He looked for some time at the stones at the bottom of a river through the rapidly flowing water, then he directed his gaze to the stones on the bank of the river; these appeared to be moving, too. That is, here was a situation in which the same objects, the stones on the river bank, appeared to be stationary at one time and moving at another. Have the stones changed or has their perception been modified? This clearly poses a problem for naive realists, who believe that reality is equated with our perceptual experience. The movement after-effect remains a phenomenon of interest to perceptual psychologists, and it can be elicited with a wide range of moving stimuli.

Philosophy has played a central role in the study of perception because the senses and their functions have been of focal importance to philosophy. Most of the basic ideas were initially expounded by Greek thinkers, and they have been elaborated upon by more modern philosophers. Thus, the distinction between innate and learned processes in perception became enshrined in nativist and empiricist philosophies, respectively. The nativists believed that we are born with the ability to perceive space, whereas the empiricists argued that we have no such knowledge of the world at birth, but we need to learn to see the spatial attributes like size, shape and distance. The modern empirical philosophy was expounded by John Locke at the end of the seventeenth century. Locke wrote:

> Let us suppose the mind to be, as we say, white paper, void of all characters, without any *ideas*: how comes it to be furnished? Whence comes it by that vast store, which the busy and boundless fancy of man has painted on it with an almost endless variety? Whence has it all the materials of reason and knowledge? To this I answer in one word, from experience: in that all our knowledge is founded, and from that it ultimately derives itself. (1690)

For Locke the mental element is the idea, which is based upon sensory experience. Ideas could be simple (like whiteness) or compound (like snow), and compound ideas are made up from associations between simple ones, by a process like 'mental chemistry'. Similar associative links can account for our ability to generalise across stimuli: for instance, to form a general idea of a triangle from many different specific instances. Thus, Locke was an empiricist and an associationist: knowledge derives from the senses and we learn to perceive the objects in the world by association.

The empiricist philosophers were not, however, empirical in their approach to perception. That is, they rarely carried out experiments to support their theory, even when they were explicitly suggested. Following the publication of Locke's *Essay Concerning Human Understanding* in 1690, an Irish student of vision, William Molyneux, wrote to Locke posing an hypothetical question: suppose someone was born blind and subsequently learned to discriminate between a sphere and a cube by touch; if their vision was later restored, would they be able to name them by sight alone? Molyneux concluded that they would not be able to name the objects appropriately, and Locke agreed with this conclusion. It was not possible to check this prediction empirically at that time, but early in the eighteenth century the oculist William Cheselden did perform cataract removals on congenitally blind patients. Unfortunately, neither his study nor the many others conducted over the last two centuries enable a clear answer to be given to Molyneux's question, largely because of the poor quality of vision initially available to the patients after the operation.

Locke charted the course for empiricism, but many of the details were provided by later philosophers, two of whom will be mentioned briefly here. Bishop Berkeley argued in *An Essay Toward a New Theory of Vision* (1709) that we learn to perceive the dimensions of space by associating muscular sensations with those of vision. For example, in order to perceive distance visually we learn the relationship between the visual stimulation and the states of the muscles controlling the eyes. The muscular and touch systems were considered to provide direct and undistorted spatial information that could be used to teach vision the dimensions of space. Berkeley also introduced the concept of unconscious inference into perception.

The Scotsman Thomas Reid (1764) made a clear distinction between sensation and perception. Thus, redness and roundness may be sensations produced by an apple, but its perception includes an appreciation of the object itself. Perceptions also involve projective aspects that are not present in sensations: the apple is perceived as being out there, but the sensations can be internal. Reid's distinction has had far reaching consequences, and it has persisted well into this century; it has pervaded our language and it even defines the categories of our enquiries. We use the term sensory to describe those areas concerned with the early stages of processing (as in sensory physiology) and the term perceptual to those dealing with later stages (as in space perception).

Empiricist philosophy was initially confined to Britain, but its widest influence has probably been through its adoption beyond Britain's shores – particularly by Helmholtz in nineteenth-century Germany and Watson in twentieth-century America. The seventeenth- and eighteenth-century empiricists challenged the rationalist Continental philosophers who argued that we obtain knowledge about the world by thinking, independently of sensory experience. René Descartes gave to the mind properties that were not shared by the body, which was treated as a machine. His mechanistic approach to the senses clarified many issues in perception, but he had the thorny problem of accounting for the interaction of the rational mind with the mechanistic body. This was a task attempted later by Immanuel Kant, a German philosopher in the eighteenth century. He did not deny that all knowledge begins with experience, but he did not believe that it all arises out of experience. He considered that certain aspects of knowledge are innate, most particularly the ideas of space and time. That is, Kant suggested that the individual is born with the ability to organise experience in both space and time. Perception is then an active organising process for Kant, rather than a passive receptive process of the type Locke proposed. Kant's influence on Continental philosophy was vast, but it also had numerous repercussions in related disciplines like physiology and psychology.

PSYCHOLOGY

Psychology, as an independent discipline, is considered to have been founded in 1879, when Wilhelm Wundt (a student of Helmholtz) opened his Psychological Institute at Leipzig University. Prior to that psychology was allied principally to philosophy, although perception was the province of sensory physiologists. Wundt saw the task of his new institute as that of studying conscious experience. What distinguished his approach from the many earlier ones addressing the same issues was the methods employed. Psychology came of age when it developed its own methodology: the problems of consciousness and perception were examined in novel ways, and psychology became an experimental discipline rather than just an observational one. Wundt rejected phenomenology, which is the oldest method of measuring perception, based upon the use of everyday language to describe experience.

Wundt incorporated precise methods for measuring detection and discrimination in his Psychological Institute, and it was in providing alternatives to phenomenology that psychology gained its independence from other disciplines. Wundt used a method we now call analytic introspection for studying consciousness, but in the area of perception he utilised the psychophysical methods that had been described a few years earlier by his compatriots Ernst Weber and Gustav Theodor Fechner. Fechner published his *Elements of Psychophysics* in 1860, and this had a profound effect on the subsequent study of perception. In it were described methods of quantifying perception, with the precision normally associated with the physical sciences. A number of psychophysical methods were introduced that measured the limits of perception – the thresholds for detecting the presence of a stimulus and for discriminating the difference between two stimuli. For example, in the context of light intensity, the detection threshold would be the physical intensity (called luminance) that could just be seen. The discrimination threshold would be the luminance difference between two stimuli that could just be seen as brighter or dimmer. Fechner described methods that could be used to determine detection and difference thresholds.

Fechner was initially a physicist and later became a philosopher; between these two states he performed many experiments on perceptual phenomena. His overriding interest was to devise a metric scale for perceptual dimensions that had a similar rigour to those measuring physical dimensions. For example, a physicist will have some arbitrary scale for measuring length (say centimetres) and a set of rules for defining it so that different lengths can be compared using the same units. We can make perceptual comparisons of lengths, we can determine that one line is longer or shorter than another, but can we apply a scale to our judgements in the way that centimetres are applied to physical measurement? Fechner did devise such a scale, based on a logarithmic series, and this has been revised more recently to comply with a power series. The scaling functions are not restricted to dimensions like length, but have been applied to judgements ranging from brightness to pain.

Wundt himself did measure thresholds, but he also invented a new method for studying conscious experience later called analytic introspection. Introspection is looking inward at mental processes and the method differed from phenomenology in that instead of using familiar object names (like book or page) only terms signifying sensory quality (colour or brightness), intensity (extension) and direction were permitted. Thus, the description of the book you are reading could take the form something like 'two white surfaces, attached along an edge with one raised with respect to the other; on each surface are black marks, slightly separated from one another horizontally but with larger spaces at irregular intervals...'. Observers had to undergo extensive training before they were considered to be skilled at analytic introspection. By using this method Wundt believed that he could determine the elements from which perceptions and thought were constructed. Wundt was a philosophical empiricist and associationist, and he had been greatly influenced by Locke's ideas about mental chemistry. Wundt was trying to isolate the basic elements and to determine the rules for their combination into more complex perceptions and thought, and this approach was called structuralism. The basic elements were taken to be the sensory attributes (like quality and extension), and these could be combined to make the molecules of perception; the combination was achieved by a process of association. Perception represented a synthesis or building up of the sensory attributes via learning by association, whereas the method analysed or broke down complex perceptions into their component sensory attributes.

Many of Wundt's contemporaries adopted his technique but few were able to obtain the same results as Wundt: analytic introspection was not a reliable means for plumbing the processes of perception. By the early twentieth century there was widespread disaffection with the method and its attendant theory, and alternatives were sought. Two major reactions that appeared in the second decade were Gestalt psychology and Behaviourism. Gestalt is a German word that can be translated approximately as configuration, but the German term is retained because of the difficulty of capturing its nuances with a single English word. The Gestalt psychologists (initially Max Wertheimer, Kurt Koffka and Wolfgang Köhler) were in the mainstream of Continental philosophy; they were nativists and phenomenologists. They were nativists because they believed that perception was unitary and reflected an innate organisation within the brain. Perception was to them an organised process that operated according to rules, and it could not be broken down into its constituent parts. They were phenomenologists because they considered that the richness of perception could only be recorded adequately by a system as rich as language. The Gestaltists' main opposition to Wundt's structuralism was theoretical – they did not accept that unitary perceptions could be analysed into smaller parts. Indeed, the cliché associated with Gestalt psychology is that 'the whole is different from the sum of its parts' – thus, the perception of a square is different from the separate effects of its four constituent sides.

John Watson launched the Behaviourist attack on structuralism in 1913. His dissatisfaction was with the method rather than the theory; in fact behaviourist theory was also empiricist and associationist. The method of analytic introspection was rejected because it was unreliable and subjective. Sensations and perceptions were inferences based upon introspections, and were not open to public scrutiny as would be expected of a science.

> Psychology as the behaviorist views it is a purely objective experimental branch of natural science. Its theoretical goal is the prediction and control of behavior. Introspection forms no essential part of its methods, nor is the scientific value of its data dependent upon the readiness with which they lend themselves to interpretation in terms of consciousness. (1913)

Watson argued that the only aspects of psychology that could be measured reliably were the stimuli presented to subjects and the responses they made. Hence, Behaviourism was often referred to as S–R theory; the organism was likened to a black box about which nothing could be known directly, but only by inference. Watson and the growing band of Behaviourists in America distrusted the study of perception generally, because it could evidently take place without any obvious response. When it was studied, it was in the context of discrimination learning, where the emphasis was more on the process of learning than on perception. Thus, the Gestaltists became the heirs to perceptual research, almost by default.

The Gestalt psychologists formulated some descriptive rules for perceptual organisation and produced a wide range of demonstrations that could be used to support them. The initial and fundamental process is the separation of a figure from its background, because all the other grouping principles can only operate with segregated figures. Normally, a figure is defined by contours that surround it completely, whereas the ground is larger or lacking a defined boundary, as in Figure 2.9a. Under certain circumstances neither of these conditions are met (see Figure 2.9b), and perceptual instability ensues – first one part and then the other is seen as figure, and this perceptual alternation continues. Most of the remaining demonstrations of Gestalt grouping principles have clearly segregated figures; they are usually line drawings, like those shown in Figure 2.10, and these are shown to observers who are asked to describe what they see. For example, Figure 2.10a is said to look like three columns or three pairs of lines. Although many alternative descriptions are possible (for instance, seven rows of dots) they are rarely given. The elements of the configuration are equally sized dots but these tend to be grouped to form vertical lines; the lines are similar in length and orientation but they differ with regard to their distance or proximity from one another. This was called grouping by proximity.

In Figure 2.10b the dots tend to be described as three columns of black and three columns of white dots. Although all the dots are equally spaced, so that proximity cannot be operating, they are grouped according to their

(a)

(b)

Figure 2.9 (a) A figure, like this black goblet-shape, has closed contours and is smaller than the background against which it is presented. (b) Rubin's crosses. Rubin (1915) examined the reversals of figure and ground that occur with a pattern like this. Two crosses, comprised of either radiating lines or concentric arcs, have common boundaries, and fluctuate between being figure and ground, but only one can be seen as figure at one time.

similarity; other things being equal, similar elements within a larger configuration will be related perceptually. The organising principles rarely operate in isolation, more frequently they complement or counteract one another. For example, in Figure 2.10c the dots are typically described as forming two symmetrical triangles, one of white dots and the other of black dots. These are symmetrical figures, and also what the Gestalt psychologists called good figures; simple geometrical shapes, like triangles, squares and circles were considered to be good figures because they could not be reduced perceptually to any simpler components. In Figure 2.10c the

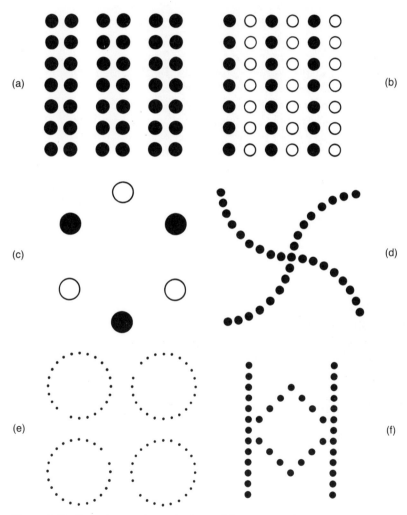

Figure 2.10 Gestalt grouping principles: (a) proximity; (b) similarity; (c) symmetry; (d) good continuation; (e) closure; (f) an example of embedded figures.

principle of symmetry is operating, but not in isolation: it is complemented by the similarity of the dots (black or white), but it is acting against the proximity of the dots.

The dots in Figure 2.10d would be most commonly described as following two intersecting curved lines, rather than alternatives like two V-shapes meeting at their points. This organising principle was referred to as good continuation – the lines are seen as maintaining some continuity of direction and not changing direction abruptly. Even the sequences of dots in Figure 2.10e display goodness of figure, in this case circularity. They also illustrate another Gestalt principle, namely that of closure. In each of the four patterns one dot is missing from the regular sequence, but it is not immediately evident. Any irregularities in good figures tend to be smoothed out perceptually.

In Figure 2.10f the various organising principles operate in a way to conceal an aspect of the pattern. This would be described generally as a diamond flanked by two vertical lines, but rarely as a letter W above a letter M. In this instance we are dealing with embedded figures, which are hidden by the grouping rules to yield alternative organisations.

Many more organising principles have been described by Gestalt psychologists, although these are the main ones. Their intention initially was to provide an alternative theory of active, innately organised perception to counter the passive, structuralist views of Wundt and his adherents. The theory was supported by these demonstrations, which drew upon phenomenology. However, it should be noted that the demonstrations themselves were not representative of normal object perception because they were based upon line drawings. That is, the evidence for the principles of organisation is based upon the manner in which two-dimensional pictures are perceived rather than three-dimensional objects. The Gestalt psychologists, and Köhler in particular, extended the theory beyond the realms of phenomenology into the brain. They did conduct more conventional experiments on phenomena like after-effects (see Figure 2.11) and illusions using responses other than verbal descriptions. The results of these experiments were used to suggest a speculative neurophysiology of vision that involved electrical fields in the brain. This strategy was not a wise one because the opponents of Gestalt could attack the physiological speculations far more easily than the robust perceptual demonstrations.

In the second quarter of this century most research in perception was conducted by Gestalt psychologists. At the same time, an alternative approach was being developed in relative isolation in Britain, and it has had a profound effect on the shape of modern perceptual research. Frederick Bartlett examined perception in realistic and dynamic situations and he represents a continuation of the British empiricist tradition with his analysis of perception as a skilled activity. Bartlett rejected the application

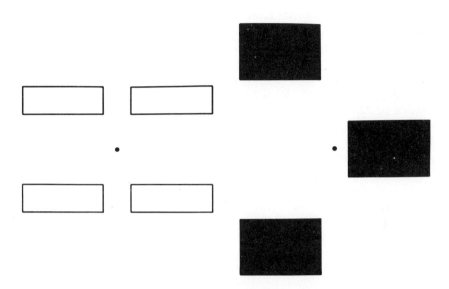

Figure 2.11 A figural after-effect can be produced by observing these patterns. Initially fixate on the left hand dot: the left and right pair of outline rectangles will appear to be equally separated from one another. Now fixate on the right hand dot for about 1 min, after which shift fixation back to the dot on the left. The outlines will no longer look equally separated – the left pair will seem nearer to one another than will the right pair. Köhler and Wallach (1944) called this a figural after-effect.

of stimulus–response interpretations of complex tasks like playing cricket or tennis because the actions were highly organised and initiated in advance of any contact with the ball. Indeed, the actions were made with respect to the position the ball would be predicted to occupy at some short time in the future. Complex activities of this type indicated that behavioural sequences had to be programmed in advance and coordinated with predictions based on perception. This led Bartlett to a cognitive theory of perception, one in which the division between perception and thought was difficult to draw. Like Helmholtz, Bartlett considered that perception was like problem solving, incorporating processes of inference but also of prediction. In order to make predictions that involve action we need to have some mental representation of the environment in which the action will take place. This concept of forming a mental model of the world in which we behave was proposed by a student of Bartlett's, Kenneth Craik, and it is one of the ideas that has proved important in the development of both cognitive and computational theories of vision. Perception is considered to be a process in which information regarding aspects of the world is analysed and utilised to plan behaviour. This information-processing approach has become widely accepted as perception can then be considered as a sequence of representations that are initially crude and become increasingly appropriate to the three-dimensional environment.

When Bartlett and Craik proposed their theories of perception relatively little was known about the brain mechanisms that mediate perception. This is one of the reasons why the Gestalt psychologists were able to propose their speculative neurophysiology of vision. In the last three decades there have been major strides in furthering our understanding of neural processes in the visual system. These discoveries have been taken to support the view that vision involves a sequence of stages in which different aspects of the stimulus, like colour and contour, are extracted. These neurophysiological advances will be described in Chapter 3, following a description of the stimulus for vision, light, and the organ that responds to it, the eye.

REFERENCE NOTES

Gardner's (1987) wide-ranging book *The Mind's New Science* on the history of the cognitive revolution provides a good link between the issues covered in Chapters 1 and 2. The philosophical precursors of cognition are essentially similar to those for perception, and Gardner provides a clear description of the conflicts between nativist and empiricist approaches to perception and thought. His account is not strictly chronological, but he does treat the major theoretical movements of the twentieth century, like Gestalt theory and Bartlett's concept of schema, as well as contrasting the theories of perception proposed by Gibson and Marr.

There are many general histories of psychology, of which Hearnshaw's (1987) *The Shaping of Modern Psychology* is recommended. It is particularly valuable in describing the influence of the life sciences on the development of psychology. Fancher's (1990) *Pioneers of Psychology* is a very readable introduction to the main streams of thought in psychology from Descartes to Freud. In addition to the chapters on philosophy and psychophysics, those concerned with the physiology of mind and the theory of evolution are especially apposite. R. I. Watson's (1968) *The Great Psychologists* concentrates on the endeavours of many of those mentioned in the present chapter. Watson (1979) has also assembled a extensive list of *Basic Writings in the History of Psychology*, in which extracts from the works of Descartes, Newton, Locke, Berkeley, Kant, Fechner, Helmholtz, Wundt, Darwin, and the Gestalt psychologists can be read. Herrnstein and Boring (1965) have also collected a useful set of historical extracts. Watson's first book is dedicated to his mentor, E. G. Boring, who wrote one of the few books dealing specifically with historical issues in perception. Boring's (1942)

Sensation and Perception in the History of Experimental Psychology presents a comprehensive account of the nature of light, of anatomical studies of the eye and nervous system, and of investigations of visual phenomena from the seventeenth to the early twentieth centuries. Miller's (1962) *Psychology. The Science of Mental Life* is also dedicated to Boring; it provides a very readable historical introduction to psychology generally, and to the work of Wundt and Fechner in particular. Earlier concepts of the senses are elucidated by Crombie (1972), and Dember (1964) presents selected extracts from a number of important books and articles on vision published in the nineteenth century. Here one has ready access to the works of Young, Bell, Müller, Helmholtz and Wheatstone.

The historical connections between optics and vision are traced by Pirenne (1970), and his book includes many pinhole camera photographs taken to illustrate the principles of optical projection in an eye or camera. He also deals extensively with the art of linear perspective, the emergence of which, in the early fifteenth century, is detailed by Edgerton (1975) and by Kemp (1990). Descartes (1637/1902, 1664/1909), writing on the eye and vision, can be found in facsimile editions, and also in translation: see Olscamp's (1965) translation of his book on optics, and Hall's (1972) translation of the *Treatise of Man*. Morgan's (1977) delightful book on *Molyneux's Question* carefully dissects the philosophical ideas underlying Locke's empiricism in the context of surgery to remove cataracts; he has also translated some articles by French philosophers who are critical of empiricism. The work of the Gestalt psychologists was originally in German, and many of the source articles are available in a collection of translations edited by Ellis (1938). Here one can find articles by Wertheimer, Köhler, and Koffka on Gestalt psychology generally, as well as on specific issues like the laws of organisation in perception. Gordon's (1989) book has chapters on psychophysics and Gestalt theory.

Chapter 3

Light and the eye

Light is the stimulus for vision and the eye is the organ which responds to light energy. This chapter will examine two contemporary developments from the heritage of perception which are actively being pursued. One concerns advances in our understanding of the nature of the stimulus – visual optics – and the other is about how the visual system responds to light – visual neurophysiology. The image-forming properties of the eye are quite well understood, and most aberrations of the eye can now be corrected optically. The performance of the human eye is remarkable considering that its optical parts are so simple. One of the ways of measuring the performance of the visual system is to treat it as a physicist would a lens, by determining how faithfully it can transmit patterns of light incident upon it. One outcome of this approach has been the suggestion that the visual system is most sensitive to sharply defined contours.

Knowledge about the neuroanatomy and neurophysiology of vision has advanced because it has proved possible to examine the structures in the visual system in greater detail. Techniques have been devised to examine structure and function at and below the cellular level. Thus there is now better understanding of how light is absorbed by pigments in the receptors, how these chemical changes modify the electrical potentials of the receptor cells, and how a nerve impulse is eventually generated. The methods of recording the electrical activity of individual nerve cells have proved particularly productive, and have demonstrated that the cells do not respond solely to the presence or absence of light, but to its patterning. Single cells in the visual cortex of animals closely related to humans (like monkeys) respond most strongly to oriented edges. Thus, similar conclusions are being reached from quite different lines of enquiry: the results from both visual optics and neurophysiology suggest that the early stages of vision involve the extraction of simple features from the light stimulating the eye. It is not surprising to find that visual psychologists have been conducting experiments to relate these findings to the phenomena they investigate.

VISUAL OPTICS

In Chapter 2, we saw how the discovery of the eye's ability to form an image of the world was a turning point in the understanding of vision. Once the principles and methods of optics could be applied to the eye, there was an immediate advance in visual science, whose consequences have remained important. Image formation is a necessary, but not sufficient condition for vision. Seeing involves a sequence of processes which are initiated by the presence of an image on the retina, so that this is only the first step. Description of retinal image formation, and of the optical characteristics of the eye, requires the use of conventions (such as diagrams showing the path of rays of light) which are very great simplifications of the true state of affairs. In particular, the retinal image is never stationary; that is, it never has the characteristics of a 'snapshot' of the world, frozen in time, but this is how it is represented in conventional diagrams. In this section we will be primarily concerned with those aspects of visual optics which have the greatest influence on perception, and thus determine why things look the way they do.

Optical functions of the eye

The environment contains objects which can emit, reflect or absorb electromagnetic radiation. Such radiation is ubiquitous, but only a small portion can be directly sensed by living organisms, and a smaller part still can be detected by the eye. Electromagnetic radiation can be considered as a wave, and as such can vary in wavelength. Wavelength is defined by the distance between successive peaks in the wave, and is measured in nanometres (nm), where 1 nm equals one billionth of a metre (10^{-9} m). The range of human vision extends from around 400 nm to around 700 nm, and this band of electromagnetic radiation is referred to as light. To someone with normal colour vision, light of different wavelengths appears coloured (Figure 3.1), making up the visible spectrum.

   Light sources in the natural world are relatively rare, and are limited to the sun and stars, lightning, fire, and biochemical processes in living organisms (bioluminescence). Of these the sun is by far the most important, and its location provides a constraint on the appearance of illuminated objects that plays a fundamental role in the perception of depth and shape. The interpretation of three-dimensional structure from shadows seems to be based on an assumption that light comes from the sky above. Our widespread use of artificial sources of illumination may cause misperception of objects if the light source is located below eye level. Objects which are not light sources can only reflect some part of the light which falls upon them. Generally, objects are neither perfect reflectors nor perfect absorbers of light. Their molecular structure causes certain wavelengths in the incident

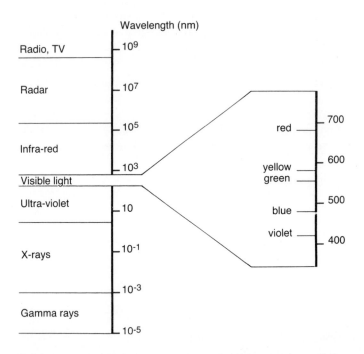

Figure 3.1 Part of the electromagnetic spectrum, showing the small proportion which corresponds to visible light. The expanded section indicates the approximate wavelengths at which certain colours are normally seen.

radiation to be absorbed, and others to be reflected. For example, a blue object appears to be this colour because it absorbs most of the incident light energy with wavelengths above around 550 nm. In practice, the perceived colour of objects is also influenced by factors such as the colour of adjacent objects and of the incident light. The light reflected from one object may in turn fall upon other objects, with their own reflective properties. Our environment is therefore filled with emitted and reflected light, which forms a field of energy carrying information about the environment's characteristics. In order to see, we must first capture a sample of this radiation, in such a way that the information it carries is not too distorted or degraded.

This sampling of the light field is the function of the image forming components of the eye. The simplest image-forming system is an enclosed hollow space, with a small aperture through which light can enter. Any device like this will form an image on the internal surface opposite the aperture, and is called a camera obscura (Figure 3.2). A sample of the light

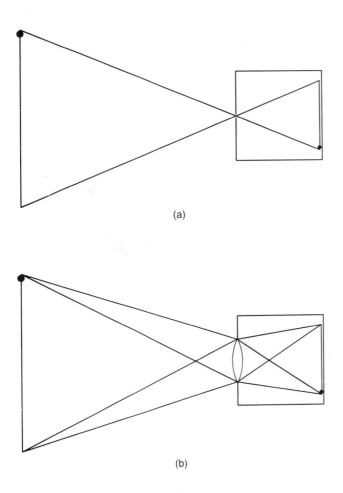

(a)

(b)

Figure 3.2 (a) The formation of an image in a camera obscura. The pinhole aperture allows certain light rays from objects in the environment to enter the camera, where they form an inverted image on the screen. In (b) the addition of a lens increases the proportion of the rays from a point on the object which are brought to a single point in the camera.

field enters the camera obscura through the aperture, and if this is small then only a small fraction of the total light energy will be able to enter. However, the rays of light will be limited to those which form an image. The quality of the image (its sharpness and brightness) depends on the size of the aperture. A small aperture will give a sharp image, but it will also be faint. A camera obscura works best when the external illumination is high,

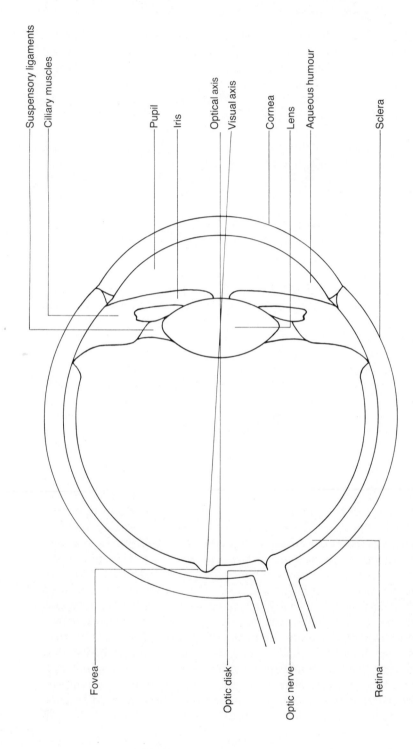

Figure 3.3 Schematic diagram of the vertebrate eye. In reality the eye is not normally a perfect sphere, but is elongated on the horizontal axis. Most of the focusing of light occurs at the curved boundary between air and the cornea. The image formed on the retina is inverted.

and the aperture is small. By the addition of some means of focusing the light from distant objects, the image quality can be maintained with a larger aperture. Focusing consists of bringing together rays of light emitted from a single point in the environment to a single point in the image. Light is emitted in all directions from objects, but if the object is far enough from the imaging device then the rays which enter it will be approximately parallel, and the object is said to be at optical infinity. This distance is conventionally taken to be 6 metres (20 feet). If the object is close then the rays from a point on it which enter the aperture are divergent, and need greater focusing, or bending, in order to be brought to a single point in the image.

These principles are embodied in the structure of the vertebrate eye (see Figure 3.3). Light first strikes the curved, transparent outer layer of the eye, called the cornea. This causes a change in the path of light rays (refraction), because the cornea has an optical density higher than that of air, and the velocity of light is reduced. The curvature of the cornea causes the rays of light from an object which strike it at varying points to be refracted by varying amounts, so that they are brought to a focus inside the eye, close to the plane of the retina. The curvature of the cornea also allows it to refract light from directions somewhat behind the observer. The full field of view extends through about 208 degrees horizontally for a forward-pointing eye, although light from this region is imaged on the extreme periphery of the retina, and is blocked by the nose and head on one side. Vertically, the field of view is about 120 deg (Figure 3.4). Note that these values define the range within which light is imaged on some part of the retina; whether or not anything is seen depends on processes that occur after the absorption of light energy by the retina. It is the difference between the optical density of the cornea and air which causes refraction, which is why vision underwater is usually less distinct; there is very little refraction at the boundary between water and the cornea so that little focusing occurs.

In fact almost all the focusing power of the eye resides in the cornea, rather than in the lens. The lens provides an adjustable fine focusing power, called accommodation, due to the fact that its shape can be changed. Its normal shape is approximately spherical, but this is changed by the application of tension by ligaments attached to the transparent sack in which the lens is contained. This tension causes the lens to become more elongated, and to apply less change to the path of light rays. The ligaments themselves are controlled by a circular ring of muscles (the ciliary muscles) which when contracted allow the ligaments to reduce the tension they apply, and the lens to assume its normal spherical shape. In its most elongated state, the lens in a normal eye will bring rays from an object at optical infinity (defined as a distance greater than 6 m) to a focus on the retina. This is referred to as the far point of accommodation. At its most nearly spherical, it will focus rays from an object at a distance of about 15

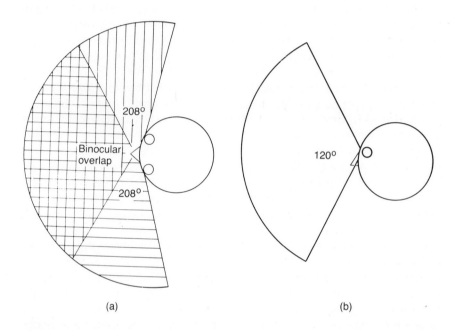

208°

Binocular overlap

208°

(a)

120°

(b)

Figure 3.4 The horizontal (a) and vertical (b) field of view. The hatched area of the horizontal field represents the area of binocular overlap between the fields of the two eyes.

cm from the eye (the near point). An emmetropic, or normal, eye is capable of adjusting accommodation within the range between these far and near points. Emmetropia is the result of the focusing power of the lens combined with the length of the eye, either of which may be inappropriate, with results that are described in the next section. When someone's lens is removed, usually due to the presence of a cataract which makes it opaque, then vision is generally little impaired, provided the illumination is high. This is due to focusing by the cornea, and to the presence of a variable aperture in the eye's optical system, called the pupil. The pupil is created by a ring of muscles (the iris), which can expand and contract to adjust the size of the pupil, and thus the amount of light entering the eye. In high light levels, the pupil contracts to a minimum diameter (about 1 mm), and it functions like the aperture in a camera obscura, by assisting in the focusing of light. More precisely, a small pupil diameter increases the depth of focus of the eye, which is the range of object distances for which a clear image can be obtained without adjustment of the lens. By maximising the depth of focus with a small pupil, someone without a lens can see clearly over a reasonable range of distances, but this is reduced in lower light levels. In addition, there is a surprising side-effect: the lens normally absorbs most of the ultra-violet radiation that strikes the eye, and if it is removed, people report being able to see deeper shades of blue beyond the limit of visiblity for normal observers. Pupil diameter can also vary for reasons other than the ambient light level. It is influenced by attention, and dilates when we try to carry out a difficult or important task. Emotions can also have an effect, as the pupil will also dilate with heightened arousal, for example due to fear. The drug atropine, which may be used to cause maximum pupil dilation before clinical examination of the eye, takes its name from the plant *Atropa Belladonna* (Deadly Nightshade) from which it can be extracted. The term *Belladonna* means 'beautiful woman' and in the past it was not uncommon for women to use eye drops made from the plant in order to create pupil dilation, and perhaps also an increase in attractiveness. Any beneficial effects may have been due to the implication of attentive interest conveyed by the size of her pupils.

The accommodation of the eye is driven by a reflex response to the retinal image, but the basis of this is not well understood. It does not seem to depend simply on the degree of blur, and is influenced by other factors such as the wavelength of the light. Feedback from the state of accommodation can act as a source of information for the visual system about the distance of objects; the more the accommodation, the closer the object. Clearly, this is limited to the range of distances between the far and near points, and will not convey much information in good illumination, when less accommodative effort is required. In experiments on depth perception it is a common practice to have observers look through an artificial pupil, which is a small aperture about 1 mm in diameter placed immediately in front of the eye. This has the effect of ensuring that the retinal image is in focus regardless of the state of accommodation, which is thereby held constant as a factor in determining the perception of distance.

Limitations of optical function

In practice, the optical functioning of the normal eye falls short of ideal in a number of ways. In addition, individuals may have various sorts of deficiency which further degrade the formation of images. Myopic (short-sighted) eyes are unable to focus rays from optical infinity on the retina, but only to a point in front of it. This is due either to the eyeball being too long, or the power of the lens being too great, or a combination of the two factors (see Figure 3.5). The far point at which myopic vision is distinct is close enough for rays from an object to be divergent, and the near point is also closer than it is for emmetropic eyes. Hypermetropic (long-sighted) eyes are the converse case; rays from optical infinity can be

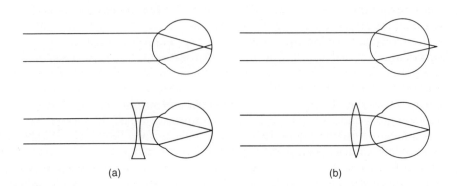

Figure 3.5 Myopic (a) and hypermetropic (b) eyes, showing the effects of optical correction. In the myopic eye, light rays from optical infinity are brought to a focus in front of the retina, which is corrected with a concave (negative) lens. The focal plane of the hypermetropic eye lies behind the retina, and this can be corrected by a convex (positive) lens.

focused, but not those from nearer objects, and the near point is further away. Both these states can be corrected by suitable lenses; myopia with a negative concave lens that makes the light rays diverge as if coming from a nearer point, and hypermetropia with a positive convex lens that causes a corresponding convergence. In the relatively unusual event that an individual has one myopic eye, and one that is emmetropic or even hypermetropic, each can be corrected with the appropriate lens. However, the resulting images in the two eyes are of different sizes, since a convex lens magnifies the image while a concave one reduces it. This condition, known as aniseikonia, causes problems for binocular vision, since it may not be possible to fuse two such different sized images, with the result that one is suppressed.

As ageing proceeds, it becomes harder to change the accommodation of the eye, largely due to a loss of elasticity in the lens. This is known as presbyopia, and it affects most people eventually to a greater or lesser extent, even if they were emmetropic as young adults. The effect of presbyopia is most marked on people who were hypermetropic, since it further restricts the range between the near and far points. By contrast, a myopic person will come closer to emmetropia as presbyopia sets in. When visual perception is impaired by presbyopia, it may be some time before the individual is aware of the extent of the impairment, or before he or she is prepared to admit to it, if good eyesight has been a source of pride. This may cause problems, particularly in the work place, as errors and accidents become more probable.

Even if the eye is emmetropic, or has been corrected by spectacles, the image formed on the retina is subject to a number of distortions. The sharpness of the image is reduced away from the centre of vision. This is a point on the retina approximately in line with the centre of the lens, which is therefore traversed by light rays without appreciable refraction. It is not surprising that the highest concentration of light-sensitive cells is found at this point. The best image is still appreciably blurred and light energy from a point in the environment is spread out across an area, called the blur circle, rather than being concentrated at a point on the retina. Different wavelengths are not focused equally; typically, the focal plane for red light lies somewhat further from the lens than that for blue light, so that if the eye accommodates to bring one wavelength into focus, others are blurred. This difference in focusing power for different wavelengths is called chromatic aberration, and it is quite marked in the human eye. With white light, only the middle, yellow, wavelengths are usually in good focus; the shorter and longer wavelengths are focused in front of and behind the retina, respectively. This means that the image of a white disc consists of a central yellow area surrounded by red and blue coloured fringes. Nevertheless we are not generally aware of chromatic aberration, and there is evidently some process of compensation in the visual system which removes its effects.

Spherical and chromatic aberrations occur even if the transparent surfaces of the eye are parts of perfect spheres. Such symmetry is rare in biological systems, and the eyes usually have optical surfaces that are not spherical. The most common form for the cornea is that the curvature differs in directions at right angles to one another. This has the effect of producing two focal points for the eye, corresponding to each of the curvatures (see Figures 3.6 and 3.7) and is known as astigmatism. Thus if a horizontal line is in focus, a vertical one will not be, and vice versa. When

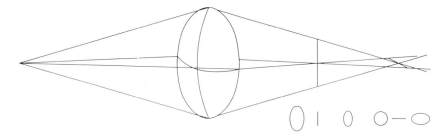

Figure 3.6 Focusing of light by an astigmatic lens. The lens shown is more curved in the horizontal than in the vertical axis. Rays from a point cannot be brought to a single point of focus. Instead there are two focal planes, corresponding to the two axes of curvature. At intermediate positions, as shown, a point source is represented by an elliptical distribution of light. Astigmatism can be corrected with a lens whose curvatures are opposite to those of the lens.

Figure 3.7 The effect of astigmatism on the appearance of lines in different
orientations. If you have an uncorrected astigmatism, it will not be possible to
bring all orientations into equally sharp focus at the same time. One set of lines in
a given orientation will appear darker than the rest. If the page is rotated, the lines
concerned will change, corresponding to their orientation with respect to the eye.

this difference is large enough to interfere with vision, it can be corrected
with a cylindrical lens that is shaped so as to focus one orientation more
strongly than another, and thus compensate for the deficiency of the eye.

In addition to these distortions imposed by the optics of the eye, various
effects are produced by the media through which the light passes. The
cornea, lens and fluids inside the eye are not perfectly transparent, and
alter the spectral composition of the light. In particular, the lens absorbs
long and short wavelengths more than middle ones, giving it a yellowish
appearance. This yellowing increases with age, leading to shifts in the
appearance of colours. The fluids in the eye may develop small areas of
opacity, where light is absorbed more strongly. These appear to an observer
as small dark blobs, called muscae volitantes or floaters, which seem to
move about as the eyes do. If not understood, these objects may be thought
to be in the outside world, and to be moving with very high velocities; some
of the reported sightings of UFOs have been traced to this source. Before
light can strike the sensitive elements in the retina, it must pass through the
layer of blood vessels and nerve fibres that lies above them. This seemingly
inefficient arrangement is probably a consequence of biological constraints
on the evolution of the eye, and it means that light is both absorbed and
scattered before it can be detected. You can in fact see the blood vessels in
the eye, by shining a small torch into the corner of the eye while in an
otherwise dark room. It helps to close the eye partially and to move the

torch around. It usually takes some practice to produce the effect for the first time, but it is very striking once seen. The blood vessels appear as a pattern of branches, like a tree, that appears and disappears as the torch is moved around. In fact you are seeing the shadows of the vessels, since less light reaches the retina behind where they lie. These and other sorts of perceptions produced by the structure of the eye itself are known as entoptic phenomena.

Since such effort is applied to the correction of individual errors in the optics of the eye, it might be thought that the quality of the image was of paramount importance to perception. In fact, most of the distortions of the image pass unnoticed, and it is remarkable how effectively we perceive despite their presence. Why then is it important for the image to be at least approximately in focus? The eye is a means of obtaining information about the outside world, and vision depends on the information available for processing. A blurred edge carries less information, since its location is less precisely specified, and although we can recognise objects when visual information is degraded, the process is slower and more prone to error. The quality of the retinal image imposes constraints on visual performance, and acts as a limiting factor on what we can see.

Measures of optical performance

In the previous sections we have examined the principles of image formation by the eye, and identified some of the common faults which can alter or reduce the information available for perception. An important area of study in vision is concerned with measuring the performance of the eye. This is important for various purposes; such as identifying and correcting anomalies, and finding out the limits of normal vision in applied settings. Most people are familiar with the techniques employed in optometry, as the result of having eye-tests. Such tests employ a type of psychophysics, modified to take account of the problems of taking measurements from a cross-section of the population. It is important to realise that measurements are usually of perceptual rather than optical performance, in that people are asked to say what they can see when looking at standardised visual patterns. Under these circumstances the response may be influenced by other factors, since even the most skilled observer cannot simply report the events that take place on the retina. Nevertheless, careful use of psychophysical methods can ensure that subjective reports are a useful indication of the quality of the information available to the eye. While most of our knowledge is obtained in this way, it is also possible to make objective assessments using instruments such as the ophthalmoscope and retinoscope. If the two sorts of measure differ, then it can be taken that this is due to the processing of information subsequent to the eye. For example, there is a condition known as amblyopia, in which an individual has

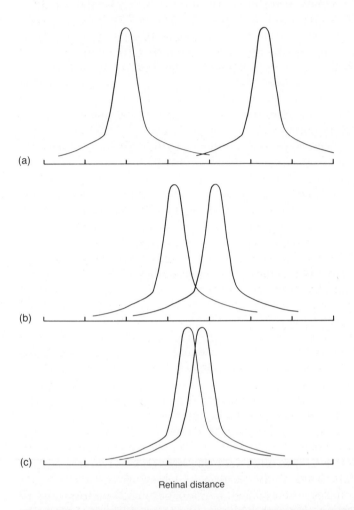

Retinal distance

Figure 3.8 Light distributions on the retina determine the resolution of adjacent image points. A point source is imaged as a spread-out distribution of light energy (the blur circle), even in an emmetropic eye. The poorer the accommodation, the more the blurring of the image. In (a) two point sources are separated by a distance sufficient to produce distributions which are easily discriminated. In (b) and (c) the two distributions increasingly overlap. At some point the observer will be unable to see that there are two objects rather than one, and this corresponds to the limit of visual acuity.

blurred vision in one eye which cannot be corrected by any optical means. Therefore, the poor acuity is not due to the optics of the eye, but to the ways the neural signals are processed in the visual system. Amblyopia is often a consequence of an uncorrected squint during childhood, leading to failure of normal binocular vision, and the suppression of information from one eye.

The standard of vision is most commonly expressed in terms of acuity, which is, at the simplest, the ability to discriminate detail. Suppose that there are two points of light on a dark background. As described in the previous section, each will be imaged on the retina with a degree of blur, even in an emmetropic eye. More precisely, this means that the light energy will be spread out over some area, and a graph of its distribution would show a central peak with a tailing off at each side. The more the blur, the more spread out this distribution will be. If the two points are physically separated by a sufficient distance, their two distributions will not overlap; that is, their representations on the retina will also be physically distinct, and are said to be optically resolved. As they are brought closer together, the two distributions of light energy will become increasingly combined, until they merge into one (Figure 3.8). If we ask an observer to indicate the minimum separation at which the points appear separate, then we have a measure of visual acuity. If the observer's eye needs optical correction, then we would expect to find that the minimum separation is larger than that for other people. Clearly, this presupposes some accepted standard of performance against which someone can be assessed, and a standardised test pattern at which to look.

Many such patterns have been proposed, and are useful under different circumstances (Figure 3.9). The familiar opticians' chart (the Snellen chart) uses letters of the alphabet of decreasing size, and tests the ability to discriminate the separate features of each letter well enough to identify them. While this has some relevance to real life visual tasks, it has the drawback that we have little knowledge of the processes that underlie the recognition of letters. A more general measure is the Landoldt C chart, which employs a test pattern consisting of a black ring with a section missing, like a letter 'C'. The ring can be shown in various orientations and the observer's task is to identify the location of the gap. As the 'C' is made progressively smaller, there comes a point at which performance in detecting the gap is no better than chance, and this is the limit of acuity. In general, visual acuity is expressed in terms of the minimum resolvable visual angle, for which the normal standard is a gap subtending 1 min (1 minute of arc or 1/60th of a degree). Acuity is stated as a fraction, relating a standard testing distance (6 metres, or 20 feet) to the distance at which a gap would subtend 1 min (minute). Thus an acuity of 6/6 (the same as 20/20) means that performance is normal, whereas 6/3 means that a gap could be resolved at 6 metres which would subtend 1 min at 3 metres, i.e. a better than normal acuity. Similarly, 6/18 means that the minimum gap that can be seen subtends 3 min at 6 metres, and performance is a third of normal. While these sorts of test have considerable practical utility, they have a number of drawbacks for scientific research on perception. Even if they are

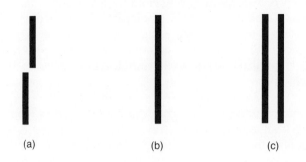

(a)   (b)   (c)

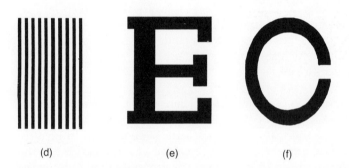

(d)   (e)   (f)

Figure 3.9 Examples of patterns used to test visual acuity. In each case the test is based on establishing the limiting conditions for discriminating a designated feature. (a) Vernier acuity. Detection of misalignment between the two line segments. This is commonly found to be very much better than would be expected from other acuity measures. (b) Detection of the presence of a single line. This depends upon the length of the line, and its orientation. (c) Two-line discrimination. The minimum separation is measured at which two lines are seen, rather than one. (d) Grating acuity. The minimum contrast at which a grating with a given spacing between the lines can be discriminated from a uniform grey field. (e) Snellen letter and (f) Landoldt 'C', as commonly used for ophthalmic assessments. The Snellen letters are read from a chart on which they appear with decreasing size. The Landoldt 'C' is shown in different orientations, with gaps of decreasing size, until a point is reached where it cannot be discriminated from a circle with a continuous circumference.

carried out under carefully controlled conditions of illumination, the fact remains that both Snellen letters and Landoldt C's are complex patterns, from which it is not easy to generalise.

One approach to specifying visual performance in the most general terms derives from measurements of acuity for grating patterns. A grating consists of a number of light and dark lines with a particular width and orientation. Grating acuity is assessed by adjusting the contrast between the light and dark lines until the grating can just be discriminated from an unpatterned grey field. If the boundary between the light and dark lines is sharp and they are equally wide, then the grating is said to have a square-wave profile. This can be seen in Figure 3.10, which shows a graph of luminance in a square-wave grating across the width of the field. A different luminance profile is produced if the change from light to dark is a gradual one. An example of this is the sine wave grating, in which luminance varies across the test field according to a sine function (see Figure 3.10). A cosine grating would have a similar profile, but shifted so

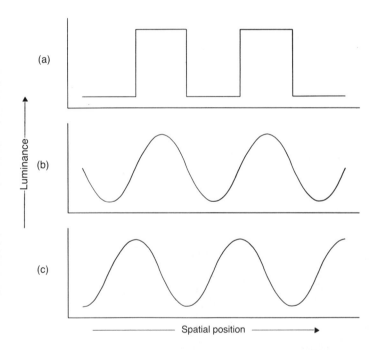

Figure 3.10 Illustration of the way in which luminance varies with spatial position for various spatial wave-forms. In (a), a square wave, there are sharp transitions from light to dark, forming a series of bars with sharp edges. In (b) a sine wave and (c) a cosine wave, the transitions are more gradual. Sine waves differ from cosine waves only in the location of the maxima and minima, i.e., in phase. A wave-form is fully described by its frequency (the number of oscillations in a given interval), its amplitude (the size of the oscillations), and its phase. Any complex wave-form can be created from a combination of sine waves with appropriate amplitudes, phases and frequencies.

Figure 3.11 A square wave and sine wave grating. Note the gradual variation in brightness of the sine wave at the transition from light to dark.

that the dark lines coincide with the middle luminance of a sine wave grating. In this case the difference is in the phase of the gratings, that is, in the relative location of the maxima and minima in luminance. Phase is expressed in terms of angles, and a cosine grating is 90 degrees out of phase with a sine wave one. The importance of sine wave gratings lies in their use as general tests of the performance of an optical system. To understand the nature and significance of this work, it is necessary to describe some basic concepts in the specification of signals, whether optical, electronic or acoustic.

In the early nineteenth century, the French mathematician Jean Fourier proposed the theorem that any complex change in the state of a system could be described in terms of the combination of simple sine wave oscillations of different frequency and amplitude. Thus a pure tone is a single frequency of vibration, whose amplitude varies sinusoidally over time. Any complex sound can be described in terms of a combination of pure tones, with suitably chosen frequencies and amplitudes. This provides a very powerful means of specifying sounds, and of testing the response to them by physical systems. By testing the response with a range of pure tones, it is possible to predict performance with any arbitrary sound that might occur. This can be applied, for example, to the specification of performance in loud-speaker systems. In order to apply these concepts to vision, it is necessary to think in terms of spatial rather than temporal frequencies. Visual stimuli have the property of being extended over space, and intensity can vary in this dimension also. Thus a static pattern which changes from light to dark according to a sine wave function constitutes a spatial, rather than temporal, frequency (Figure 3.11).

Any optical system can be tested with a range of such spatial frequencies in order to find out how well they are transmitted. The relevant measure is the contrast of the test pattern emerging from the optical system, compared to that which is fed in. Loss of contrast shows up as a reduction in the difference between the light and dark areas. The overall optical performance is expressed as a modulation transfer function (MTF), which is the relationship between contrast transmission and spatial frequency. Direct measurements of the MTF for the human eye might be made by measuring the contrast of gratings projected onto the retinal surface, for example with an ophthalmoscope and a photodetector. More simply, an observer can be asked to report when the contrast of a sine-wave grating with a certain spatial frequency is sufficient for it to be just visible. In this case the measurement is of the MTF of the observer, treated as a single system, and it incorporates the effects of neural as well as optical processes. Such an MTF is called a contrast sensitivity function (CSF), and an example is shown in Figure 3.12.

The human CSF clearly shows a differential response to different spatial frequencies. For example, there is a rapid drop in response above about 12

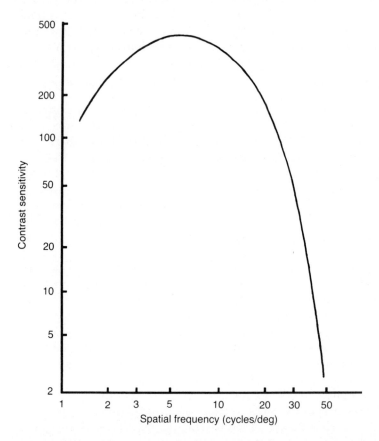

Figure 3.12 A typical human contrast sensitivity function. Contrast is measured by the ratio of the difference between the luminances of lightest and darkest parts of the grating, divided by their sum. Contrast sensitivity is the reciprocal of the contrast at which a grating of a given spatial frequency is just discriminable from a uniform grey field. Peak sensitivity occurs at around 5 cycles/deg. (After Barlow and Mollon, 1982)

cycles per degree, and a more gradual decline below about 6 cycles per degree. The high frequency cut-off is probably due to the optical characteristics of the eye, and is related to the diameter of the pupil. It is in fact very close to the ideal performance of an optical system with the dimensions of the eye. The low frequency cut-off is more influenced by signal processing later in the visual system. Note that the scale of spatial frequency is logarithmic, which can give a somewhat misleading impression of the shape of the function. The CSF is an MTF for gratings at threshold contrast, and other techniques can be used to find MTF's for supra-threshold gratings, although this is more difficult. The application of Fourier analysis, and the use of visual stimuli in the form of sinusoidal gratings with a defined spatial frequency, has led to the development of theories regarding the processing of visual information by the brain.

VISUAL NEUROPHYSIOLOGY

Vision, like all other aspects of experience and behaviour, is mediated by activity in the brain. It also depends upon activity in highly specialised cells in the sense organs called receptors. A full understanding of vision will include an appreciation of the neurophysiological processes that are initiated by the activity of light on receptors in the eye. These involve the modification of light energy into nerve impulses and their transmission to the areas at the back of the brain where they are analysed. Tremendous advances have recently been made in our knowledge about the neural processes underlying vision, and many of these will be touched upon in the following sections.

Psychology has constantly tried to link observable function (behaviour) with underlying structure (anatomy, physiology, genetics etc.), and these attempts are often considered to have been most successful in the area of perception. Some visual phenomena can be reduced to known neurophysiological processes. Reductionism, describing phenomena at one level in terms of concepts at a simpler level, has been one of the main motivations for scientific enquiry generally. It is certainly a powerful force in visual science. Paradoxically, we do not know a great deal about the neurophysiology of human vision, but we do know a lot about that in some of our nearest biological neighbours. Much of the material described below is based upon experiments on other species, particularly monkeys. We assume that equivalent processes occur in the human visual system because of the many biological similarities that exist: the receptors in the eyes, the pathways from the eyes to the brain, and the anatomy of the visual areas of the brain are all strikingly similar. Therefore, it does seem justified to relate the wealth of perceptual data on humans to the neurophysiological evidence from other species. In this way it is possible to interpret visual phenomena in terms of the brain events that might give rise to them. First, it is necessary to outline the principal features of the visual system.

Receptors

All sensory systems function by transducing some type of environmental energy into a form that can be analysed by the cells in the central nervous system (CNS). The general structure of nerve cells (neurons) is shown schematically in Figure 3.13. Neurons communicate electro-chemically: they transmit signals along the nerve fibres in pulses of fixed amplitude,

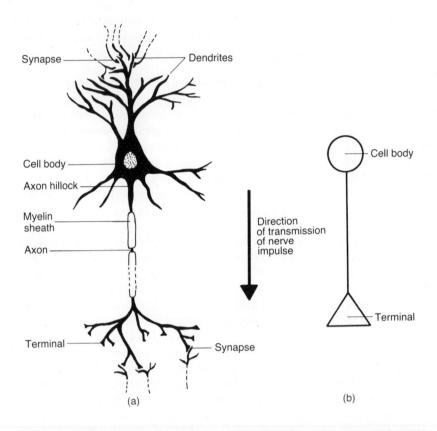

Figure 3.13 The main structures in a typical nerve cell. (a) The dendrites receive inputs, transmitted chemically across the synapses, from many other nerve cells; inputs can be excitatory and inhibitory. If the net activity passes some threshold then an action potential or nerve impulse is initiated in the axon hillock and it is transmitted along the axon to the terminals of the neuron, thereby influencing other neurons. The transmission of the action potential along the axon is facilitated by the myelin sheath, which acts as an insulator. (b) A schematic nerve cell of the type that will be used to indicate the direction of neural transmission in some of the following illustrations. (After Kandel and Schwartz, 1985)

hence the term nerve impulse. Neurons do not make direct contacts with one another, and the activity of one neuron influences others chemically across synapses via neurotransmitters. Receptors, like other nerve cells, have a resting potential difference between the inside and outside of the cell. Processes in the membrane surrounding the nerve cell retain negatively charged molecules (negative ions) within the cell so that the interior is negatively charged (by about 70 millivolts) with respect to the extracellular ions.

The transduction process usually involves a modification of the potential, so that the potential difference is reduced; this is called depolaris- ation. These electrical changes are graded, i.e., they will vary with the intensity of the environmental energy stimulating the receptor. The process of vision is initiated by light falling on specialised receptors in the retina (Figure 3.14). The retinal receptors contain light-sensitive pigments that are modified chemically by absorbing light. However, unlike other receptors they hyperpolarise when light falls on them: the potential differ- ence between the inside and outside of the receptor cells increases. Before describing the physiological processes at the retinal level, a little more should be said about the structure of the retina itself.

The retina is an outgrowth of the CNS and the receptors are directed towards the back of the eye. Therefore, before the light strikes the receptors it passes through the various neural structures in the retina and also the blood vessels that supply them. There are two types of receptor in the human retina, and they are called rods and cones because of their appear- ance under the microscope; rods have a cylindrical outer segment (which contains the photosensitive pigment molecules) and cones have tapered outer segments. The retina is estimated to consist of about 130 million receptors, the vast majority (over 120 million) of which are rods with about 6 million cones. The distributions of the rods and cones differ in a system- atic way. The cones are concentrated in and around a central region of the retina, where there is a shallow depression called the fovea. There are decreasing numbers of cones as the distance from the fovea increases, and there are none in the peripheral regions of the retina (Figure 3.15).

One part of each eye is devoid of any receptors, and it is called the blind spot (or optic disc). It is located about 17 deg towards the nasal side of each fovea, and it is the exit pathway of the nerves from the retina (the optic nerve), as well as the region where the arteries enter and veins leave the eye. We are usually unaware of this small area of blindness in each eye, because it corresponds to different parts of the visual field of each eye. Even when we use one eye alone we generally overlook this blind spot, and it is only when we employ some specific procedure, like following the instructions to observe Figure 3.16 that we can locate it.

The light-absorbing pigment molecules in the receptors are distributed in the photosensitive membrane in their outer segments (Figure 3.17). In rods the photosensitive membrane consists of separate discs stacked on top of one another, rather like a pile of coins. The photosensitive membrane in cones has a different structure: it consists of a single surface folded successively over on itself. All rods contain the same visual pigment, which is a complex protein molecule called rhodopsin. There are three different

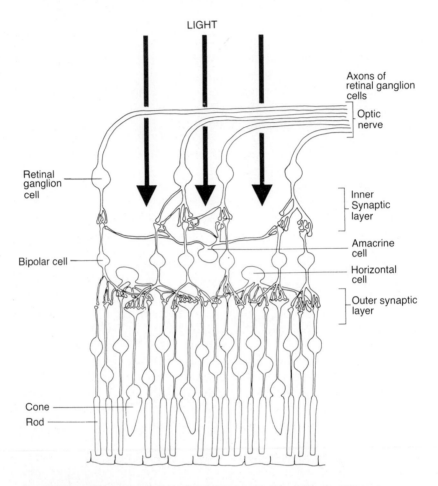

Figure 3.14 The neural structure of the retina. Light passes through the neural layers before striking the receptors (rods and cones) which contain the photosensitive pigments. The vertical organisation of the retina is from receptor to bipolar cell to retinal ganglion cell. The horizontal organisation is mediated by horizontal cells at the receptor-bipolar (outer) synaptic layer and by the amacrine cells at the bipolar-retinal ganglion cell (inner) synaptic layer. (After Cornsweet, 1970)

types of cones each with a different light-sensitive pigment. The cone pigments can absorb light throughout the visible spectrum, but one type is most sensitive to low wavelengths of light (around 430 nm), another to the middle region of the spectrum (around 530 nm), and the third to slightly longer wavelengths (around 560 nm).

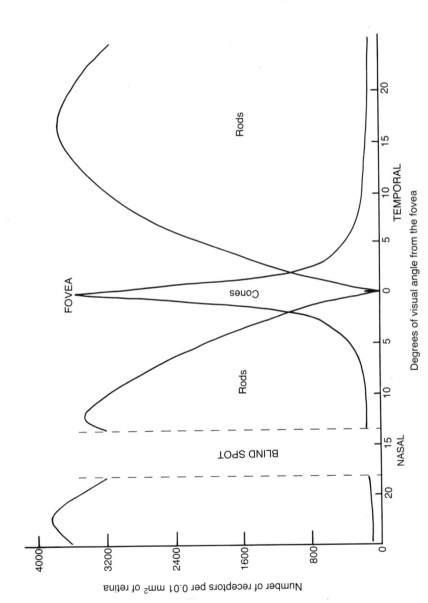

Figure 3.15 Distribution of rods and cones over a horizontal region of the retina passing through the fovea and blind spot.

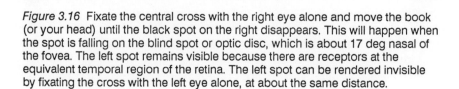

Figure 3.16 Fixate the central cross with the right eye alone and move the book (or your head) until the black spot on the right disappears. This will happen when the spot is falling on the blind spot or optic disc, which is about 17 deg nasal of the fovea. The left spot remains visible because there are receptors at the equivalent temporal region of the retina. The left spot can be rendered invisible by fixating the cross with the left eye alone, at about the same distance.

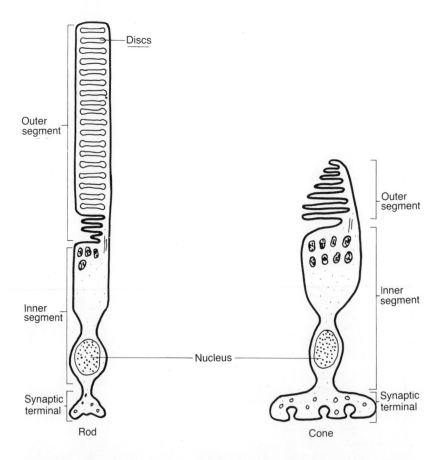

Figure 3.17 Detailed structure of rod and cone receptors. The light-sensitive pigments are located in the outer segments – stacked discs for rods and a single folded surface for cones. The inner segment is concerned with the metabolic functions of the cells. (After Kandel and Schwartz, 1985)

Duplicity theory

With all these differences in mind, it is not surprising that the rods and cones operate under different conditions of light stimulation. The rods are more sensitive than the cones and respond in twilight or moonlight; rods become overloaded in daylight and are unable to function. The cones require the intense illumination of daylight to function. This difference in sensitivity is indicated in Figure 3.18. The rods are so sensitive that an individual rod can register the absorption of a single photon of light, but the activity of a single rod does not provide an impression of light. Under

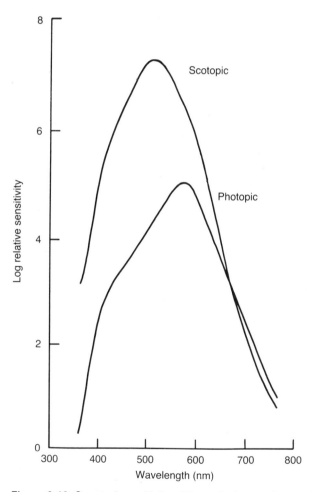

Figure 3.18 Spectral sensitivity of the rods (scotopic curve) and cones (photopic curve). The rods can detect light at lower intensities than the cones, and their peak sensitivity is for lower wavelengths of light. (After Kaufman, 1974)

ideal conditions a human observer can detect a light when less than 10 photons are absorbed. The increased sensitivity of rods is combined with a slow response to light; it is estimated that a rod receptor takes about 0.3 s (seconds) to signal the absorption of a photon. The cones require more light to function, but their response is about four times faster than rods. There is, therefore, a trade-off between sensitivity and response time in rods and cones. Figure 3.18 also illustrates another aspect of rod and cone function: in dim light rods respond to the whole visible spectrum but they are most sensitive to wavelengths around 500 nm; the spectral sensitivity under bright conditions is somewhat different, showing a peak at around 555 nm. This could be the basis for some differences in our sensitivities to colours under dim or bright light conditions. Bluish-green objects appear to be brighter in dim light than they do in daylight, and conversely greenish-yellow objects appear brighter in daylight than under dim conditions. This is called the Purkinje shift, after the physiologist who first described it in 1825. We are most sensitive to light of around 500 nm in low illumination (reflecting the function of rods) and around 555 nm in bright conditions (reflecting cone function).

Another feature of this distinction is the time taken for the receptors to recover from intense light adaptation. When we have been exposed to bright daylight and then enter a dark environment (like a cinema) we are initially unable to distinguish any detail, but gradually our sensitivity improves until after about 30 min we can see quite well. It is referred to as dark adaptation; it can be measured accurately by adapting the observer to bright light for a few minutes, then placing them in darkness and measuring the detection threshold for light at regular intervals. The resulting dark adaptation curve (Figure 3.19) has two components, the initial phase shows the recovery of the cones and the final phase the slower recovery of the rods. If the detection threshold is measured with a small red spot presented to the fovea then only the initial component will be found, because the spot would stimulate cones alone. Some individuals do not have any cones in the retina, and their dark adaptation curves would have the second phase alone.

Any photoreceptor can only signal the absorption of photons of light. The signals delivered will depend upon the wavelength of the light as well as its intensity, because of the differences in spectral sensitivity described above. Therefore, the same signal can result from a wide range of combinations between intensity and wavelength, and no photoreceptor can distinguish between these two dimensions. This is referred to as the principle of univariance. This principle is important when discussing differences in wavelength sensitivity between rods and cones because it applies to both of them. All rods contain the same visual pigment and so they could not discriminate on the basis of wavelength. The same is true for any given type of cone: it can only respond in one dimension, by

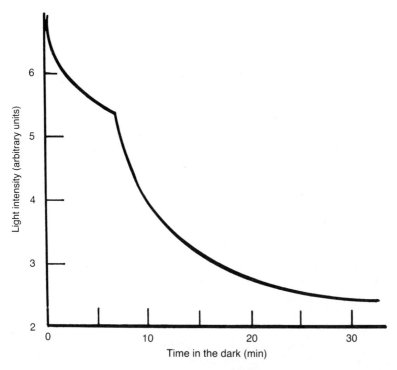

Figure 3.19 Dark adaptation or the recovery from light adaptation. The curve represents the increasing sensitivity (or decreasing thresholds) for light detection with time in the dark. The initial rapid phase reflects the recovery of the cones and the slower phase that of the rods. An asymptote is reached after about 30 min in darkness.

hyperpolarising by some amount. However, there are three different types of cone, and their combined activities can mediate wavelength discrimination or colour vision. It is now considered that colour vision is based upon signals from the three cone types being combined at subsequent neural stages. This is demonstrated with regard to our ability to see colours in different regions of the visual field. Colour vision is best in and around the fovea. However, in the peripheral retina, where there are rods but no cones, we are all colour blind (Figure 3.20).

The differences in function described above are attributable to the characteristics of rods and cones, and this is referred to as duplicity theory. However, we should be cautious of treating the rods and cones alone as the bases for the effects described; the effects are the consequence of activity occurring throughout the visual system, not just at the initial stages. The activity of the rods and cones defines the limiting light conditions under

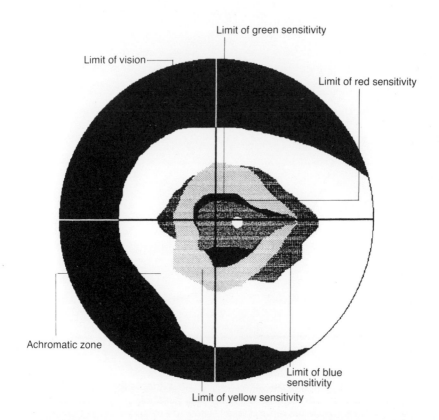

Limit of green sensitivity

Limit of vision

Limit of red sensitivity

Achromatic zone

Limit of blue sensitivity

Limit of yellow sensitivity

Figure 3.20 Colour regions of the right eye. Colour sensitivity can be determined by means of an instrument called a perimeter, which can present coloured spots of light to peripheral regions of the retina. All colours can be detected in the central area of the retina. The areas for red and green sensitivity are similar but smaller than are those for blue and yellow.

which vision is possible. Beyond these the manner in which neural information is processed will be of importance, and therefore it is necessary to examine the neural interactions within the retina and the pathways to the brain.

Retinal structure

The retina is a complex neural structure, as was evident from Figure 3.14. An even more simplified and schematic diagram of its structure is shown in Figure 3.21. It can be thought of as having both a vertical and a horizontal organisation: the vertical organisation corresponds to the connections

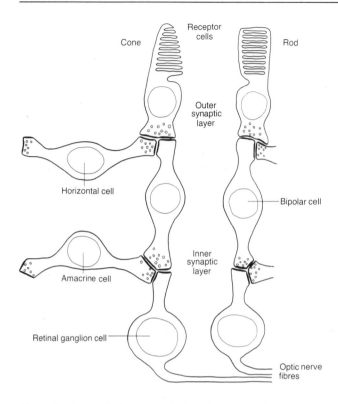

Figure 3.21 Detailed representation of the neural structures in the retina. At the outer synaptic layer the receptors can influence the activity of the bipolar and horizontal cells, and the horizontal cells can affect the receptor and bipolar cells. At the inner synaptic layer the bipolar cells can influence the activity of both the retinal ganglion and amacrine cells, and the amacrine cells can in turn affect the bipolar and retinal ganglion cells. (After Werblin, 1976)

leading to the brain, and these have horizontal (or lateral) connections between them. Receptors make synaptic connections with bipolar cells, which in turn make synaptic contact with retinal ganglion cells. The ganglion cells are much larger than receptors or bipolar cells; their cell bodies are in the retina, but their axons (or nerve fibres) leave the retina to form the optic nerve. There are about 1 million axons in each optic nerve, so an enormous neural convergence has taken place in the retina – from about 130 million receptors to 1 million ganglion cells. This convergence is not evenly distributed over the retina, and is least for the foveal region. Here individual cones often synapse with a single bipolar cell, which synapses with a single ganglion cell. Conversely, the convergence is much greater than average in the peripheral retina. The horizontal or lateral connections occur at the first and second synaptic layers. At the first

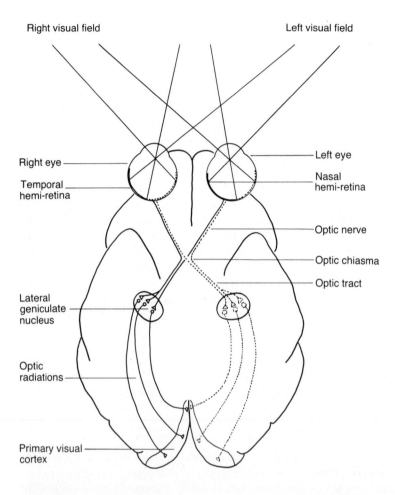

Right visual field

Left visual field

Right eye

Temporal hemi-retina

Left eye

Nasal hemi-retina

Optic nerve

Optic chiasma

Optic tract

Lateral geniculate nucleus

Optic radiations

Primary visual cortex

Figure 3.22 Pathways from the eyes to the visual cortex, viewed from below. The axons of the retinal ganglion cells form the optic nerves which pass under the frontal lobes of the brain. Fibres from the nasal halves of each retina cross over to the opposite hemisphere, while those from the temporal halves project to the hemisphere on the same side. This partial decussation occurs at the optic chiasma, and it results in signals from the same regions of the visual field projecting to the same hemispheres. The optic tracts consist of fibres from both eyes, and the axons terminate in a large subcortical body called the lateral geniculate nucleus (LGN). The cells from the LGN project to the primary visual cortex, also called V1.

synaptic layer, between receptors and bipolar cells, there are horizontal cells, and at the second layer, between bipolar and retinal ganglion cells, there are amacrine cells.

Visual pathways

The axons of the retinal ganglion cells leave the eye forming the optic nerve. This nerve is situated at the base of the brain, and the two optic nerves travel towards one another and appear to meet at the optic chiasma (see Figure 3.22); it was so called by the early anatomists because it resembled the shape of the Greek letter *chi*. The axons do not in fact meet, but they project to different cerebral hemispheres according to the area of the retina from which they originate: axons from the temporal side of each retina (the left half-retina for the left eye and the right half-retina for the right eye) project to the ipsilateral hemisphere (on the same side), and the axons from the nasal halves of the retinae cross over and project to the contralateral hemisphere. There is a narrow vertical strip in the centre of both retinae, subtending about 1 deg, that projects to both hemispheres. Animals that have lateral rather than frontal eyes, with little or no binocular overlap of their two visual fields, have almost complete crossover at the optic chiasma. The partial crossover of fibres in humans results in the transmission of signals from equivalent parts of the visual field to the same hemispheres. Thus, the right half of the visual field projects to the left halves of the retinae, and they in turn send neural signals to the left hemisphere.

The axons from the retinal ganglion cells continue beyond the optic chiasma as the optic tract, and they form synaptic connections in the thalamus, in a structure called the lateral geniculate nucleus (LGN). The LGN consists of six concentric layers, rather like an onion. The fibres from the contralateral eye project to layers 1, 4 and 6, and those from the ipsilateral eye to layers 2, 3 and 5 (see Figure 3.23). The cell bodies in layers 1 and 2 are larger than those in layers 3 to 6; the former are called magnocellular layers and the latter parvocellular layers.

Axons from the LGN cells project to the visual cortex, which is situated at the back of the brain. The visual cortex also has a vertical and a horizontal cellular organisation (Figure 3.24). Vertically (perpendicular to the cortical surface) it can be divided into six layers, on the basis of the cell types that can be distinguished microscopically. The horizontal organisation is in terms of the lateral fibre connections.

Neural activity in the retina

Having outlined the structure of the retina and the pathways to the brain, we can examine the activities of these cells. The initial stages of light

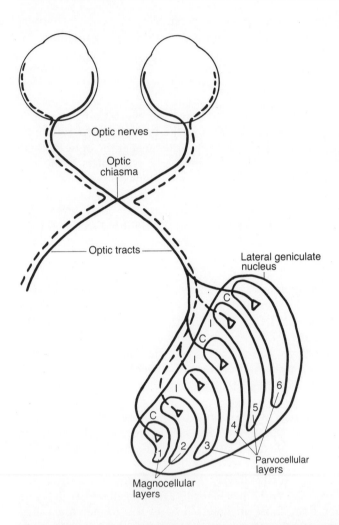

Figure 3.23 The lateral geniculate nucleus (LGN) consists of six layers. The cell bodies in layers 1 and 2 are larger than those in layers 3–6; the former are called magnocellular and the latter parvocellular layers. Projections from the contra-lateral (C) eye synapse in layers 1, 4 and 6, and those from the ipsilateral (I) eye synapse in layers 2, 3 and 5. (After Kandel and Schwartz, 1985)

absorption in the receptors results in hyperpolarisation. The measurement of such small graded electrical changes is possible by the use of minute pipettes (micropipettes) in contact with the surface of the cells or inserted into the cells themselves. The amount of hyperpolarisation that occurs is proportional to the light energy absorbed. The receptors form synaptic

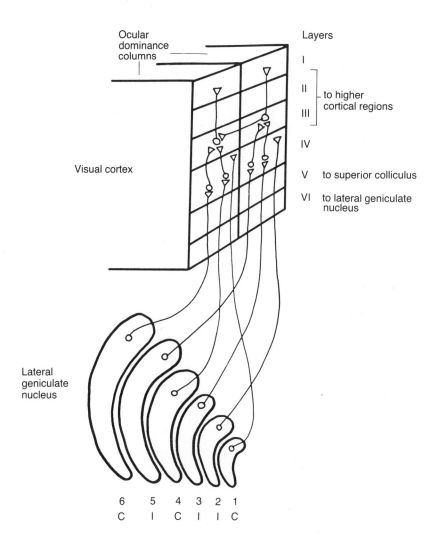

Figure 3.24 Projections from the LGN to the primary visual cortex (V1). All cells project to layer IV of V1; those from the magnocellular layers project to higher locations in layer IV. Fibres from the ipsi- and contralateral layers of LGN project initially to adjacent regions of V1, maintaining a distinction based on the eye stimulated. There are also lateral connections between these adjacent regions. V1 has six distinct layers. Incoming fibres to layer IV project upwards to layers III, II and I, and are concerned with analysing the visual signals. Layers V and VI send signals back to subcortical structures, like to LGN from layer VI. (After Kandel and Schwartz, 1985)

connections with bipolar cells and horizontal cells. The electrical activity of the bipolar cells depends on the source of stimulation: direct influence from the receptor cell results in hyperpolarisation, whereas indirect influence from horizontal cells produces depolarisation. The horizontal cells in synaptic contact with receptors also hyperpolarise. All these electrical events are graded, that is, they vary on a continuous scale according to the intensity of stimulation.

Quite a different electrical response can be recorded from the amacrine and retinal ganglion cells: they produce action potentials (or nerve impulses) which can be measured extra-cellularly with micro-electrodes. Action potentials are all-or-none electro-chemical events that have a fixed amplitude; they are the rapid depolarisations that occur along the axons of nerves. Much more is known about the activity of retinal ganglion cells (and subsequent stages in the visual pathway) because extra-cellular recording has been technically possible for longer than has intra-cellular recording. Indeed, the activity of retinal ganglion cells can be measured without entering the retina – by recording from single axons in the optic nerve or optic tract. This technique has generally been applied to experimental animals like cats and monkeys, and it has furnished us with important information concerning the ways in which patterns of light are coded in the visual system.

Prior to the use of micro-electrode recording it was thought that the cells in the visual pathway were excited simply by the presence of light. Now it is known that it is the pattern of light that is of importance, not solely its presence. This is evident at the retinal ganglion cell level. When experiments were performed to determine the adequate or appropriate stimulus for these cells it was found that they did not fire (produce nerve impulses) when the whole eye was stimulated by diffuse light. Firstly, light had to be presented to a particular part of the retina, and secondly it had to have specific dimensions. Some retinal ganglion cells could be excited by small spots of light, but they ceased firing when the spot was increased in size (Figure 3.25). These are called on-centre cells, as they are characterised by excitation when the centre is stimulated by light and by inhibition when the annular surround is also stimulated. Retinal ganglion cells, like other neurons, have a resting discharge rate, i.e., they continue to produce nerve impulses at irregular intervals in the absence of light. Neural inhibition can be demonstrated by stimulating the surround alone with light, as the resting discharge rate then declines. Other retinal ganglion cells display the opposite pattern of activity: they are excited by the presence of light in the annular surround and inhibited by its presence in the centre. These are called off-centre cells.

The activity of each retinal ganglion cell can be influenced by a particular pattern of light falling on the appropriate part of the retina. This region is called the receptive field for that cell. All retinal ganglion cells have

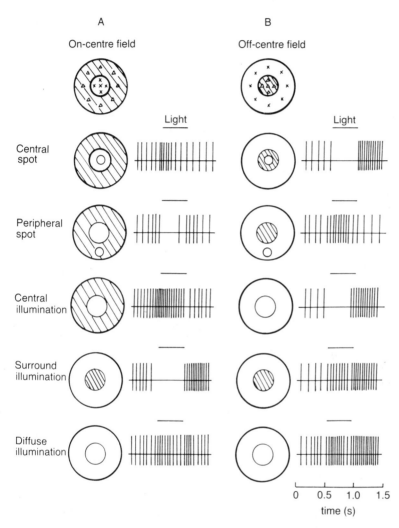

Figure 3.25 Responses of on-and off-centre retinal ganglion cells to a variety of light patterns falling on their receptive fields. The cross symbols in the upper figures refer to excitatory influences and the triangles signify inhibition.

concentric receptive fields. That is, central and surrounding regions that are antagonistic in their function. Thus, the processes of neural excitation and inhibition are vital in determining the ways in which cells in the visual system respond to the patterns of light falling on the retina. The retinal ganglion cells respond to changes in the pattern of illumination, rather than to steady states of uniform illumination. These changes can be spatial and temporal. So far we have described the spatial characteristics – the centre–surround receptive fields, but there are differences in the responses of retinal ganglion cells to the duration of stimulation. Prolonged stimulation (for a few seconds) of some ganglion cells results in an initial reduction of the firing rate, levelling off to a steady rate. These are called X (or sustained) cells because they continue to discharge at above their resting rate with prolonged stimulation. Others respond only to the onset or cessation of stimulation, and then revert rapidly to the resting discharge rate even if stimulation is continued; these are Y (or transient) cells. The X cells occur predominantly in and around the fovea, where visual acuity is best, and they have smaller receptive fields than the Y cells, which are distributed more evenly throughout the retina.

The receptive fields of retinal ganglion cells are antagonistic with the centre stimulated by the opposite characteristics to the surround. Some code luminance differences between centre and surround whereas others code wavelength differences. For example, some are excited when long wavelength light (referred to here as red for convenience) falls on the centre and inhibited when the complementary (green) falls on the surround. All excitatory and inhibitory combinations of these colour opponent cells have been found with pairings between long and medium (red–green) and short and medium-long (blue–yellow) wavelengths. It has recently been discovered that the sizes of the retinal ganglion cells are related to colour opponency: only small ganglion cells have this property, whereas large ganglion cells respond on the basis of luminance differences alone, and not colour differences.

The excitatory and inhibitory interconnections in the retina are the basis for the receptive field properties of the retinal ganglion cells. The antagonistic interaction between centre and surround also determines the type of stimulus that will produce a response in these cells. As we have seen, the maximum response is elicited by a small white or dark spot, but large responses will also be produced by the grating stimuli described in the previous section. That is, the light bar of a grating will produce a large response if its projected width on the retina corresponds to the dimensions of the on-centre receptive field; conversely, a dark bar of the grating would produce a large response in an off-centre retinal ganglion cell with a receptive field of the appropriate dimensions.

Contrast phenomena

The lateral inhibitory interactions within the retina act to increase the differences between neural signals for edges or boundaries in the stimulus. Therefore, the neural coding of light falling on the retina depends on changes in its spatial distribution over time; these changes are enhanced by the neural machinery within the retina. Indeed, the enhancement is such that it can lead to the visibility of patterns that are not present physically in the stimulus. Mach bands are one phenomenon of this type; they are named after the physicist Ernst Mach who described them in the nineteenth century (Figure 3.26). The areas of constant luminance on the left and right are separated by a ramp of increasing luminance: if a light meter was passed horizontally across the pattern it would register a constant level then a gradual increase followed by another constant (but higher) level of luminance. This does not correspond with what is seen in the pattern, as there appears to be a dark vertical band on the left side of the ramp and a light band on the right, which are the Mach bands.

Shortly after Mach had described his phenomenon (in 1865), a related effect was reported by Hermann when looking at a grid of black squares on a white background (Figure 3.27): the background does not appear uniformly white, but dark grey dots are apparent at all the intersections apart from the one fixated. The reverse occurs with white squares on a black

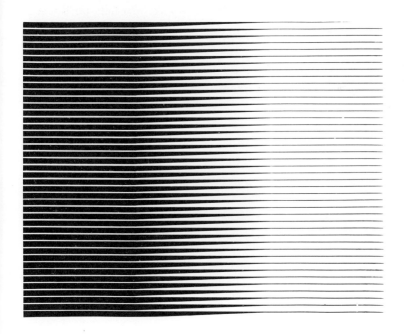

Figure 3.26 Mach bands refer to the light and dark bands that can be seen flanking the boundaries between the luminance ramp. A dark band is visible on the darker side of the ramp and a light band on the lighter side, despite the absence of such differences in the pattern when measured with a light meter.

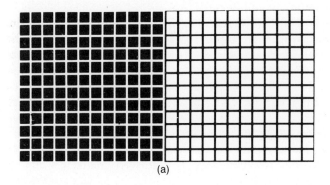

(a)

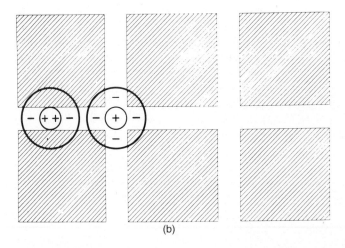

(b)

Figure 3.27 Hermann–Hering grid. (a) Dark grey dots appear at the white intersections on the left and light dots are visible at the black intersections on the right. Note that these might not be apparent at the intersection you fixate upon. (b) The interpretation of the Hermann grid effect in terms of on-centre receptive fields. The surround inhibition is greater at the intersections of the white lines than between the squares, because more of the surround is exposed to light. A similar interpretation of the Hering grid can be given in terms of off-centre cells.

background, as was reported by Hering in 1878. These are now referred to as the Hermann–Hering grids, and they have been related to the properties of concentric receptive fields in the retina. Consider two equivalent on-centre receptive fields stimulated by different parts of the white background in a Hermann grid (see Figure 3.27). The one that falls between the intersections would be inhibited by a smaller white area surrounding it than will the one falling at an intersection.

The dimensions of concentric receptive fields are smallest in the retinal ganglion cells receiving their input from the central fovea, and they increase in size with increasing distance from the fovea. This is probably the reason why the Hermann–Hering dots are not visible at the fixated intersection: both the centre and surround would fall between the squares and within the intersections, so that there would be no differential response from them, and no illusory dots. If the separations are made sufficiently small then the dots can be seen at the fixated intersections. In fact, measuring the limiting dimensions of grids that yield the illusory dots has been used to estimate the sizes of receptive fields at different eccentricities in human vision.

Mach bands and Hermann–Hering grids can be encompassed within a wider class of phenomena, namely simultaneous contrast effects. These generally refer to the apparent brightness or colour of one region in a pattern when it is surrounded by another having a different brightness or colour. For example, in Figure 3.28 the central grey squares all reflect the same amount of light, i.e., they have the same physical luminance, but there is a difference in their brightnesses. This difference in brightness (a perceptual dimension) where there is no difference in luminance (a physical dimension) is due to the surrounding regions in each case. When the surround is lighter than the central grey square it appears darker than when the surround is darker than it. If the surrounds were coloured then the central grey areas would also appear slightly coloured, but in the complementary colour of the surround. For instance, if the surround was red then the physically grey centre would appear greenish; if it was blue then the centre would appear yellowish. These effects have often been manipulated systematically in art, particularly in the Pointilliste paintings of Georges Seurat.

Neural activity in Lateral Geniculate Nucleus

This distinction between large and small retinal ganglion cells mentioned above is amplified in the projection to the LGN (refer back to Figure 3.23): the small colour-opponent retinal ganglion cells project to the parvocellular region (layers 3–6) and the large cells project to the magnocellular region (layers 1 and 2). Therefore the large and small cells that were intermingled in the optic tract project to separate sites in the LGN. Moreover, these separate pathways (referred to as the parvo and magno systems) display other functional differences in addition to wavelength sensitivity: parvo cells respond (a) more slowly (b) to higher spatial frequencies and (c) with less sensitivity to luminance contrast than magno cells. These are also differences that have been used to define X and

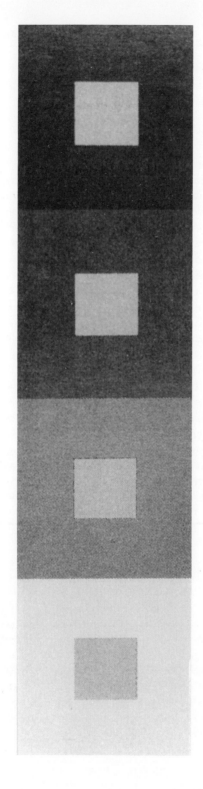

Figure 3.28 Simultaneous brightness contrast. The central squares are all the same luminance, but their brightnesses are influenced by the area surrounding them. If the surround is darker then the grey square looks brighter, and vice versa.

Y cells, and there presently remains some confusion over whether the physiological distinctions between parvo and magno might be the same as those between X and Y cells.

Neural activity in visual cortex

The axons from the LGN project to visual area 1 (V1) of the visual cortex, and enter it in layer IV (refer back to Figure 3.24). Again the distinction between the parvo and magno projections is preserved, with the parvo fibres terminating in the lower and the magno in the upper half of layer IV. The cells form synaptic connections with neurons projecting vertically to upper layers of V1. In addition to separate regions in layers I–III receiving input from parvo and magno systems there is another which receives input from both. The regions are shown up by specific staining procedures as oval blobs separated from one another, and micro-electrode recordings show that cells in these regions have quite different receptive field properties. In fact, almost all the cells in the visual cortex have receptive field character- istics that differ from the concentric organisation found at earlier stages in the visual system. The neurons in the blobs receive inputs from both the parvo and magno systems: they can be excited by coloured or white light falling on the retina, but they are not as sensitive to its precise position on the retina. The cells in the interblob regions receive inputs from the parvo system: they are excited by edges or bars in a particular orientation, but are relatively insensitive to wavelength. That is, a cell will respond to a line at a specific orientation no matter what its wavelength or intensity, but it will not respond to lines that are inclined away from the preferred orientation (Figure 3.29). The cells in layer IV that receive their inputs from the magno pathway are excited by lines or edges in a specific orientation, particularly if they are moving; they are not selective for wavelength. For example, a given cell might respond most strongly when a horizontal line moved vertically.

These orientation-selective neurons were, until recently, considered to make up the majority of cells in the visual cortex. Indeed, such was the interest elicited after their discovery, by David Hubel and Torsten Wiesel in 1959, that they became called feature detectors. This was because the cortical neurons were selectively tuned to extract certain features contained in the pattern of retinal stimulation – in this case orientation. Direction of edge motion is another feature extracted. The orientation-selective neurons have a highly ordered organisation over V1, both perpendicular to the cortical surface and parallel to it, as is shown in Figure 3.30. If a micro- electrode is inserted at right angles to the surface and all orientation cells encountered are recorded, then they will have the same preferred orientation, say 45 deg. This has been called a cortical column. An equivalent insertion in the neighbouring column will record a slightly

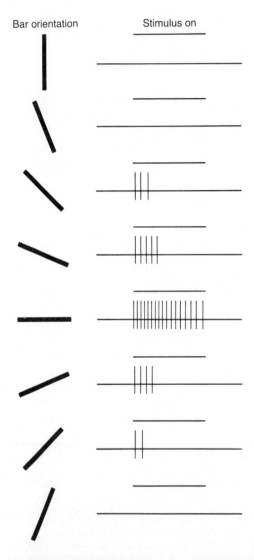

Figure 3.29 Receptive field properties of a cortical orientation detector. The orientation at which a bar is presented to a specific part of the retina is shown on the left. On the right the upper horizontal lines indicate when the stimulus (a black bar on a light background) is presented, and the vertical lines denote nerve impulses. For this cortical cell the firing rate is highest for a horizontal bar, and it declines sharply when the orientation differs from horizontal, not responding at all for bars at right angles to the preferred orientation. Neighbouring cells respond most strongly to different orientations, so that all orientations are represented for all retinal regions. (After Kandel and Schwartz, 1985)

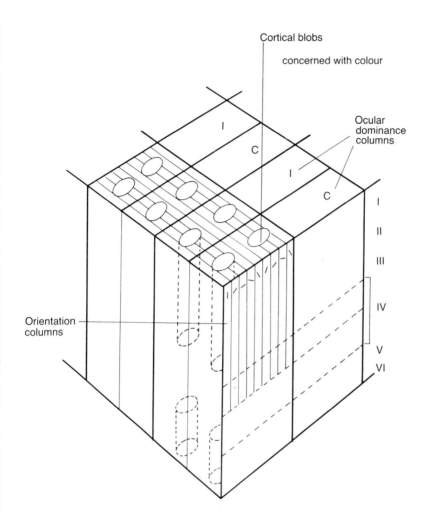

Figure 3.30 The organisation of cells in the primary visual cortex (V1). Cells in layers I, II, III and the upper part of layer IV respond to contours in specific orientations. A column, perpendicular to the surface of the cortex, contains cells having the same receptive field orientations, and are referred to as orientation columns. Neighbouring columns display a shift of preferred orientation of about 15 deg. There are also cortical blobs, receiving inputs from both magno and parvo cells in LGN, that respond to the wavelength of the original light stimulus. Projections from the ipsilateral (I) and contralateral (C) eyes remain separate in V1, resulting in a larger horizontal organisation based on ocular dominance. Within cortical areas of about 1 mm^2 both eyes and all orientations are represented for a small region of the visual field. Hubel and Wiesel referred to these as hypercolumns. (After Kandel and Schwartz, 1985)

different orientation selectivity, say 30 deg; the next column would have cells displaying a preferred orientation of around 15 deg, and so on, each column differing by about 15 deg from its immediate neighbour. In fact, the orientation selectivity of the cortical cells is not quite as precise as might have been suggested here; there is a particular orientation that will produce the maximum response from each neuron, but it will also respond, though with decreasing intensity, to lines within 10–20 deg of the preferred orientation. Accordingly, a given line falling on the retina will excite a range of orientation-selective neurons, but to varying extents. It is clear that area V1 has a vertical organisation in terms of orientation selectivity, and a horizontal organisation in terms of orientation change. This results in all orientations being represented for a given retinal region.

So far, nothing has been said about combining signals from the two eyes. The fibres in the optic tract are from similar halves of both eyes, but they project to different layers in the LGN. The first stage at which binocular integration of the neural signals occurs is in V1. The cortical neurons can be excited by appropriate stimulation of either eye, although one eye will generally have a greater influence than the other. This aspect of eye preference represents yet another horizontal organisation over the surface of V1: neighbouring orientation-columns tend to have the same eye preference. However, at intervals of about 0.5 mm the eye preference changes abruptly to the other eye, and the sequence of orientation-selective columns is repeated, as is represented schematically in Figure 3.30. Figure 3.31 shows the pattern of eye preference regions that have been established in monkey visual cortex. The eye-preference slabs can be identified by

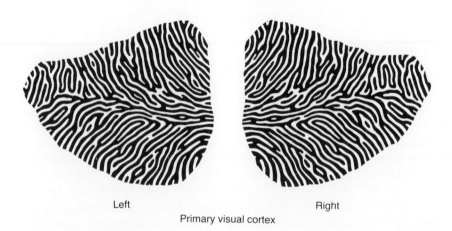

Left   Right
Primary visual cortex

Figure 3.31 The pattern of ocular dominance columns, represented by black and white areas, over the left and right hemispheric regions of V1. (After Hubel and Wiesel, 1979)

particular staining procedures and they are striped, rather like the stripes on a zebra. All the cells in the regions shown in white have one eye preference and those shown in black have a preference for the other eye. The combination of binocular signals to furnish information about relative depth (stereopsis) takes place at the next visual area.

Area V1 is, therefore, a highly organised structure. It appears to break down the pattern of light falling on the eye into discrete features, like retinal location, orientation, movement and wavelength, as well as maintaining a difference between the signals from the two eyes. These features are further differentiated in the subsequent cortical processing. Axons from neurons in V1 project to a variety of other visual areas in the cortex, as shown in Figure 3.32c. The adjacent visual area (V2) receives inputs from the three receptive field types in V1, but subsequent visual areas appear to specialise in the processing of particular features extracted in V1. The binocular combination in V1 is primarily for inputs from corresponding areas of each eye. That is, most binocular V1 neurons are excited by cells from the two eyes with equivalent receptive field characteristics and equivalent retinal locations. In V2 there are binocular cells that respond most strongly when the receptive field characteristics are slightly different. The inputs from each eye would have the same orientation selectivity, but the retinal locations associated with the receptive fields would be slightly different. These have been called disparity detectors because they appear to be responding to specific disparities (or horizontal retinal separations) between the stimulating edges in each eye. There are some disparity detectors at the level of V1. In addition to the analysis of retinal disparity further specialisations can be found in visual cortical areas. For example, area V4 is principally concerned with the analysis of colour, with cells in areas V5 and MT processing movement. There are even cells in a more central area that can process complex stimuli like faces.

The projections from the retina to the LGN and onwards to the multiple visual areas retain the basic mapping of the retinal surface: adjacent regions on the retina project to adjacent regions in LGN, V1, V2, etc. This is called retinotopic projection because the distribution of stimulation on the retina is preserved at more central sites. In turn, the pattern of retinal stimulation is geometrically related to the layout of objects in space. While adjacent regions on the retina project to adjacent regions in the visual cortex, the precise separations are not retained. The fovea is only a small area in the retina, but its projection to the cortex is disproportionately large. Conversely, the large peripheral areas of the retina are represented by small areas in the cortex (see Figure 3.32a and b). If you think of the retinal surface as a balloon with a very weak central area (analogous to the fovea) then inflating it results in a huge expansion of the central region, but relatively little of the surrounding area. Neighbouring regions are still adjacent, as in

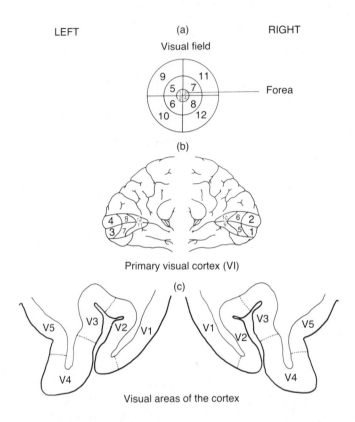

LEFT   (a)   RIGHT
                    Visual field

                                              Forea

                         (b)

Primary visual cortex (VI)

                         (c)

Visual areas of the cortex

Figure 3.32 (a) The visual field considered schematically as 12 regions, centred on the fovea. (b) The cortical representations of these regions. The diagram represents the posterior portions of the occipital cortex spread apart, exposing area V1. Note the inverted and reversed relationship between the visual field and its cortical representation, and also the cortical magnification: the largest areas of V1 process signals from the small foveal area of the retina, corresponding to areas 1–4 in (a). (c) A horizontal section through the occipital cortex showing visual areas 1–5. Signals from LGN are processed in V1; V2 is principally involved in processing retinal disparities, V4 with wavelength and V5 with movement. ((a) and (b) after Kandel and Schwartz, 1985; (c) after Barlow and Mollon, 1982)

retinotopic projection, but the relative separations are changed. This is a general scheme found in the cortical projections of sensory systems: those parts of the sensory surface that have the greatest sensitivity also have the greatest cortical projection. For example, the cortical representation of the sensitive fingers is far more extensive than that of the arms, even though the area of the skin surface is much less. Similarly with vision, the retinal region serving the sharpest acuity (in and around the fovea) also has the largest cortical representation. It has been estimated that the central 10 degrees of the retinal surface is represented by about 80 per cent of the cells in the visual cortex. This concentration of cortical processing to the central visual field would present a problem if the eyes remained stationary, because stimuli of significance could move out of the region where acuity is highest. In fact, the problem does not arise because of our exquisite control over eye movements, so that we can pursue moving objects to keep them projecting to the fovea or we can move our eyes rapidly and accurately to locate novel objects in the visual field. These control processes are mediated by pathways in the mid-brain that have not yet been mentioned.

Midbrain structures associated with vision

The discovery of multiple mapping in visual areas of the cortex is relatively recent, and as many as twenty such areas have now been found in monkey cortex. However, the concept of a second visual system was first proposed in the 1960s. Unlike the multiple maps in the cortex, this one is subcortical and older in evolutionary terms. The pathways that have been described so far comprise the classical projection system. Some fibres branch off the optic tract before the LGN to make synaptic connections in a structure in the mid-brain called the superior colliculus (Figure 3.33). The paired superior colliculi also receive inputs from layer V of V1. In evolutionary terms the superior colliculus is far older than the visual cortex. In many animals, like reptiles, all visual processing occurs in the optic tectum (which is equivalent to the superior colliculus in mammals), as there is no cortex present. In mammals its function is related to localising objects in peripheral vision and directing eye movements towards them. Experimental animals that have had the visual cortex removed can still locate objects on the basis of collicular activity, but they are unable to recognise them.

The mid-brain also contains a number of oculomotor nuclei that control the movements of the extraocular muscles within the orbit. All eye movements are rotations generated by the coordinated activities of pairs of muscles attached to the eye ball. There are three pairs of muscles which can rotate the eye in the three dimensions of space (Figure 3.34). We commonly refer to eye movements in terms of the directions the eyes point rather than the axis around which they rotate. The most frequent movements are up and down, and right and left. The former are coordinated in the two eyes, i.e., both move up and down in the same way.

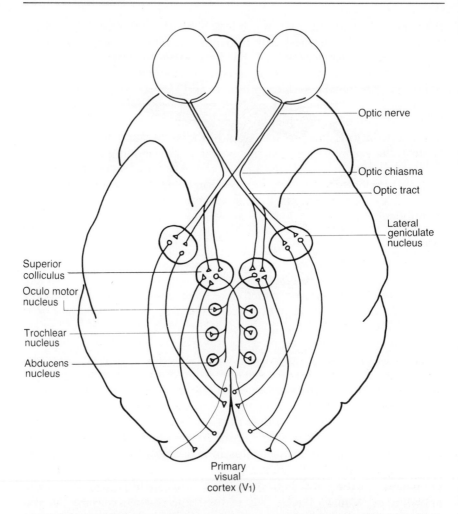

Figure 3.33 The classical projection pathway from the eyes to the brain via LGN, and the older pathway, in evolutionary terms, to the superior colliculus. Fibres from the optic tract synapse in the superior colliculus, and the collicular fibres project to three nuclei concerned with the control of eye movements. Note that the superior colliculus also receives feedback from (layer V of) V1.

Neurophysiological interpretations of visual phenomena

Very little is known about the neurophysiology of the human visual system. The experimental findings summarised above have been derived from experiments on many animals, but principally cats and monkeys. It might be the case that the human visual system behaves in quite a different way. This is, however, very unlikely. The anatomy of the visual system in

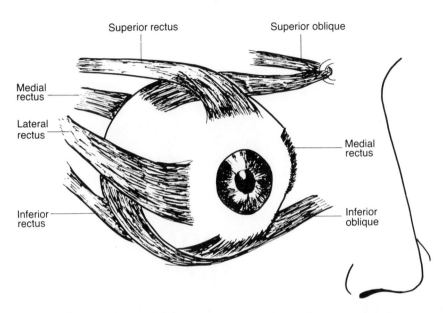

Figure 3.34 Extraocular muscles of the right eye. Rotations of the eye about a vertical axis (left and right) are controlled by the medial and lateral rectus muscles, those about a horizontal axis (up and down) by the superior and inferior rectus muscles, and those about the optical axis (torsion) by the superior and inferior oblique muscles. (After Sekuler and Blake, 1990)

humans is very similar to that of monkeys, and some species (e.g., rhesus monkeys) have about the same colour discrimination as humans. Therefore, we assume that the physiological processes measured in related species also applies to our visual systems. This extrapolation seems reasonable because the processes in cats and monkeys are closely comparable, even though the differences between their brain structures is greater than those between humans and monkeys. Some phenomena have already been described in terms of the physiological processes that give rise to them. For instance, the phases of dark adaptation were attributed to differences in rod and cone recovery times, or Hermann–Hering grid effects were related to differences in surround inhibition operating on the receptive fields of retinal ganglion cells. In attributing the phenomena to these particular processes we should not think that the phenomena are experienced at the levels these processes occur; the phenomena require those retinal processes but they can only be experienced if the information is transmitted to more central sites. In order to sustain neurophysiological interpretations we need to assume that changes coded at one level in the visual pathway are retained throughout subsequent processing. The search for neurophysiological interpretations of visual phenomena has proved to be a driving force in vision research over the last few decades, especially since the discovery of feature detectors in the visual cortex. The phenomena interpreted in this way tend to be rather simple, and they reflect the operation of the relevant stimulus dimension (like orientation or motion) in isolation.

Under normal circumstances we can judge orientation very accurately. Even in a darkened room we can adjust a light line to within about 1 deg of the vertical. This accuracy in perceiving the vertical can be biased by observation of a non-vertical pattern. For example, the gratings on the left in Figure 3.35 will initially appear to be vertical and aligned. Following inspection of the pattern on the right for about 1 min, the gratings on the left will appear neither vertical nor aligned. This is called the tilt after-effect, and it has been interpreted in terms of orientation selective cortical

Figure 3.35 Stimuli for producing a tilt after-effect. Initially look at the black spot on the left: the gratings above and below it will appear to be vertical and aligned. Then inspect the figure on the right by looking at the black rectangle for about 1 min; move your eyes slowly back and forth along the rectangle to avoid generating an after-image. Looking back at the spot on the left will result in the lines appearing slightly tilted with respect to one another: the upper grating will look tilted anti-clockwise, and the lower one clockwise. This after-effect will only last for a few seconds after which the gratings will again look vertical and aligned.

neurons. According to this interpretation, a vertical grating will stimulate a range of orientation-selective cells in the visual cortex – those with preferred orientations inclined slightly away from the vertical as well as those for vertical (see Figure 3.36). Initially the balance for those inclined clockwise of the vertical will match that for those inclined anti-clockwise. During inspection of the inclined grating an overlapping distribution of orientation-selective cells will be stimulated. However, since the inspection is prolonged these will undergo adaptation, i.e., their firing rates will be reduced by constant stimulation, and the cells will require some time to return to their original sensitivity. When the original pattern is observed again, the balance between the clockwise and anti-clockwise influences will be disturbed and shifted in the opposite direction to the inspection orientation. This shift in the distribution has been used to account for the shift in orientation that we can see. The effects of adaptation are relatively short lived, and so the two gratings return to alignment after a few seconds.

The tilt after-effect represents an example of successive biasing: some orientation-selective cells are adapted and the recovery from this adaptation is evident in the misjudgement of orientation. Related orientation biases can be induced simultaneously in patterns like that in Figure 3.37. The gratings in the two circular regions are vertical and aligned, but they do not appear so because of the inclined gratings surrounding them: they appear to be tilted in the opposite direction to their surrounding contours. This tilt illusion has been interpreted in terms of inhibition between orientation-selective cells in the cortex.

The motion after-effect has been interpreted in a similar way to the tilt after-effect, but incorporating motion detecting cortical cells rather than orientation-detecting cells. Studies of tilt and movement after-effects have also provided evidence for the ways in which signals from the two eyes interact. If a moving pattern is observed by one eye and a stationary pattern is subsequently observed by the other then the movement after-effect can still be measured, but it only lasts for about 60 per cent as long as adapting and testing the same eye. This is called the interocular transfer of the after-effect, and it has been used to infer the nature of binocular interaction in the human visual system. For example, the fact that interocular transfer occurs at all suggests that there are binocular cells that share the same information: they can be stimulated equivalently by either eye. The fact that transfer is less than complete suggests that there are also some monocular cells contributing to the perception.

In addition to the binocular cells that are excited if either eye is stimulated there are others that are only excited if both eyes are stimulated at the same time. Some of these respond only when contours fall on corresponding locations in each eye, that is, when the receptive fields in each eye are exactly in register. Such binocular cells probably mediate binocular single vision – the perceptual experience of a single world. Other

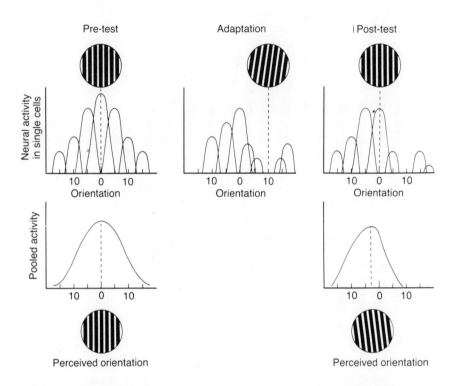

Figure 3.36 An interpretation of the tilt after-effect based on adaptation of cortical orientation-selective cells. The vertical pre-test grating has the maximum neural effect on those cortical cells with vertically oriented receptive fields, but there will be smaller effects on other cortical cells having receptive fields within about 15 deg clockwise and anti-clockwise of the vertical. The pooled activity of these cells is shown on the lower left. The effects are symmetrically distributed around the vertical, and it is assumed that the peak of this distribution represents the perceived orientation of the grating. During adaptation to a grating inclined 10 deg clockwise of the vertical the cortical responses will adapt as shown in the central figure. On post-test, the vertical grating will stimulate some cells (clockwise of the vertical) which have been adapted and others (anti-clockwise of the vertical) that have not. The resulting pooled distribution of activity (shown on the lower right) has its peak biased in an anti-clockwise direction, with a consequent shift in perceived orientation. The adapted cells recover quite rapidly to their normal sensitivity and so the after-effect also dissipates. (After Blakemore, 1973)

cortical cells respond only when there are small horizontal displacements between the locations of stimulation on each retina. These are called disparity detectors because they may be implicated in stereoscopic depth

Figure 3.37 Tilt illusion. The central lines are parallel to the edges of the page, but they look tilted clockwise because of the surrounding anti-clockwise lines.

perception or stereopsis. Binocular single vision and stereopsis will be discussed in Chapter 4. Interest in stereopsis has increased in recent years because neurophysiologists have found regions in the brain like V2, which appears to extract and process retinal disparities in comparative isolation. Other brain regions process features like colour and movement. However, we know relatively little about the ways in which these 'feature maps' are subsequently integrated to provide us with unified percepts of objects having a particular shape, size, texture and location in space.

Neurophysiological investigations are conducted under conditions that are far more controlled than those operating in perceptual experiments. The animals are generally immobilised so that the experimenters can define precisely both the area of the retina stimulated by light and the response that is elicited in the brain. Perceptual experiments, involving active and intact subjects, are open to much greater variability. The eyes move around resulting in the stimulation of a range of retinal regions, and the responses, like pressing a switch, are much more complex. There are a number of strategies that can be adopted to accommodate these differences. One is to try to simplify the stimulus and response conditions in perceptual experiments to match, as closely as is feasible, those obtaining in neuro-physiological experiments. This is the approach that has been adopted in the study of spatial after-effects described above. It has the advantage of proposing and testing explicit hypotheses linking neurophysiological and psychophysical data. The disadvantage is that the phenomena investigated are very simple, and the conditions of their occurrence are far removed from perception of objects in the world. Another strategy, and the one adopted in this book, is to examine functional aspects of perception, like location, motion and recognition, and to draw on the neurophysiological evidence when it is pertinent. This will enable the investigation of both simple and complex phenomena, but with respect to the latter it is more difficult to draw on our knowledge of neurophysiological processes underlying perception.

REFERENCE NOTES

Pirenne's (1967) book *Vision and the Eye* provides a bridge between Chapters 2 and 3. Initially he deals with the retinal image in an historical context and then covers most of the essential information relating optical and retinal characteristics of the eye to very basic visual phenomena like accommodation, dark adaptation, spectral sensitivity and visual acuity. Many textbooks on perception have good sections on the eye as an optical instrument and on the physiological processes both in the retina and in the brain that follow from light stimulation. For example, Barlow and Mollon's (1982) book *The Senses* provides a solid introduction to the anatomy and physiology of the visual system, and there are two particularly good chapters on the optics of the eye; the use of gratings as stimuli for probing the visual system is explained, and various perceptual phenomena are interpreted in terms of the underlying physiological processes. The text-books by Sekuler and Blake (1990) and by Goldstein (1989) are also recommended for their coverage of the visual physiology and of spatial frequency analysis. Similarly, textbooks on physiological psychology usually have a chapter on the visual system; Bloom and Lazerson's (1988) *Brain, Mind, and Behavior* presents many drawings that attempt to represent the three-dimensional locations of structures in the brain. A more detailed and thorough account of the visual system and neurophysiology generally can be found in Kandel and Schwartz's (1985) *Principles of Neural Science*.

The excitement of research in the area of visual physiology is often conveyed in the many well-illustrated articles on this topic that appear occasionally in the *Scientific American*. Fortunately, there are a number of collections of these articles in book form, which provide a very good introduction to the subject. Held and Richards have edited two sets of readings: *Perception: Mechanisms and Models* (1972) and *Recent Progress in Perception* (1976). The former contains articles on 'Eye and Camera', 'Visual Pigments in Man', 'Inhibition in Visual Systems', 'How Cells Receive Stimuli', 'Retinal Processing of Visual Images' and 'The Visual Cortex of the Brain'. The latter reprints papers on 'Contour and Contrast', 'The Control of Sensitivity in the Retina', 'Contrast and Spatial Frequency', 'The Neurophysiology of Binocular Vision' and 'The Superior Colliculus of the Brain'. There is also a Scientific American book, edited by Hubel (1979), devoted to *The Brain*, which has an excellent article on 'Brain Mechanisms of Vision' by Hubel and Wiesel, as well as others on 'The Neuron', 'The Development of the Brain' and 'The Chemistry of the Brain'. Interpretations of visual neurophysiology are undergoing constant revision, and the views presented in all these readings are now a little dated. Emphasis is shifting to processing information in parallel streams, and this can be seen from more recent articles, like those by Livingstone (1988) and Schnapf and Baylor (1987). This concern with parallel processing is very evident in an eclectic and up-to-date review of the relationship between vision and neurophysiology, edited by Spillmann and Werner (1990).

Chapter 4

Location

Virtually all our perception is dependent upon the adequate location of objects in the environment. The example of crossing the road, described in Chapter 1, illustrated the many ways in which the perception of location is necessary before other aspects of a scene, like motion or recognition, are processed. Our perceptual-motor coordination relies upon localising objects accurately, so that we can step over them, reach for them, avoid them or orient appropriately to them. Perception is a platform for action, and actions take place in a three-dimensional environment. It is necessary, therefore, for spatial perception to share the three-dimensional coordinate system in which behaviour occurs. The aspect of visual perception that will be examined in this chapter is location. Specifying the location of an object requires information for its direction and distance. Direction and distance will be considered separately in this chapter, although they always function in tandem: to have information that an object was a given distance away would be of little assistance to guiding behaviour if its direction was not also detected, and vice versa. Both direction and distance can be described in many ways, according to the frame of reference that is adopted. When discussing any aspects of space or spatial perception it is necessary to define the frame of reference relative to which measures are made.

FRAMES OF REFERENCE

The concept of a frame of reference is critically important for understanding the issues in this and subsequent chapters. It can be illustrated using a familiar system, namely, points drawn on graph paper. Figure 4.1a shows a graph with the axes marked. Using a Cartesian system (with X and Y axes) a point can be specified; here it is at values X = 2 and Y = 2, and it is marked by a circle. The location of the coordinate axes defines a frame of reference, relative to which the point is located. Figure 4.1b represents a similar graph with the point (marked by a square) at the same location (X = 2 and Y = 2) with respect to them. If we take the axes as the frame of reference in each case then the points have the same locations. The intersection of the X and

Y axes defines the point relative to which all other points are plotted. It is only when a further frame of reference is adopted that a measure of the enclosed one can be taken. For instance, the graphs represented in Figure 4.1 are positioned differently on the printed page: if the page is taken as a frame of reference then the locations of the two graphs on it can be measured, and differences between them can be described. Therefore, taking the page as the frame of reference the circle and square symbols have different locations, even though their coordinate values (2, 2) are the same. The page itself can be in different positions, but this can only be measured if a larger frame of reference still is adopted, like the surface of the earth. In such a descriptive system no information about locations with respect to one frame of reference is lost by moving up to another one; rather information that was not available is introduced by adopting a superordinate frame of reference.

Statements about location are restricted to the highest frame of reference in operation. For example, at the level of the graph in Figure 4.1a, the coordinates of the circular symbol can be specified, but no statements can be made about the location of the axes, because they define the frame of reference relative to which all other points are specified. It is only when a higher frame of reference is adopted, like the page, that the location of the axes can be described, and the location of the page can only be specified if we consider a frame of reference relative to which it can be located, like the surface of the earth. The earth is not the final frame of reference, of course, because its location could be determined with respect to the solar system.

This example is conceptually similar to what is happening in spatial perception, because the perceiver has many articulating parts: the eye in the orbit, one eye with respect to the other, the head on the shoulders and the

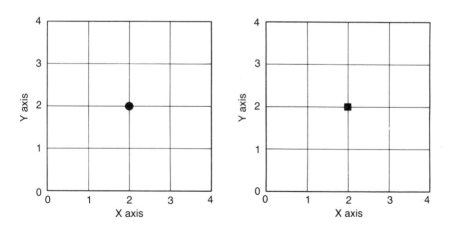

Figure 4.1 Two graphs with circular and square symbols at the same X and Y coordinate values (2,2).

body on the ground. The retina in one eye is somewhat like the drawn X and Y axes on the graph paper; different points on the retinal surface can be stimulated, but they can only be measured with respect to the retina itself. The second sheet of graph paper is like the other eye. The information about locations on each eye could be derived by adopting a similar frame of reference for both, like the coordinate axes of the two graphs. In the example that we have drawn in Figure 4.1, the coordinates on each graph are (2, 2) and (2, 2); if the the axes of the two graphs were superimposed on one another, then the points would be in correspondence. The page can be likened to the head; whenever the page moves the two graphs move with it. Similarly, whenever the head moves the two eyes are displaced in space. Therefore, changes in retinal stimulation can be produced by movements of the eye with a fixed head, by movements of the head without eye movements, or by a combination of the two. The changes in position of the page (or head) occur with respect to a larger frame of reference, namely the surface of the earth. For all practical purposes, the surface of the earth will be taken as the final frame of reference and will accordingly be defined as stationary.

VISUAL DIRECTION

Visual direction can be considered as a line extending from a point in the perceiver. We will start our treatment of visual direction by considering simplified situations, like a stationary observer. This has the advantage of building up a scheme of spatial representation in a systematic way. The information available at early stages (like the retina) is inadequate for guiding behaviour, and it needs to be amplified successively by other sources of information (like eye and body positions) in order to achieve a representation of three-dimensional space.

Retinocentric direction

Suppose a point of light in an otherwise dark room is observed by a single, stationary eye. How can observers determine its direction? One of the sources of information that must be used is the location on the retina that was stimulated. This is referred to as a local sign. Essentially, a local sign can be considered as a two-dimensional coordinate reference on the retina itself. It is likely that the fovea acts as the origin for the retinal frame of reference, and positions with respect to it can be discussed in terms of the familiar Cartesian coordinate system (see Figure 4.2), although other co-ordinate systems could equally well apply. We will refer to this aspect of the coding of direction as retinocentric, that is, with respect to the coordinate system provided by the retina. Within the retinocentric frame of reference there is no information about the position of the retina itself, only about points on it. If one eye moved slightly, as is illustrated schematically

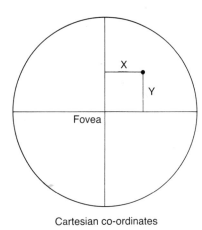

Cartesian co-ordinates

Figure 4.2 Circular schematic of a retina representing a point at a given location in terms of Cartesian coordinates. The fovea is taken as the origin for the coordinate system.

in Figure 4.3, then different retinal coordinates (or local signs) would be stimulated. At the retinocentric level there would be no means of determining whether this was a consequence of motion of the point or displacement of the eye.

Now consider a situation in which two points of light are present in an otherwise dark room. If the directions of each point are determined independently then their directions with respect to one another could also be computed. This is essentially the comparison of the two retinocentric values (see Figure 4.4). Thus, the coordinates of one point $(x1, y1)$ could be subtracted from those of the second point $(x2, y2)$ to determine their separation. It would also be possible to derive the relational directions of the two points without determining their retinocentric values: one could be so many retinal units away from the other, so that their separation alone was coded. For example, in Figure 4.4 one point $(x1, y1)$ could be taken as the origin of a coordinate system and the separation from $(x2, y2)$ would be given by its coordinates; alternatively, the second point could act as the origin. Such a relational system (which we call patterncentric) can take either point as the frame of reference for the other. So, for example, point A could be the origin and point B is separated from it, or vice versa. With just two points there are no advantages in taking A or B as the relational frame of reference. It is difficult to present an illustration of such a patterncentric scheme because the page on which it would be printed provides an implicit frame of reference! That is, the directions of one light source with respect

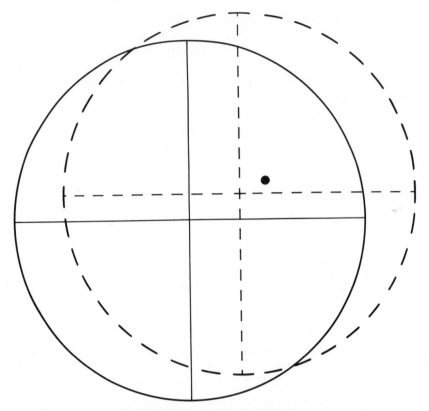

Figure 4.3 A point (the black dot) located at a constant position in space would stimulate different local signs (retinal coordinate values) if the eye moved, as indicated by its position relative to the solid and dashed circles.

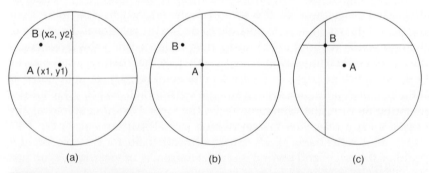

Figure 4.4 (a) Two points (A and B) could be described by their Cartesian coordinates (x1, y1 and x2, y2), and their locations relative to one another could be determined from the difference between the coordinates. Alternatively, (b) point A could act as an origin and define a patterncentric frame of reference, (c) as could point B.

to the other are described independently of their local sign values (their locations on the retina) – they could be anywhere as long as both were imaged in the eye. The relational values would code separation independently of direction or orientation.

Such a relational system operating on its own could not account for our ability to determine the directions of isolated lights, but we will see later that the joint operation of retinocentric and patterncentric values assists in the interpretation of several movement phenomena.

When an isolated target is presented to the peripheral part of the retina it initiates a fixation reflex – the eye moves automatically to locate the target on the fovea. Indeed, the adequate perception of the spatial detail is dependent upon light from the object falling on the central region of the eye, because acuity is best in and around the fovea. Therefore, we need to be able to direct our eyes to objects that require more detailed spatial resolution in order to determine whether they are of interest to us. In order for this to occur the retinocentric coordinates must be involved in the control of eye movements. For example, the retinocentric coordinates corresponding to an isolated point of light could be $x1, y1$, and these values are used to bring the point onto retinocentric coordinates of $0, 0$.

We can determine the visual direction of a point falling on the fovea (with retinocentric values of $0, 0$). A different visual direction is perceived if the eyes have to rotate to fixate the point on the fovea, and the retinocentric signals remain $(0, 0)$. Thus, different visual directions can arise from stimulation of the same retinocentric coordinates. Clearly, the difference in visual direction could not be registered at the retinocentric level. However, there are signals for the position of the eye in the orbit, and if these eye position signals are combined with the retinocentric signals then differences in the direction of points could be discriminated. This influence of eye movement control on visual direction is supported by a simple demonstration: when a light moves around the darkened room, the changes in visual direction can be perceived if the eye remains stationary and also if the eye pursues the target. In the first instance there would be changes in retinocentric values as the target moved, but in the second case the retinocentric values would remain unchanged. In order for direction to be perceived in the latter instance the retinocentric values alone would not suffice, and signals from eye movements would need to be used in the computation of visual direction. Therefore, visual direction is dependent upon both retinocentric and eye movement information.

Egocentric direction

So far, we have considered situations in which a target is observed with one eye, whereas normal vision is binocular. When we rotate an open eye the closed one rotates, too. This can easily be demonstrated. Close one eye and

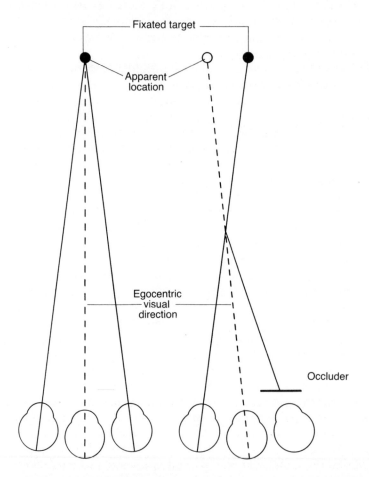

Figure 4.5 The change in visual direction when one eye is occluded. When one eye is occluded it rotates inwards, thereby modifying the egocentric visual direction of the target. (After Ono, 1990)

gently place the index finger of one hand on the upper eyelid. Look at the other outstretched index finger with the open eye, and follow its movements. You will feel the closed eye rotating in its orbit, yoked to the movements of the open eye: the two eyes work as one. This principle was stated by the German physiologist Ewald Hering, and it is known as Hering's law of equal innervation: 'The two eyes are so related to one another that one cannot be moved independently of the other; rather, the musculature of both eyes reacts simultaneously to one and the same impulse of will' (Hering, 1868/1942).

The integration of eye movements between the two eyes affects visual direction, too, because the direction in which a stationary monocular target is seen depends on the position of the occluded eye. When one eye is occluded, it tends to rotate inwards, towards the nose, and this rotation of the closed eye results in changes in the visual direction of the target seen with the open eye, as is illustrated in Figure 4.5. Moreover, when both eyes fixate on a target its visual direction does not correspond to the retinocentric direction of either eye alone, but it assumes an intermediate direction, midway between the eyes. Not only do the two eyes work as one, but the visual direction of a target appears aligned with a single central eye, rather like the mythological cyclops. Indeed, this position between the eyes is often referred to as the cyclopean eye, as well as the egocentre. This can easily be demonstrated with the aid of a sheet of paper and two coloured pens. Make two marks at one end of the sheet separated by about 60 mm (somewhat less than the distance between the eyes) and join one to a central fixation point at the opposite end using a red pen and the other using a green pen (see Figure 4.6a). Now, place the sheet slightly below eye level and fixate the point at which the lines intersect. Although each line is pointing directly at one eye, the impression is of a single line pointing between the eyes (to the cyclopean eye), with two flanking lines pointing wide of the left and right eyes. The central line might also appear to fluctuate between red and green, as a consequence of binocular rivalry.

An even simpler demonstration of the same general point can be made with a single line drawn on a sheet of paper (see Figure 4.6b). If the line is aligned with a point midway between the eyes and the far point is fixated with both eyes then two lines will be visible, one directed at each eye. In this case, the central line appears to be directed to the opposite eye, as can be ascertained by closing the eyes in turn.

The initial registration of direction is dependent upon a retinocentric frame of reference, but any judgements made by an observer are dependent on the integrated activity of both eyes. We refer to this as the egocentric frame of reference, as it yields a single visual direction with respect to the egocentre or cyclopean eye. One of the most fundamental aspects of vision is the integration of information from the two eyes to provide a single percept of the world. We have described above how the two sets of eye muscles operate like a single unit; does the same apply to the two sets of retinocentric signals? The evidence suggests that the signals from both retinae are combined independently of those for eye movements. The egocentric frame of reference is based upon information derived from the combination of a binocular retinocentric signal and a binocular eye movement signal.

If the information from each eye is equally weighted the egocentre is located midway between the two eyes. This is not always so, because one eye can have a greater influence than the other. For example, if the influence of the right eye is stronger than that of the left then the egocentre

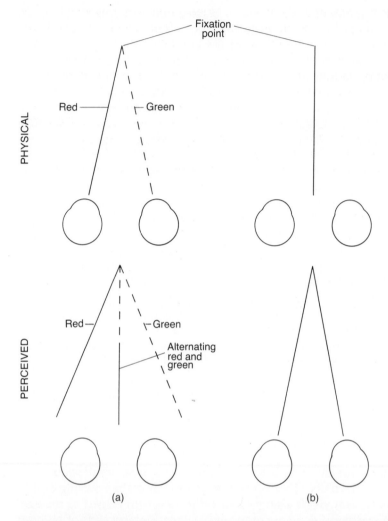

Figure 4.6 (a) The visual direction of red and green lines directed along the optic axes of each eye. (b) The visual direction of a single line in the median plane. (After Ono, 1990)

would be shifted towards the right eye. It was noted on p. 84 that the neural signals from each eye go to adjacent eye preference slabs in the visual cortex, and so the possibility of the eyes contributing differentially to ego-centric direction is present in the processing of information in the visual system. In fact one of the oldest tests of eye dominance is based upon assessing visual direction. It was described by a Neapolitan natural philo-sopher called Porta in 1593. If you look with both eyes at an object a few metres away and then point at it with your index finger, the finger will appear somewhat blurred but pointing at the target. While keeping the head and finger still, alternately close one eye and then the other. The finger will remain aligned when one eye is open, but not when the other is used. This is a test of sighting eye dominance. It can be refined somewhat by carrying out the task not by pointing a finger but by locating the target in a hole in the centre of a card held in both hands; this avoids problems associated with changing fixation from the far object to the nearer finger, as well as a possible bias from using the preferred hand. About 65 per cent of the population are right eye sighting dominant, 30 per cent are left eye dominant, and the remainder do not have a preferred sighting eye. The hole-in-the-card test places an impossible demand on the observer: usually, the card is raised to align the target with the egocentre, but then light from the target would not reach either eye. Because the egocentre is generally displaced slightly to one side of the midpoint between the eyes, the card is then moved to the nearer eye to locate the target optically in the hole (see Figure 4.7). Porta believed that right-handed people were also right-eyed, but there is no simple link between hand and eye preference.

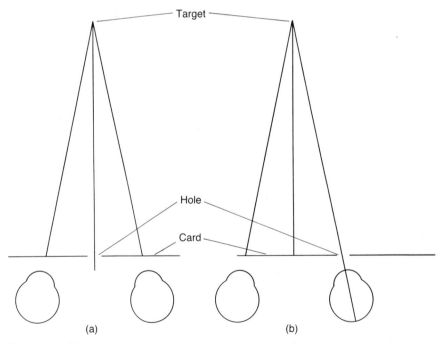

Figure 4.7 Sighting dominance determined with the hole-in-the-card test. (a) The hole is initially aligned with the egocentre, but no light from the target can then strike either eye. (b) The egocentre is usually displaced slightly towards a particular eye, and the hole is moved in that direction so that the target can be seen.

Binocular single vision

Porta also proposed an intriguingly simple theory to account for binocular single vision. He suggested that we only use one eye at a time! We know that such permanent suppression of signals from one eye does occur in about 4 per cent of the population, usually arising as a consequence of an uncorrected squint in childhood. These individuals can see with each eye alone, although the acuity is much poorer in the deviating eye. When both eyes are open they are functionally monocular, in that neural signals from the normal eye suppress those from the deviating one, as though they only had one eye open. A similar form of suppression can be demonstrated in people with normal binocular vision. The vertical and horizontal gratings shown in Figure 4.8 have different visual directions upon initial inspection. However, if you look at the tip of a finger held between the patterns and your eyes it will appear to point towards the vertical grating when the right eye is open and to the horizontal grating with the left eye. Move the finger until you find a position that is aligned with the base of the centre of the vertical grating with the right eye and the horizontal grating with the left. Keeping your finger as steady as possible fixate its tip with both eyes. Initially the gratings will appear a little blurred, because the state of accommodation is closely linked to the degree of convergence between the eyes. If you persevere for a minute or so the vertical and horizontal gratings will have the same visual directions, but they will not both be visible at the same time: occasionally only one grating will be seen, but more often a complex mosaic made up of local vertical and horizontal regions will be visible. The mosaic is itself dynamic, undergoing constant changes in its composition. This phenomenon, which is called binocular rivalry, is of particular interest because we do not see a stable grid, but rather an alternation between parts of the two differently oriented gratings. Binocular rivalry also occurs when different colours are presented to each eye – rather than seeing an additive combination of the colours (as would be produced by projecting them independently onto a screen) we see an alternation between them.

The mosaic patterns that we see are made up from local regions in one eye that are suppressing the corresponding regions in the other eye. The fact that such percepts occur at all contradicts Porta's theory, but it does indicate that binocular vision involves aspects of competition as well as co-operation. Competition, or rivalry, takes place when corresponding regions of each eye are presented with different patterns. This provides yet another means for determining eye dominance. If rivalling patterns are viewed for some fixed duration, say 1 min, and the duration for which each pattern is completely visible is measured, then the two durations could be compared. The eye receiving the pattern that was seen longer is called rivalry dominant and, surprisingly, it is not necessarily the same as the sighting

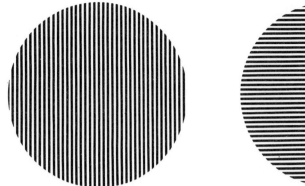

Figure 4.8 Rivalry patterns. Binocular rivalry can be seen with suitable observation of these gratings. If your eyes converge on a point between you and the gratings then the latter can both appear to have the same visual direction. Some people can achieve this without any assistance, for others it is necessary to align, say, a finger-tip with the vertical grating when using the right eye and the horizontal grating when using the left eye. When this is achieved three gratings will be visible – vertical on the left (as seen by the left eye alone), horizontal on the right (as seen by the right eye alone) and the central area where they overlap. Binocular rivalry occurs in this central region, resulting in the fluctuating appearance of the gratings.

dominant eye. That is, sighting and rivalry measures reflect different aspects of eye dominance.

The alternative theoretical view concerning binocular single vision to Porta's was proposed at about the same time – at the beginning of the seventeenth century. It was that objects are seen as single when they have the same visual direction, and that visual direction results from stimulation of corresponding points on the two retinae. Corresponding points have the same retinocentric coordinate values with respect to the foveas: if the two retinae were exactly superimposed on top of one another then contacting points would be corresponding. Returning to the example of the graphs mentioned earlier, the origins of the two graphs are like the foveas in the two retinae, and the two points on the graphs would be corresponding because they have the same coordinates (2, 2) with respect to the origin. Corresponding points can also be described geometrically: with fixation on a given point, all other points lying on a circle passing through the fixation point and the optical centres of each eye fall on corresponding points. This definition of corresponding points was formulated over 170 years ago by two German physiologists, Vieth and Müller, and it is now referred to as the Vieth–Müller circle. The geometrical values of the projections to each

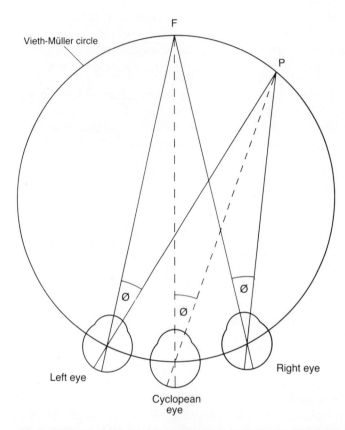

Figure 4.9 Vieth–Müller circle. With binocular fixation on a point (F) a circle can be described that passes through the point and the optical centres of each eye. Any other point (like P) on the circumference of the circle will stimulate corresponding points in each eye. The angle subtended by the two points will be the same at each eye, and also at the cyclopean eye. (After Howard, 1982)

eye also apply to the egocentre (see Figure 4.9). The geometrical definition is too restrictive in practice; it would predict that only those objects falling on the Vieth–Müller circle would be seen as single and having the same visual directions for each eye.

As the distance of the fixated object from the eyes increases the Vieth–Müller circle becomes very large, and for all intents and purposes it can be thought of as a plane, and so corresponding points lie on a fronto-parallel plane (at right angles to the straight ahead). In fact, the conditions that have been mentioned above approximate stimulation in a fronto-parallel or frontal plane. When we fixate on an object in the frontal plane we can still see objects singly when they are slightly in front or behind it; however, they do not then share the same visual directions for each eye, and neither of these correspond to the egocentric visual direction. That is, we see the objects separated in depth with respect to the fixated object, and in directions defined with respect to the egocentre.

There is a limit to the disparity that can be processed to yield depth perception. Only stimuli quite close to the Vieth–Müller circle, in a region referred to as Panum's fusional area, can be seen in depth on the basis of disparity alone. Beyond the range where noncorresponding stimulation results in perceived singleness and depth, it would be expected that objects would be seen as having two visual directions. However, we are rarely aware of seeing double images, even though the conditions for their visibility occur constantly. Whenever you fixate on a near object, more distant ones can have radically different alignments for each eye, but they are not often seen double. This can easily be demonstrated by fixating a finger, held about 20 cm from the eyes, and then closing each eye altern-ately. You will probably be surprised at the large differences in alignment that are evident, and yet they pose few problems for normal perception. One of the reasons for this is likely to be that the non-fixated objects are slightly out of focus because of the state of accommodation required for viewing the near finger. Another factor is the operation of binocular rivalry: the corresponding regions of each eye will be stimulated by quite different patterns, and so singleness can be served by suppressing one or the other in local regions.

A single target is seen singly when it falls on both foveas, but under circumstances like observing the rivalling patterns in Figure 4.9, it is possible for a single target to be seen double, i.e., for one object to have two different visual directions. When the vertical and horizontal patterns were projecting to corresponding retinal regions, by converging on a point between them and the eyes, three patterns were visible – a vertical grating on the left, the rivalling patterns in the centre and a horizontal grating on the right. Another way in which a single object can have two visual directions is by passively moving one of the eyes. Passive movement of an eye means it is displaced by means other than the extraocular muscles themselves. If you look at an object that is in relative isolation (like a clock on the wall) then gently press the corner of one eye, you will probably see two objects; one remains steady and the other appears to move as the eye is passively displaced. As soon as the pressure is removed from one eye the object appears single again. Passive eye movements of this type are distin-guished from active or voluntary eye movements because the former do not modify our perception of direction in the way voluntary eye movements do. Voluntary eye movements are recorded internally and can be used to compensate for retinal image motions that occur as a consequence of them. No such compensation occurs for passive eye movements.

The outcome of the computations based upon patterncentric, retinocentric and eye movement information from both eyes provide a representation of egocentric visual direction. This is a representation of the line along which a single target can be located or an angle between two targets. The lines or angles do not locate the targets unambiguously because their distances have not been determined.

VISUAL DISTANCE

Information about the direction of objects with respect to the perceiver is clearly important, but insufficient by itself to control anything but very simple sorts of behaviour, like guiding oneself towards a target. For example, the tendency (called tropism) of plants and animals to grow or move towards certain sorts of stimulation, and away from others, can be based on a sensory estimate of the direction in which the stimulation is strongest. However, an object could lie anywhere along a line of visual direction, and for most behaviour it is necessary to know the distance as well as the direction of objects in the environment. Together, distance and direction specify the location of an object in three-dimensional space. The size of an object cannot be known from direction alone, either. Lines of visual direction, which define the boundaries of an object, could cor-respond to any of a large number of identically shaped objects, with different sizes and distances. All that would be known is the angular size of the object, and this would not generally be sufficient for recognition or appropriate action. For human behaviour, and probably that of most vertebrates also, perception involves recovering both the direction and the distance of objects in the environment, so that their location is specified unambiguously.

Egocentric distance is the distance separating the observer from some environmental feature. This is sometimes misleadingly called absolute distance, although it is in fact relative to the observer. Just as with the specification of direction, there is always a frame of reference to define any distance, and it needs to be made explicit. Relative distance is the term normally given to the separation in space of one object with respect to another. If the objects are stationary, their relative distance remains constant, despite any movement by an observer. As will be seen, one of the critical requirements of the visual system is to recover relative distances and directions in the environment despite movements of the observers' eyes, head and body.

We are familiar with ways of measuring both egocentric and relative distances, using physical devices like rulers and tape-measures, and scales with units like inches and feet, or centimetres and metres. These scales provide metric distance information, which conveys not only the order of objects in depth, but the actual distances between them. One reason these are needed is that experience teaches us not to rely on judgements of distance 'by eye', if accuracy is required. Nevertheless, we obviously do perceive distances, whether accurately or not, and it is reasonable to ask what units the perceptual system might use. Most people can apply familiar units to express their perception of distances, and are able to report how far away something appears, for example in centimetres. No doubt this is due to our constant use of such scales since childhood. However the guide dog which featured in Chapter 1 would have no such familiarity, but could still perceive distances and act accordingly. Essentially, the requirement for a perceptual system is that the metric representation of distance in the nervous system should be lawfully related to physical distances in the outside world; that is, the perception of distance produced by an object at two metres should be double that from an object at one metre, and half that from one at four metres. All this means is that an adequate perceptual system must conform to the nature of the three-dimensional space in which we live, at least for the range of distances which cover the space where we can carry out actions. It is striking that many of our units of distance have their origin in human anatomy, like the length of the forearm or foot, or the stride when walking. Possibly, in the absence of verbal scales, distance information may be expressed in terms of the muscular effort needed to reach a given point in the environment. Even someone who had difficulty in stating the apparent distance of a target might be quite good at reaching out and touching it. Human distance perception is poor at longer ranges, such as more than a few metres, as is well known to drivers, pilots, mountaineers and golfers. Clearly our ability to represent distances decreases outside the normal range of action.

The fundamental importance of distance perception is shown by the way in which other perceptual characteristics depend upon it. An error in distance perception may affect whether or not an object appears to move, what colour or brightness it appears to have, and what size and shape it appears to be. How do we come to perceive distance at all? This question has been at the heart of perceptual investigation for centuries, and it is generally answered by description of the various sources of information about distance which are available to us. These sources of information are known as cues, and their identification and analysis has been an important achievement, although primarily on the part of artists rather than psychologists. There are a number of these cues, which under normal circumstances give rise to a reliable perception of distance. When failures occur it is generally because of the lack of strong cues to distance, which causes inaccurate perceptions. The major cues to distance are described in the following two sections, in terms of their contribution to the perception of egocentric and relative distance.

Egocentric distance

Suppose that you are seated in a dark room, and a small illuminated disc appears in front of you. The disc will be at a particular physical distance, but at what egocentric distance, if any, will it be perceived? Under such reduced conditions, your perception of distance may be quite inaccurate, but the disc will still appear to be at some distance, even if this is erroneous. In fact, even if all sources of distance information are eliminated, observers will still see an object at a particular distance, generally around 1.5–2 m, regardless of its physical distance. This has been called the specific distance tendency by the American psychologist Walter Gogel, whose work has demonstrated the importance of distance perception in many visual processes. The specific distance tendency ensures that some value of perceived distance will be present in the perception of any object. Generally, we are not strongly influenced by the specific distance tendency, because there are other cues available. One of these, accommodation, was described in Chapter 3. In principle, the accommodative state of the eye could provide information about distance, although as was discussed earlier this will be confounded with the light level in the environment and with the wavelength of the light. The question of whether, and to what extent, accommodation actually does play a part in determining perceived distance remains controversial. Probably it is at best a weak cue, which comes into play mainly at short egocentric distances, or when other sources of distance information are reduced.

Distance can be determined from ocular convergence provided the distance separating the two eyes is known (see Figure 4.10). This interocular distance (IOD) averages around 65 mm in adults, but varies quite considerably between individuals. It also changes within individuals as the result of growth, but presumably any changes are slow enough for us to adapt to them as they occur. Provided an object is straight ahead, its distance can be found from the ratio of the convergence angle to the IOD. More precisely, for this case, the distance is equal to half the IOD divided by the tangent of the angle by which each eye deviates from the straight ahead position. For objects away from the straight ahead position, the relationship is more complex, but still solvable. It is not likely that the nervous system actually performs the operation of taking the tangent of an angle, but rather that there is in practice a consistent relationship between the state of the muscles that move the eyes, and the distance of centrally fixated objects. Such a relationship would be established as the result of visual and manipulative experience with objects, and the nervous system is good at detecting and recording the way in which one sensory event is correlated with another.

There is some disagreement as to exactly how information about ocular convergence might be obtained; the alternatives are either feedback from detectors in the ocular muscles themselves, or more likely, a copy of the commands sent to the muscles from the brain. In either case, for

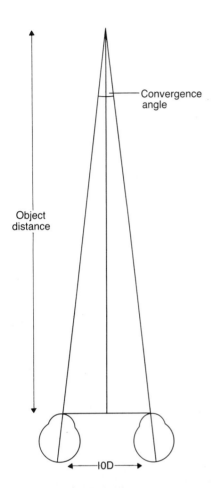

Object
distance

Convergence
angle

|OD

Figure 4.10 The geometry of ocular convergence and distance. The physical distance to the point on which the eyes are converged can be found from the ratio of the interocular distance (IOD) to the angle by which each eye deviates from the straight-ahead position. More precisely, the distance is equal to the IOD divided by two times the tangent of the convergence angle. This equation is only approximate if convergence is to a point which is not straight ahead; beyond around 6 m the optic axes are effectively parallel for all points of fixation.

convergence to be an effective cue to distance, such information must be available, from whatever source. In order to show that convergence affects perceived distance, it is necessary to devise experimental conditions in which convergence can be controlled and altered, and other cues are eliminated or held constant.

Changes in convergence can lead to paradoxical effects on the perception of distance and size, which have caused some controversy as to whether convergence is a reliable cue to egocentric distance at all. Typically, if convergence is reduced so as to correspond to a greater distance, while the physical distance to the target remains constant, the perceived size of an object also increases. Similarly, perceived size decreases if convergence is increased. The paradoxical effect is that an observer may not also report that the perceived distance has changed, when the convergence does. Possibly we modify our judgement of distance on the basis of perceived size. An object which appears larger may be judged to be nearer, even though the information from convergence, which has determined the perceived size, indicates the opposite.

Eye movements, called vergence movements, change the state of convergence to different egocentric distances. Vergence movements are equal in extent, but opposite in direction, in the two eyes. In addition, as discussed earlier, the eyes may move so as to change the point of fixation to a different egocentric direction. Such version movements cause the eyes to move through equal extents in the same direction. Both vergence and version obey Hering's Law, which states that the eyes act as a single functional unit, whose movements are always of the same extent – in the opposite direction for vergence, and in the same direction for version. Hering's Law applies independently to vergence and version, which seem to be controlled independently. This can be seen clearly if fixation is shifted from one target to another at a different distance and in a different direction, which requires a change in both vergence and version. The latency for vergence movements is slightly shorter than that for version, so there is an initial change in vergence towards the distance of the new target. However, vergence movements are relatively slow compared to version, and before the new state of convergence has been reached, a rapid change in version takes place, appropriate to the direction of the new target. The vergence movement then continues until the target is imaged on the fovea in each eye. In each phase, eye movements obey Hering's Law, although the overall result may be that each eye has moved by a different amount in order to change fixation.

Information which is geometrically equivalent to convergence can also be obtained by viewing an object from different directions, for instance when the head is moved from side to side. The change in an object's egocentric direction when viewed from two positions could be used to find the object's distance, if the extent of the head movement is known. There is some evidence that this cue of egocentric motion parallax can be used by human perceivers.

It is also possible that we are sensitive to the differential vertical magnification of images in the two eyes. When an object is beyond about 6 m, it projects images whose vertical size on the retina is effectively the same

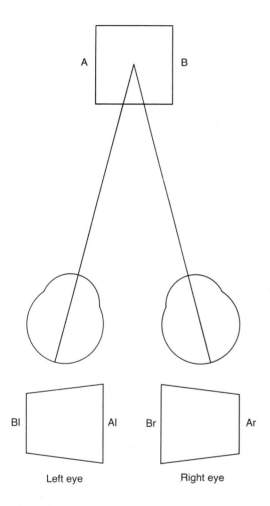

Figure 4.11 Vertical disparity produced by convergence. The stimulus is a square with equal sides, but its optical projection to each eye is unequal. The trapezoids represent the left and right retinal images of the square, and show that the temporal vertical sides are longer than the nasal ones. Binocular fusion takes place between Al and Ar, and between Bl and Br. The difference in the projected lengths of these pairs constitutes the vertical disparity. This provides a cue to the distance of the stimulus, since it varies with convergence.

for both eyes. However as an object is brought closer, the eyes must converge if the object is to be centred on both the left and right eye foveas. As a result there is a difference between the vertical extent of the retinal images in each eye. Imagine that the object is an outline square, perhaps drawn on a piece of paper. If the eyes are appreciably converged, the retinal images will be trapezoidal, with the vertical nearest the nose shorter than the vertical nearest the temples. As can be seen from Figure 4.11 however, the nasal and temporal lines represent opposite sides of the square in each eye. Thus the nasal vertical in the left eye corresponds to the temporal vertical in the right eye. This difference between the vertical extent of images falling on corresponding regions of each eye increases as an object is brought closer. It is a purely optical source of information about distance, in that although it arises as the result of convergence, its interpretation does not require information about the positions of the eyes.

One question raised by the above discussion is how we are able to see the distances of objects beyond around 6 m. Conventionally, rays of light emanating from a source at 6 m or more are said to lie at optical infinity, because they are effectively parallel to the optical axis. There will therefore be no appreciable convergence of the eyes when viewing an object at or beyond this distance. Clearly, the world does not appear to collapse into two dimensions as cues to egocentric distance are reduced, so there must be additional processes at work. One possibility would be the familiar size of objects. If the things we see at a distance are familiar from past experience, such as people, buildings or vehicles, then we might base the perception of their distance on our knowledge of their true physical size. This would require that the perceived size of the object is compared to some representation in memory of how big the object actually is. The ratio of perceived size to remembered physical size could then be used to derive the distance. The role of familiar size in distance perception has been the subject of many experiments. What seems to be the case is that the perceived size of objects, whether or not they are familiar, is based on their retinal size and their perceived distance. This gives a perceived size which may or may not correspond to familiar, remembered size. If there is a discrepancy between the size that a familiar object appears to be, and the size which we know it to have, then we may alter what we say we think its distance is. If you look down from a tall building towards people on the ground, there is very little distance information available. The people below will look small, despite our knowledge that they are not likely to be abnormal in this respect. Thus our perceptions will not be altered by our past knowledge, but our verbal interpretations and possibly our actions may be.

Relative distance

The various cues that indicate the relative distance between objects enable us to extend the perception of distance in the environment beyond the range of egocentric cues, and also to obtain information about the three-dimensional structure of objects. In themselves these cues cannot give an egocentric scale of distance or depth; they can indicate the relative separations of objects and parts of objects, but the scaling of the separation is ambiguous. Given three points at different distances, relative cues would enable an observer to state that the distance from A to B is twice that from B to C, but not to give metric information about these separations. If the points A, B and C lie on the surface of a solid object, relative cues will correctly specify its shape, but not its overall size. That is, it would be possible to recover the three-dimensional shape of a car, and recognise it as such, but not to say what size it was, or even whether it was a real car or a toy. However, if the egocentric distance to any one point is known, perhaps from convergence, then this allows relative distances to be scaled unambiguously. This means that relative cues can provide distance information extending out to a greater range than is possible with egocentric cues alone. All that is needed is the egocentric distance to one nearby point, to act as a stepping-stone for the rest of the visual scene. In principle the relative distances between objects could be obtained from a series of egocentric distances; if the distances to A and B are known independently, the distance from A to B could be given by subtraction. In practice, as we have seen, egocentric distance information is not available much beyond the range of physical action, and its primary role seems to be to provide a metric for interpreting the cues that specify relative distances directly.

The first people to understand the importance of cues to relative distance were painters, rather than scientists. During the fifteenth century, initially in Florence, artists began to make use of techniques which increased the apparent realism of their paintings by giving them three-dimensional characteristics. The most important of these techniques was perspective, the laws of which were formally set out by Alberti in 1435. Nowadays we take perspective in pictures for granted, but it is only necessary to look at paintings from earlier times to see that pictorial representations of three-dimensional space have not always incorporated this feature. Other cues to distance may well be present, such as the obscuring of a distant object by a nearer one, and the placing of more distant objects higher up within the pictured scene, but to an extent these are unavoidable if the picture is to be interpreted at all. At other times and in other cultures, realism has been less important. For example, a picture may have been valued primarily for its symbolism of religous or social beliefs, and not for its verisimilitude. Nevertheless, when it became possible to create images which engendered in the viewer something akin to the perceptual experience produced by a real scene, this was adopted enthusiastically by artists, and it remains an ability which is valued and admired.

The problem is to establish how far such pictorial cues to distance are important for normal perception. Clearly, to the extent that they work in pictures, they are able to influence perception. What is more doubtful is whether we should regard the perception of pictures as representative of

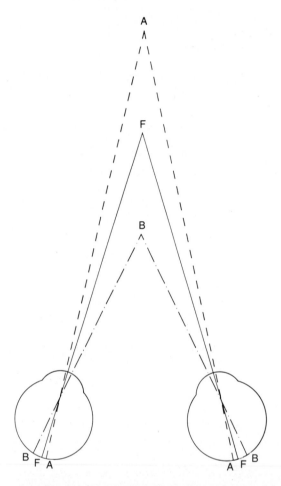

Figure 4.12 The geometry of retinal disparity. Both eyes fixate on point F, so that its image falls on the fovea of each eye. The images of points A and B, which are respectively further and nearer than F, fall on non-corresponding points. These differences in the projections from the two points are referred to as retinal disparities. If the disparities are not too great they can be processed in the visual system to provide information for relative distance, called stereoscopic depth perception or stereopsis. The sign of disparity depends on whether the non-fixated point is nearer or further than the fixation distance. Disparities can be described in terms of visual directions. Point A appears to the right of F when viewed by the right eye alone, and to the left with the left eye; this is called uncrossed disparity. Conversely, point B appears to the left of F when viewed by the right eye, and to the right with the left eye; this is referred to as crossed disparity. These differences in visual direction can easily be demonstrated. Hold both index fingers straight ahead of the egocentre, with one a few centimetres higher and further away from the other. If you fixate on the nearer one the far one will have uncrossed disparity, whereas fixation on the further one will result in crossed disparity for the nearer one.

normal perception. This might be reasonable if the retinal image were a single static 'snapshot' of the external world, like a picture, but in fact it is not. Not only does perception derive, in those with two eyes, from the combination of two different images, but these images are in constant motion as the result of eye movements and head movements. Many textbook descriptions of distance and depth perception are primarily accounts of the perception of pictures, and this leaves out all the information that is available to an active, moving perceiver.

In principle, the effectiveness of a relative cue to distance can be measured by presenting it in isolation, and assessing the extent to which it creates a perception of depth. In practice, experimental techniques cannot eliminate all information about depth other than the cue being studied. There is therefore a cue conflict, and the actual perception of distance is a compromise between the various sources of information, depending on their strength. A good example of this is the perception of depth in pictures. A picture may incorporate a number of cues to relative depth, such as overlap, height in the picture plane, perspective and shadowing. All these cues can indicate consistent depth, and need not conflict with each other. However they do conflict with other information that specifies a flat plane, arising from the picture surface, its frame and surroundings. The depth that we see therefore depends on a compromise between the various cues. Cues to the flatness of a picture can be reduced, for example by creating an image on a surface without a visible texture and without a clearcut frame. If so, the impression of depth in a picture can be markedly increased, as is the case with large screen projections in the cinema.

The most compelling cue to relative depth arises when the images of an object fall upon different retinal areas in the left and right eyes (Figure 4.12). As described above, stimulation of corresponding retinal locations gives rise to single vision and perception of a single visual direction. If the stimulated locations are very different, double vision results. Between these two extremes, there is a range where stimulation of noncor-responding points causes single vision and the appearance of depth. The process that gives rise to depth in this way is called stereopsis, and it is probably the most intensively investigated phenomenon in the history of vision research.

The geometry of binocular disparity was described long before the function that it serves was appreciated. In fact, the link between disparity and stereopsis was not described until 1838, when the physicist Charles Wheatstone published his account of the stereoscope and the experiments he had conducted with it. A stereoscope is an instrument that permits presentation of slightly different figures to each eye independently. If the figures have the characteristics of the left and right eye views of an object, then the impression obtained is of a solid or three-dimensional figure rather than a flat one. There are several ways in which this can be achieved

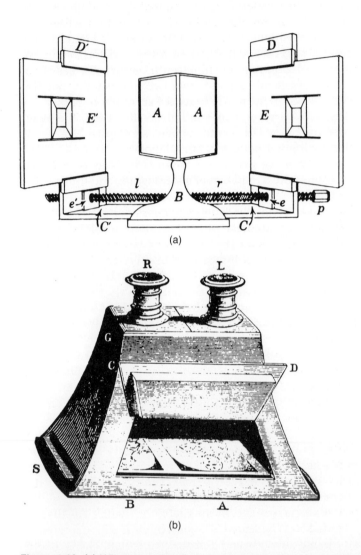

(a)

(b)

Figure 4.13 (a) Wheatstone's mirror stereoscope. The two slightly different perspective drawings of a solid object are placed on the side panels and their images are reflected to each eye via the mirrors (A). (b) Brewster's lenticular stereoscope. Half-lenses are located in the viewing tubes and act as magnifiers and prisms, so that the two pictures (A and B) appear to be straight ahead. This type of stereoscope was particularly popular in the latter half of the nineteenth century for combining stereophotographs.

optically. Wheatstone's stereoscope consisted of two plane mirrors, at right angles to one another, which reflect figures mounted appropriately on the side arms (see Figure 4.13a). An alternative model based on lenses was devised in 1849 by a Scottish physicist, David Brewster (see Figure 4.13b), and it was this type of stereoscope that graced many a Victorian parlour. The popularity of the stereoscope in the nineteenth century was based not only on the impression of depth derived from two flat pictures, but also because it could be married to the newly invented art of photography.

In addition to systems based on lenses or mirrors, there are other ways of viewing a stereogram in order to obtain stereopsis. The basic requirement is that a different pattern of stimulation can be presented to each eye independently. Some people can voluntarily alter their ocular convergence so as to fuse the two halves of a stereogram, and thus see the represented depth. This free fusion becomes easier with practice, and it can be tried with Figure 4.14. Anaglyphs are stereograms in which the left and right eye images are superimposed, but printed in different colours, such as red and green. When seen with a red filter over one eye and a green one over the other, the combined image is separated into a red and black image to one eye with a green and black image to the other, and binocular fusion may take place between the disparate black images. This method is also effective with projected images, and has been the basis of so-called 3-D films. While stereopsis in moving images is impressive, the anaglyph method is not entirely satisfactory because of the instability of binocular fusion with monocular images of different colours. The same result, but without the colour separation, can be achieved with polarising filters. The left and right eye images are projected through vertically and horizontally polarised filters, and are viewed with corresponding filters in front of the eyes.

The inventors of the original stereoscopes, Wheatstone and Brewster, engaged in a bitter public argument over the priority of invention. Brewster contended that the principles of stereoscopic vision had been known for centuries, and that a stereoscope had been made in the sixteenth century. Wheatstone described the perception of depth based on two flat but dissimilar pictures as 'a new fact in the theory of vision'. The dispute was eventually decided in Wheatstone's favour, but it is still of interest in the context of examining direction and distance perception. The geometry of binocular projections, as shown in Figure 4.12, was known and illustrated in the sixteenth and seventeenth centuries, but binocular vision was considered solely in terms of visual directions. Thus, an object that was further away than the point of binocular fixation appeared directed to the right side when using the right eye alone, and to the left side when using the left eye alone. This is now called uncrossed disparity. Conversely, a nearer object is said to have crossed disparity, because it appears directed

Figure 4.14 Stereophotograph of a stereoscope. The method for combining images in different locations, described in the legend to Figure 4.8, can be used to fuse this stereopair. The left and right images have been arranged so that the one on the left should be viewed by the right eye, and the one on the right by the left eye. If these photographs were combined with a stereoscope, so that the left one went to the left eye, then the disparities would be reversed, as would the perceived depth.

to the left of the fixated object when using the right eye and to the right when using the left eye. Binocular disparities were initially defined in terms of visual directions, and descriptions like this can be found in the writing of Galen around 200 AD. Prior to Wheatstone, the principal problem in the study of binocular vision was that of singleness of vision: how is the world seen as single when we have two different views of it? The generally accepted answer was that only objects with the same visual directions would be seen as single. In the terminology of visual direction (see pp. 107–9), only objects stimulating corresponding points (or falling on the Vieth–Müller circle) would be seen as single, all others would be double. Wheatstone demonstrated experimentally with the stereoscope that this was false: the stimulation of slightly non-corresponding points can yield singleness of vision, but it also results in the perception of depth. Accordingly, Wheatstone established for the first time that binocular vision is concerned with distance as well as direction, and it is for this reason that the instrument he invented and the experiments he conducted with it are so important.

Binocular or retinal disparity is a relative cue, because it applies to situations where one object is fixated (and therefore stimulates corresponding retinal points) while one or more other objects at different distances project to different regions of each eye. As can be seen from Fig. 4.12, disparity can be produced either if an object is nearer than the plane of fixation, or further away. For an object of fixed size the disparity will vary with egocentric distance. Wheatstone described the changes that occur when an object approaches the eyes (or when an observer approaches an object): there are increases in retinal size, retinal disparity, convergence and accommodation. Despite these changes the object appears to remain the same size. Wheatstone conducted experiments to manipulate these cues independently, and of particular interest was the relationship between disparity and convergence. When retinal disparity was kept constant and convergence increased, perceived depth decreased. Conversely, when convergence was held constant and disparity was increased perceived depth increased. Therefore, under normal circumstances there is a trade-off between increasing retinal disparity and increasing convergence which serves to maintain the constancy of perceived depth.

These points can be emphasised by means of an example. Suppose that an object such as a pencil is held at a slant so that the point is towards you, and that you are fixating on the point. There is a disparity between the retinal images of the other end of the pencil, which alters as the whole pencil is moved towards or away from you. The relationship follows an inverse square law; the disparity is proportional to the inverse of the egocentric distance squared. Thus if the egocentric distance to the point of the pencil is doubled, the disparity of the far end will be a quarter of its original value. Because of this, in order to perceive that an object in depth is a constant length, it is necessary to scale the disparity with the perceived distance. Errors in perceived distance will produce errors in the perceived depth from disparity. The IOD also determines disparity; for any given physical depth interval, the disparity will be larger if the eyes are further apart. As with egocentric distance from convergence, the IOD must be available to the visual system.

Recently it has been established that stereopsis can be obtained if the left and right eye images are separated by being presented alternately in rapid succession; typically around 20 times per second for each eye. The technique requires electronic shutters in front of each eye that can be opened and closed in succession and in synchrony with successive images presented on a screen. Fast liquid crystal shutters have been developed that can be driven by a computer, which also creates the images. The depth that results can be as compelling as that produced by optical separation or filtering, and lends itself to interactive computer driven representations of three-dimensional scenes. The closest approximation to natural viewing is obtained with separate, miniature displays for each eye, mounted on a helmet. With computer generated images, the user can seem to interact with a simulated three-dimensional environment. These techniques are currently being developed for pilot training and similar purposes, but may become more widespread.

While it is obviously necessary to view the world with two eyes in order to detect disparity, there is a functionally similar cue available to monocular vision, if the head moves from side to side. This cue is relative motion parallax, and its geometrical basis can be seen from Figure 4.15. This figure is identical to Figure 4.12, except that the two eyes have been replaced by a head, moving sideways through some distance. It is evident that the successive projections of objects on a single retina carry similar information about relative depth as does binocular disparity. If you move your head to the right so that your left eye is located in exactly the position previously occupied by your right eye, then the successive retinal projections to your left eye are identical to those that were available to your left and right eyes, with your head in its original position. Experiments have shown that the depth produced in this way is very similar, if not identical to stereopsis, and it is possible that both patterns of stimulation activate the same cortical mechanisms. For example, prolonged viewing of a stereogram of a corrugated surface produces an after-effect in which a flat surface appears to be corrugated in the opposite direction, and this also occurs with depth due to motion parallax.

Motion parallax consists of relative motion between the retinal images of objects at different distances, and is created by lateral motions of the observer's head. The kinetic depth effect shows that relative motion may also act as a cue to depth even if seen by a stationary observer. Suppose an object is placed behind a back projection screen, and illuminated by a

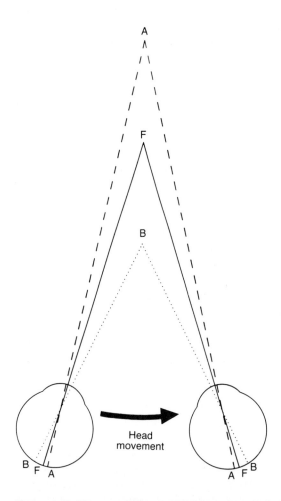

Figure 4.15 The geometry of relative motion parallax. The observer maintains fixation on point F, while moving his head from left to right through the distance shown by the arrow. The images of points A and B, which are respectively further and nearer than F, are displaced across the retina, by an amount which depends on the extent of the movement and the distance of the points relative to the plane of fixation. The distances AF and BF can be recovered if the egocentric distance to F and the extent of the movement are known. The pattern of stimulation, and the necessary sources of information, are analogous to the binocular disparity produced by static observation with two eyes (compare Figure 4.12).

source of light such as a projector. If the object is stationary, its two-dimensional shadow projected on the screen will convey little or no information about the three-dimensional shape of the object. However, if the object is rotated, an observer will report the appearance of a solid object, rather than relative motions between parts of a flat shadow.

If one eye is covered, and the head is kept still, the visual world does not suddenly cease to appear three-dimensional. The cues available in this situation are primarily those which were referred to above as pictorial, because of their use in graphical representations. Despite the term, however, they are also present in natural scenes, which is why they are also effective in pictures. Several such cues have their origin in the fact that the retinal projection of any object or surface decreases in angular size with increasing distance. This fact of geometry means that natural scenes contain perspective due to differences in relative retinal size between similar objects at different distances. Also, more distant objects on a ground plane are located higher in the visual field than nearer ones. Most natural surfaces have a visible texture, and man-made ones commonly have either decorative patterns or a regularly repeating structure. When seen at a slant such surfaces therefore display a gradual change in the density of the texture. Such texture gradients provide information not only about relative distance between the nearest and furthest parts, but also about the rate of change of distance; that is, edges, steps, corners and other surface features. Relative size may also change over time. If an object approaches you, its retinal projection increases in angular size. That this can act as a cue to relative distance is shown by the fact that observation of images undergoing expansion and contraction produces a compelling perception that the represented object is moving in depth, towards and away from the observer. The constraints of optical geometry also ensure that opaque objects obscure more distant ones where they overlap, or modify the colour or brightness of the transmitted light if they are transparent. If the observer moves, different portions of obscured objects become visible, and this revealing or obscuring of texture can itself function as a cue to distance.

Over very long distances in the natural environment the colour of surfaces tends to become bluer. This effect, known as aerial perspective, is due to the absorption and scattering of shorter wavelengths by dust and moisture particles in the atmosphere, and gives a sense of receding panorama to a landscape. In very dry or clear air aerial perspective is reduced, and it may be hard to judge the distance and size of landscape features. Aircraft pilots and mariners report problems with navigation as a result. The importance of the various cues to distance in the natural environment is shown when they are reduced or eliminated; the perception of space then becomes very uncertain. In the absence of strong cues to distance, adjacent areas of the field of view tend to take on similar apparent distances, a phenomenon which is called the equidistance tendency. This can be quite pronounced if a distant scene is observed through a nearby frame, like a window. The strong cues available for the frame tend to make the whole scene appear to be at the same distance. Good examples of the problems caused by poor distance perception are given by the descriptions of Arctic travellers of the results of losing spatial perception in an environment without significant contrast and little surface texture. As a result object recognition can be impaired: in one case a Swedish explorer had just completed a description in his notebook of a distant headland with two curving symmetrical glaciers, when he discovered he had been observing a walrus!

It is common for textbooks to include an illustration showing the various cues to relative distance. We feel that this may be misleading, since the impression of depth in pictures is complex, and invariably based on a number of conflicting cues. Alternatively, the cues mentioned above can all be seen by observing your own visual envirnonment. If you look at a nearby object, such as a pen held at arm's length, you can note the difference between the views of the object available to each eye, by opening and closing each eye alternately. Using both eyes, converge on a surface about one metre beyond the pen, and you will see the double images of it, since they have too great a degree of crossed disparity to be fused. If you reduce the distance between the pen and the further surface, the double images will disappear and you should see a single pen and the background separated in depth. Now observe with one eye only, but move your head from side to side through about 10 cm. The depth should reappear, this time from motion parallax. With a stationary head and with one eye covered, look at the room you are in, or out of a window if possible. If there is enough distance, you can observe the presence of perspective in the texture of walls, floors or ceilings, and in the convergence of actually parallel contours. If there are a number of objects in view, some will partially obscure others, providing the cue of interposition. Note the presence of shadows; we generally tend to ignore their presence, but they carry information about the shape of the objects that cast them, or the surface on which they fall, if the location of the light source is known. Paradoxically, the fact that you can see these effects with monocular observation and a stationary head means that they are at best partially effective as cues to distance. If they were wholly effective, then they would cause the modification of perceived size to correspond to the actual physical distance, and no differences in relative size would be apparent.

REFERENCE NOTES

The material covered in this chapter is diverse, and not usually drawn together in the manner which we have adopted. Howard's (1982) *Human Visual Orientation* is a very important sourcebook, which provides detailed analyses of a wide range of experimental findings concerned with the perception of spatial location. He emphasises the importance of defining frames of reference, and the interrelation of information from vision and other sensory systems. It is a remarkable and comprehensive synthesis of knowledge about many aspects of vision, and is an indispensable source of further information about many of the topics covered in this chapter. The earlier *Human Spatial Orientation* by Howard and Templeton (1966) covers a broader range, including non-visual processes of localisation and orientation, and is also useful. Visual direction and the concept of the cyclopean eye are clearly discussed by Ono in his chapter in Regan (1990) *Vision and Visual Dysfunction: Binocular Vision*. The nature and control of eye movements, and the significance of Hering's Law are also included here. Ono (1981) gives a historical account of the development of ideas about visual direction and singleness of vision.

The perception of distance is covered in most textbooks on vision, but often confined to a discussion of pictorial cues. Gogel's chapter in Epstein (1977) *Stability and Constancy in Visual Perception* describes the basis of egocentric distance perception. In the same volume, the chapter by Ono and Comerford provides an analysis of depth constancy and the geometry of binocular disparity. Gogel's approach to the role of distance perception in vision is well illustrated by his chapter with Mertz in Hershenson's (1989) *The Moon Illusion*, a collection which demonstrates the longevity of some issues in perception. The illusion concerned has been discussed since classical times, and is still not resolved. Kaufman's (1974) *Sight and Mind* gives a very clear exposition of cues to distance. Haber and Hershenson's (1980) *The Psychology of Visual Perception* is also recommended. The discovery of the stereoscope, and the rivalry between Brewster and Wheatstone can be studied in Wade's (1983) *Brewster and Wheatstone on Vision*. Papers on vision by both these Victorian scientists are reprinted here, and their respective contributions assessed. Further discussion of the historical development of ideas about binocular vision can be found in Wade (1987). Another useful source is Spillmann and Wooten's (1984) *Sensory Experience, Adaptation and Perception*. This is a collection of chapters by many of those currently active in visual science, in honor of the Austrian psychologist Ivo Kohler. The chapter by Rogers and Graham describes the measurement of depth from motion parallax, and its relationship to depth from stereopsis. The arctic explorer's confusion between a glacier and a walrus is recounted by Lopez (1986).

Chapter 5

Motion

We need not only to locate objects in space but also in time. Without the temporal dimension spatial location alone would be of little use to us. Of course, the change in spatial location over time is motion. Retinal image motion can be a consequence of displacement either of the object relative to a stationary environment or of the observer relative to a stationary object. In addition both object and observer could move together. All these conditions result in changes in the pattern of stimulation at the eyes, but despite these we retain an appropriate representation of both our position in space as well as that of the object. Occasionally, errors do occur in our perception of motion, and these can be very instructive in understanding the nature of motion perception.

One example that most people have experienced is the false allocation of motion that can occur when seated in a stationary train as a neighbouring train pulls slowly away from the station. We initially perceive the carriage in which we are seated to be moving, and this false allocation is only later replaced by the veridical percept when the other train is moving faster. Why does this happen? In order to understand it we need to examine the frames of reference that are present. First consider the situation when the train in which we are seated moves out of a station. There is a relative displacement of the platform with respect to the windows of the carriage. Some aspects that were initially visible disappear from view and others that were previously occluded become visible. The rate of these changes increases as the velocity of the train increases. Any stable environment will produce such an optic flow (to use one of Gibson's terms) with respect to a moving vehicle, and so it is the characteristic that usually defines vehicular motion. In the case where the neighbouring train starts to move the optic flow produced is ambiguous – it could be a consequence of either train moving, but it is more common for the motion of the whole visual field to specify self motion rather than motion of the environment. The illusion of motion only occurs if the neighbouring train is close enough to occupy the whole of the view visible through a large window; if it is several tracks away, so that other parts of the station are visible, then there is no illusion.

One of the reasons that we cease to experience motion of our own carriage after some seconds is that the illusory motion is not accompanied by the slight carriage motions that do occur when our train is actually moving. We can register these via receptors in the inner ear (in the vestibular system) that signal body motion through space. There is, then, a conflict between visual information signalling self motion and vestibular information signalling that the body is stationary; initially vision is dominant but it is later modified by the vestibular signals for stability. However, the situation is rather more complicated than this, because the eyes rarely remain fixed with respect to the surrounding environment. During the illusory motion we can look around the carriage and perceive that it is stable. Thus, some motions over the eyes (due to eye movements) result in perceptual stability of the carriage whereas others (due to motions relative to the window frame) produce an illusion of motion.

It is clear from this example that there are many aspects to motion perception – motion with respect to the eyes due to eye movements, motions of the head, and relational motions within the visual field. It is for this reason that we will treat motion perception in a similar way to that adopted for the perception of location, namely by starting with simple situations and building up to more complex ones that more typically reflect our normal perception in a well-structured environment. The first stage will be to consider motion with respect to a single, stationary eye, then eye movements will be introduced, and finally head and body motions will be included. The resulting perception is of motion with respect to the stable frame of reference of the earth's surface. Our representation of location and motion is with respect to this stable frame of reference, which we refer to as geocentric. It might not appear so from many experiments concerned with motion perception, because they are often conducted under unnatural conditions involving a fixed head, and sometimes with stimuli that are presented for such short intervals that the eyes cannot move over them.

The example that we have chosen to illustrate an illusion of motion is also unnatural. Our species, like all others, has evolved to process motions that occur in the natural environment and to compensate for the consequences of our own biological motions. These latter involve rotations of the eyes, and translations of the head produced by walking, running, jumping and turning. We have not evolved to compensate for the vagaries of vehicular travel, although we do so successfully most of the time. Similarly, we have not evolved to process briefly presented sequences of still pictures, like those produced on television and in films, although we do derive a compelling illusion of motion from them. Many experiments on motion perception have focused on this type of apparent motion, to the detriment of research on what is called real motion. We will try to redress the balance a little by concentrating on object and observer motions.

SOURCES OF MOTION STIMULATION

One of the paradoxes of visual motion perception is that movement over the retina is not a necessary condition for its occurrence. This has been established most clearly in laboratory experiments, but it can also be demonstrated in a number of naturally occurring phenomena. When the moon is observed on a cloudless night it appears to be stationary. However, when clouds pass near or over the moon it appears to move, even when we maintain fixation on it. This is called induced movement, and it is a clear instance of visual motion without retinal displacement. We will return to the phenomenon of induced movement later in this chapter, but for the moment it suffices to indicate that we need to consider more than retinal motion if we are to understand the perception of motion.

Motion over the retina can be produced in a wide variety of ways, because of the complex motions that observers can make with respect to a stationary environment, as well as the motions of objects in that environment. In this section we will outline the major sources of motion stimulation that follow from observer and object motions, and we will also describe some of the motion phenomena that are studied by visual scientists.

Observer motions

Observer motions can be considered in terms of the principal articulations that change the position of the eyes in space. The most basic level is that of eye movements. All eye movements are rotations. The centre of rotation is located about 13.5 mm behind the cornea, and rotations can occur around a vertical axis (towards and away from the nose), around the horizontal axis between the eyes (elevation and depression) and around the optical axis of the eye (torsion). The rotations can be slow and smooth, as when pursuing a moving object, or they can be very brief and ballistic.

Many eye rotations occur as a consequence of head movements, and their function is to maintain fixation on environmental stimuli despite the change in head position. Such compensatory eye movements result from stimulation of receptors in the vestibular system, and they take place both quickly and with precision; they are referred to as vestibulo-ocular reflexes. Amongst these are the 'doll's eye reflexes' – when the head rotates upward and backward about a horizontal axis the eyes retain the same direction with respect to the environment. That is, they rotate in the opposite direction to the head, as occurs with many dolls which have movable eyes. There are similar compensatory eye rotations for the other rotations of the head in space.

The head undergoes translations as well as rotations in space. The translations can be very complex because of the many articulations that are possible with other body parts – the head on the trunk, rotations of the torso, and bending at the hips and knees. Many of these articulations are a function of locomotion, and the motion of the head during walking and running is more uniform than that of other body parts. This can be seen most clearly in animals with lateral eyes: if you watch the head of a bird, like a seagull, when it is walking, its head remains relatively fixed in space and then moves rapidly forward, remaining there until another rapid forward movement is made. When we walk the head motion follows a path that is more nearly horizontal, despite the appreciable vertical movements of other parts of our body. We do not have the jerky head movements that are common in birds because both our eyes are pointing in the direction of motion. We can fixate on some distant object straight ahead and maintain fixation during locomotion.

The optical consequences of head movements can be distinguished from those produced by eye movements. When a single eye rotates all objects in a scene that are aligned in one eye position remain aligned following a rotation. You can easily ascertain that this is so. Keeping your head still, and closing one eye, look at some objects that are in the same direction but at different distances from you; when you rotate the eye they will remain aligned. Another characteristic of eye rotation is that some parts of the scene that were formerly visible disappear, and others that were not initially visible are disclosed. This occurs symmetrically for elevations and depressions, but not quite so symmetrically for rotations about a vertical axis. The visual field is not evenly bounded on the nasal and temporal sides, and so turning the eye in a nasal direction results in the nose obscuring a larger part of the visual field than is the case when the eye rotates temporally. All these features are unique to rotations of an eye, and they can be contrasted to the consequences of head rotations and translations.

Head rotations, as in turning to the left or right, involve translations of the eye as well as changes in direction. This results in the relative displacements of objects at different distances. Again, you can easily demonstrate for yourself. Try to keep the position of the single open eye constant in the orbit and rotate the head: objects no longer retain the same alignments, and near objects can occlude parts of more distant ones that were formerly visible or, conversely, disclose parts that were formerly hidden from view. Moreover, the occlusion and disclosure at the left and right boundaries of the visual field does not change the proportion of the field occupied by the nose. Thus, the pattern of visual stimulation can serve to differentiate between rotations of the head and of the eye.

Head movements can also be translations in the three dimensions of space. Forward movement results in a radial expansion of the visual field; if the gaze is straight ahead, then objects at the extremities of the visual field are lost from sight, and distant ones are enlarged. Movement towards a large object results in it occluding more of the background, and the optical expansion increases greatly with impending contact. Sideways movement produces a horizontal optic flow, and upward movement results in a vertical flow. In each case there is a symmetrical change at the extremities of the field, and objects at different distances undergo relative displacements.

Object motions

All the retinal motions described above have been considered with respect to a stable and stationary environment. Additional retinal displacements follow from object motion. When a rigid object moves with respect to a stationary background certain transformations in the optic array occur which can be used to determine the path of object motion. Suppose a rectangular object moves in a frontal plane, then parts of the background will become occluded by the leading edge, other parts will be disclosed by the trailing edge, and there will be shearing along the edges parallel to the motion. You can produce such motion with this book, by holding it at arm's length and moving it horizontally and vertically; note the displacements of the book with respect to objects in the background. This pattern of relative displacements will apply whatever orientation the book is held in, as long as its motion path is in the frontal plane. If, however, the book is rotated in the frontal plane a different pattern of transformations will ensue. Some small part of the background remains occluded continuously, whereas other parts (those in close alignment to the edges of the book) are systematically and symmetrically occluded and disclosed. Yet other transformations follow from varying the angle of the book to the line of sight (rotating it about a vertical axis). The maximum amount of background is occluded when the book is in the frontal plane and the minimum amount when it is in the median plane (with its spine either towards or away from you); between these two extremes, the approaching edge expands optically and the receding edge contracts. Thus, there is optical information available in the patterns of transformation for the paths along which rigid objects move. These three situations are illustrated schematically in Figure 5.1.

In these examples of object translations and rotations we have considered the transformations with respect to the visible background. What would be seen if the background were not visible? This situation is difficult to examine if an object like a book is visible, but it can be studied by attaching points of light to the four corners of the cover of a book and observing them in an otherwise dark room. Motion of the four points in a horizontal direction would not produce any changes in their relative position nor in their relative orientation (see Figure 5.2a). Under these circumstances the motion might not even be detected at all. If it was, it would be due to information from the eyes derived from pursuing the points. This is a situation that we refer to as uniform motion, and it will be discussed in more detail in the following sections. Rotation of the points in

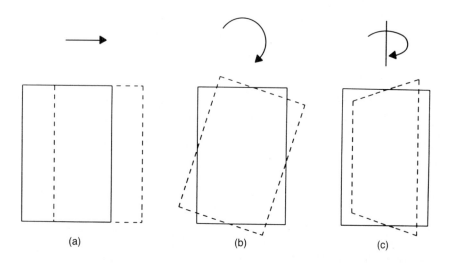

Figure 5.1 Optical transformations produced by a rectangular object (a) moving horizontally in the frontal plane, (b) rotating in the frontal plane, and (c) rotating about a vertical axis. In addition to the optical transformations of the object itself, different aspects of the background are occluded and disclosed by each one.

the frontal plane would not change the relative orientation of the points – they would remain in a rectangular configuration – but their orientation with respect to gravity would be changed (see Figure 5.2b). We can perceive motion accurately under these conditions, which indicates how important object orientation is in determining our perception of location and motion. The third transformation, rotation about a vertical axis, modifies both the relative separations and the relative orientations of the points. The lights on the receding edge would remain vertical but their separation would decrease while those on the approaching edge would increase and remain vertical; the separations of the upper and lower points would decrease as would their relative orientations (see Figure 5.2c). These complex transformations are typically seen as a surface changing its bearing with respect to the observer.

The Swedish psychologist Gunnar Johansson has examined these conditions experimentally. Rather than attach light points to the corners of a book he has simulated the transformations on a flat screen, so that only the four points are visible. He even made more subtle transformations than the ones described above. If just one of the points moves with respect to the others observers report that a surface, like a sheet of paper, is bending. As a consequence of these and many other experiments Johansson has

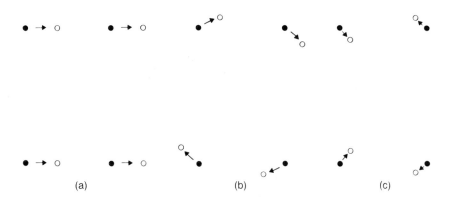

Figure 5.2 Optical transformations produced by four lights at the extremities of a rectangular object (a) moving horizontally in the frontal plane, (b) rotating in the frontal plane, and (c) rotating about a vertical axis.

proposed that 'the visual system spontaneously abstracts relational invariances in the optic flow and constructs percepts of rigid objects moving in three-dimensional space'. Similar rigidity assumptions lie at the heart of computational approaches to motion perception. That is, transformations over time between imaged points will be interpreted as changes in the orientation of a rigid surface with respect to the position of observation.

Support for the rigidity assumption derives from research Johansson initiated on biological motion. These experiments are just like the situation described above with placing lights on the extremities of a book. However, lights were placed on the joints of moving humans so that the many articulating parts would change the relative positions of the lights. Figure 5.3 illustrates a static view of lights placed on the shoulders, elbows, wrists, hips, knees and ankles of a walking person; not all twelve light sources are necessarily seen because some are occluded by the unseen body. Without some prior knowledge (such as you now have) it would be difficult to discern the nature of the object so illuminated. As soon as the array undergoes movement the object is recognised as a person, and the nature of their movement can also be discriminated – whether running or walking, dancing or drinking. It is unfortunate that this dramatic conversion from a static jumble of dots to a coherent perception of action cannot be illustrated in a book.

The facility for making fine discriminations of biological motions has received considerable experimental attention. With film sequences, human

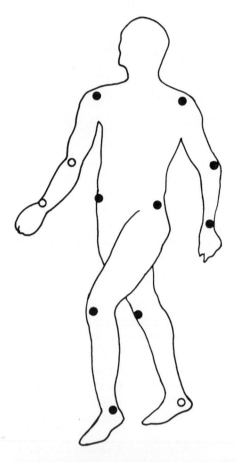

Figure 5.3 Six pairs of lights attached to the major articulations of the body; the filled dots would be visible and the unfilled ones would not be seen in the posture shown here. When a single static array is seen it is not recognised, but as soon as movement is added the lights are recognised as being attached to a person. (After Johansson, 1976)

motion can be recognised in as little as 1/10 s, that is, from just two frames of film. Reliable estimates of the gender of the lighted subject can be made, largely on the basis of differences in the centres of movement (the point in the body relative to which all movements are related); it is higher in females than males. With lights on the hips, knees, ankles and toes it is possible to distinguish between a walking male or female from a single step. Observers can estimate the weight of unseen objects on the basis of the relational dynamics of the points on the lifter. Thus, not only is the optic flow to a moving observer transformed in systematic ways, but the articulations of observed humans can be readily perceived.

MOTION PHENOMENA

It is evident from the above discussion that motion over the retina can be produced in a wide variety of ways, many of which are a consequence of eye and head movements. These complex and dynamic patterns of stimulation might be thought of as making motion perception incredibly complicated, but we do not experience it as such. We perceive the world as stable despite all these perturbations; in fact, we are not usually aware that a problem exists. Psychologists hold differing views about both the nature of and the solution to the problem of perceiving moving and stationary objects. The description of optic flows above reflects Gibson's approach to motion perception. He has drawn attention to the lawfulness of the transformations that take place with eye and object motions and he suggests that we use them to determine both our posture and the motion of objects in the world. In spite of the promise of this approach, relatively little research has been addressed to it. Instead, the history of research on motion perception has focused on simple phenomena that can be studied in the laboratory. Motion phenomena do have a longer history than many other phenomena in visual perception. This is probably because certain aspects of motion perception in the natural world are paradoxical. One was mentioned above, namely, the induced motion of the moon when clouds pass near it. The problem this posed to students of vision was whether the perceived motion was a consequence of physical motion of the moon or of some disturbance in our perception. This seems a strange contrast to us because we understand the laws of planetary motion, but before they were established the possiblity that the moon moved when clouds passed by it was a reasonable alternative. Even after planetary motion was described scientifically a false interpretation was applied to another aspect of motion perceived in heavenly bodies. In 1799, during his voyage around South America, the great German naturalist, Alexander von Humboldt, recorded that a certain star appeared to wander about haphazardly in the night sky. He even called the phenomenon 'Sternschwankung' or 'star wandering'. Other observers were able to see the phenomenon, too, though they did not all describe the haphazard movements in a similar way. A debate arose about the precise nature of the star movements, and it was decided that the star should be observed independently by several astronomers at the same time, and the reports of the motion paths could then be compared. When there was no consistency in the motions of the same star seen at the same time, it became clear that they were dealing with a perceptual rather than a physical phenomenon. The German physiologist Herman Aubert called this the autokinetic phenomenon in 1861, and it is not confined to stars. If you look at a stationary and very dim light (like a glowing cigarette end) in an otherwise totally dark room it will appear to wander about haphazardly, like the star that Humboldt observed.

The first half of the nineteenth century was a particularly rich period for describing novel motion phenomena. One that has been examined almost continually since its description in 1834 is the waterfall illusion. The phenomenon must have been seen countless times, but it was described initially by Robert Addams, a London chemist, during a tour of the Scottish Highlands. Addams observed the Falls of Foyers (Figure 5.4), which descend into Loch Ness, from a platform located on a level with the centre of the waterfall:

> Having steadfastly looked for a few seconds at a particular part of the cascade, admiring the confluence and decussation of the currents forming the liquid drapery of waters, and then suddenly directed my eyes to the left, to observe the face of the sombre age-worn rocks immediately contiguous to the water-fall, I saw the rocky surface as if in motion upwards, and with an apparent velocity equal to that of the descending water, which the moment before had prepared my eyes to behold that singular deception.

Thus, rocks that were initially seen as stationary could appear to ascend following observation of descending water. We now call this a movement after-effect, because it is not confined to waterfalls. It can be produced by prolonged inspection of almost any uniformly moving surface, but it is frequently studied in the laboratory with stimuli like those shown in Figure 5.5. The after-effect is restricted to the area of the retina exposed to the real motion and it decays relatively quickly. Following inspection for around 30 s, motion in a stationary stimulus can be seen for up to 20 s; initially the velocity is high and then it decreases until the stimulus appears stationary once more. The motion seen as an after-effect is itself somewhat paradoxical – the stationary stimulus appears to move but not to change position! For example, the rocks by the waterfall seem to ascend but they remain in the same position with respect to neighbouring rocks that are not subject to the apparent motion. Any real motion of objects involves changes in location over time. The motion after-effect is a negative after-effect, like that for tilt described on p. 90; that is, the appearance of motion in the stationary field is in the opposite direction to the real movement previously observed.

Induced movement can also be studied with a wide range of stimuli, like those illustrated in Figure 5.6. The motion can be linear or circular, and the induced motion is always in the direction opposite to the inducing movement. It is possible to move the inducing component so slowly that it cannot be detected, but it can still induce motion in the stationary component. Induced movement is a simultaneous disturbance of motion

Figure 5.4 Photograph of the Falls of Foyers

perception, rather than a successive one like the motion after-effect.

The extension of the range of novel motion phenomena described in the early nineteenth century was not solely a consequence of a growing interest in motion perception, but also because of the invention of instruments to present stimuli in novel and artificial ways. Prominent amongst these was one, invented independently by three visual scientists around 1830, which forms the basis of modern motion pictures. It presented stimuli discretely, briefly, and in succession; that is, a sequence of drawings differing slightly from one another were viewed successively through slits in a rotating disc (Figure 5.7). To the astonishment of the observer, the

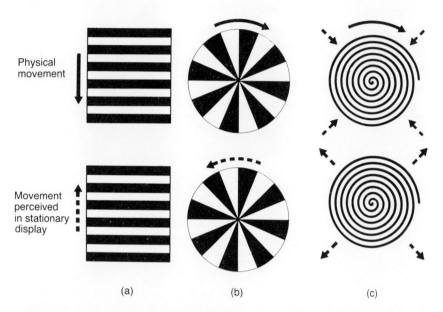

Physical movement

Movement perceived in stationary display

(a)   (b)   (c)

Figure 5.5 Laboratory stimuli that are used to produce movement after-effects. (a) Linear motion of a grating, (b) rotation of a sectored disc, and (c) rotation of a spiral. The physically stationary patterns are initially seen as stationary. During the physical motion the movement is perceived as shown by the solid arrows, but the spiral also appears to contract. Following about 30 s adaptation the stationary patterns appear to move in the directions indicated by the dashed lines.

represented figures appeared to move: perceived motion was synthesised from a sequence of still pictures.

The apparent motion seen with the phenakistoscope (or stroboscopic disc as it was also called), and in films, is based on two phenomena – visual persistence and stroboscopic motion. Visual persistence was described and even measured by Newton. He noted that a glowing ember at the end of a stick could be seen as a circle if the stick was rotated with sufficient speed. That is, the visual response to light outlasts the duration of physical stimulation. Much of our artificial lighting is intermittent rather than continuous, but we are generally unaware of this because of visual persistence; fluorescent tubes flicker with the frequency of the alternating current supply, but we only notice the intermittency when they become faulty. Stroboscopic motion was a new phenomenon: when two successive stimuli are presented in slightly different locations motion is seen, within certain temporal limits. If the blank interval between the briefly presented stimuli

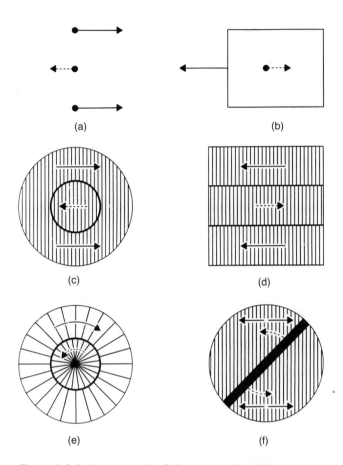

Figure 5.6 Laboratory stimuli that are used to induce movement in a stationary target. In all cases the physically moving parts are shown by solid lines and the dashed lines indicate the induced motion of the stationary components. (a) Two moving dots, (b) dot and rectangle, (c) annular movement of a grating, (d) flanking movement of gratings, (e) rotary motion of a radial annulus, and (f) line rotation induced by optical expansion of a grating. Linear induced motion is produced by (a)–(d), rotary induced motion by (e), and a combination of linear and rotary induced motion in (f).

is too short then they appear to be visible simultaneously; if it is too long they appear to be successive, and at around 100–200 msec (milliseconds) motion appears. It is possible to satisfy the conditions for stroboscopic motion independently of those for visual persistence. This is what

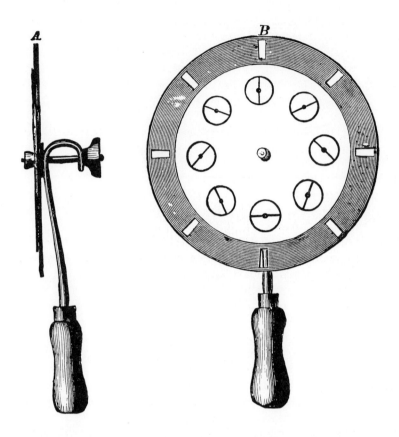

Figure 5.7 A phenakistoscope or stroboscopic disc. A side view is shown on the left, and the disc could be rotated by turning the central knob. The front face is shown on the right. The disc is rotated while facing a mirror. Its reflection is observed through the slits around the circumference. Each slit is opposite a slightly different drawing – here a set of diameters – which are seen in succession, creating an impression of a rotating diameter. (From Helmholtz, 1924)

happened in the early days of the cinema. Films were taken and projected at 16 frames per second; this satisfies the criteria for stroboscopic motion, but it is rather slow for visual persistence, and so the pictures appeared to flicker – hence 'the flicks'. The problem was overcome by both increasing the frame rate to 24 per second, and illuminating each frame with three pulses of light, so that the flicker rate is 72 per second, which is well above our flicker threshold.

The rail system was also developing rapidly in the early nineteenth century, and rail travel exposed people to patterns of visual motion that were outwith the natural range. It is not surprising, therefore, that there are phenomena, like those mentioned in the introduction to the chapter, particularly associated with vehicular stimulation. The false motion that is attributed to the carriage in which we are seated is, again, one case of many that can be studied in a laboratory. The experience of self motion as a consequence of visual movement is called vection, and it can occur in the three dimensions of space. That is, we can experience forward body motion when the optic flow is artificially modified to mimic this, or forward tilt or sideways rotation if the visual environment is appropriately manipulated. These effects are not confined to vehicles and laboratories, as they have a venerable history in the fairground. Many fairground attractions involve abnormal patterns of motion, both vestibular and visual, and so it is not surprising to find that the desire for abnormal stimulation should have exploited vection, too. There is a venerable and fiendish device called the witch's swing, on which an individual stands and experiences considerable self motion although little occurs. The visible room surrounding the person is not anchored to the ground, but swings about. This induces the impression of self motion in the opposite directions to those of the room; such impressions are intensified when allied with an unstable platform on which the hapless individual stands.

The phenomena of motion perception, like those in other areas of vision, tend to be those cases where errors are made in the allocation of motion. These errors occur under natural conditions as well as artificial ones, and we can learn a lot from studying them. They should not, however, deflect us from examining the wider range of instances in which our perception does correspond to the physical motions in the environment. In the following sections of this chapter we will outline an approach to motion perception that builds on the concepts described in the previous chapter for the perception of direction and distance. That is, we will commence by considering motion with respect to a retinocentric frame of reference, and then proceed through the egocentric and geocentric levels.

RETINOCENTRIC MOTION

The physical definition of motion is the change of position over time. Position is a relative term and its measurement requires the specification of a frame of reference. The first frame of reference we will examine is that of the retina itself. Visual motion is mediated by stimulation of the retina, but motion perception is not synonymous with retinal motion. Initially, we will examine the simplified situation of a single eye that is stationary with respect to the head, which in its turn is stationary with respect to the environment. If the eye is fixed in space then object motion would produce motion over the retina. We will consider two conditions of object motion – with and without any background visible. When an object moves in isolation (without any visible background) the only source of information for its motion derives from the displacement over the retina; this is called uniform motion. When a background is also visible, there is information for its uniform motion and also for its displacement relative to the background; this is referred to as relational motion.

Around the middle of the nineteenth century, Aubert measured the thresholds for detecting uniform and relational motions. When a target moved in isolation its motion could be detected when it reached a velocity of about 0.3 deg/s (degrees per second). When a patterned background was visible the threshold was approximately 0.03 deg/s. Therefore, the threshold for relational motion is much less than that for uniform motion. We will, however, consider uniform motion initially.

Uniform motion

When a target, like a point of light, moves over the retina it stimulates a sequence of local signs. In order for the sequence to be registered as motion there would need to be some temporal integration between the neighbouring local signs. Visual persistence provides evidence that such temporal integration does occur. That is, if the neural effects of stimulation at neighbouring local signs outlast the duration of stimulation, then they will be active at the same time even though the physical stimulation is successive. Temporal integration only operates within certain limits: if the motion is too slow it will be registered as successive; if it is too fast it will be registered as simultaneous. Thus, the angular motion of a point could be registered by a retinal motion signal, as is shown in Figure 5.8. Note that in the figure the same retinal motion signal would be produced by the different motion paths shown, provided that the angular velocity with respect to the eye was the same. This is called a retinocentric motion signal.

The retinocentric frame of reference is not confined to the retina, but is constrained by the retinal coordinate system. Neurophysiologists have demonstrated that the cells in the visual cortex are coded retinocentrically; that is, they respond when particular regions of the retina are stimulated, regardless of the direction the eyes are pointing. Many cells in the visual cortex are specifically responsive to motion in a particular direction and also at a particular velocity (see pp. 81–5). For example, one cell might respond to a horizontally oriented edge moving downwards over a particular region of the retina; it would also respond to a stationary horizontal edge in the same region, but not as strongly as to the downward motion; upward motion of a horizontal edge over the same region would have very little influence on the cell's activity. Another cell can have the opposite pattern of activity. In this way, different cells will respond to all orientations and directions of motion. Cortical cells could only respond in these ways if there were temporal integration over retinal local signs.

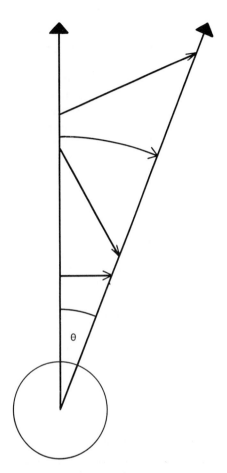

Figure 5.8 Retinocentric motion. All the different motion paths shown by the arrowed lines could result in the same rate of change of visual angle with respect to the retina.

Some visual motion phenomena have been interpreted in terms of retinocentric processes like motion detectors. One such is the motion after-effect mentioned above. Consider what happens when an observer initially looks at the rocks by the side of a waterfall: the stationary rocks will have many contours which will stimulate physiological edge detectors. Many of these edge detectors will respond more strongly to motion in one direction than in the other. For example, horizontal contours will excite motion detectors for downward and upward movement, but the net effect of these would cancel. Thus, the perception of stationariness is dependent upon the

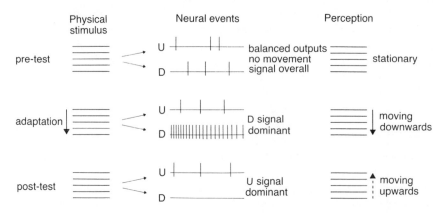

Figure 5.9 An interpretation of the movement after-effect based upon adaptation of cortical motion detectors. In the pre-test a stationary grating will excite motion detectors for upward (U) and downward (D) direction equally, and so the net activity will favour neither, resulting in its stationary appearance. During adaptation the downward direction detectors are strongly excited resulting in a neural signal for that direction, which is reflected in perception. In the post-test the stationary grating is presented again. The downward direction detectors have been adapted due to prolonged stimulation and so are not responsive. The upward detectors signal as before, but since there is no balancing output from the downward detectors the net activity signals upward motion, and the stationary grating is seen as ascending. (After Frisby, 1979)

balanced activity of motion detectors coding opposite directions of motion (Figure 5.9). When the waterfall is observed the downward motion detectors will be strongly stimulated; if this stimulation is prolonged, the motion detectors will adapt or fatigue. Subsequent observation of the stationary rocks will produce a different net effect: the fatigued downward motion detectors will exert less influence than the unadapted upward motion detectors. Therefore, the signal from the stationary rocks would be similar to one produced by contours moving slowly upwards, and that corresponds to what is seen. The effect is considered to be retinocentric because the motion after-effect is confined to the region of the retina that has been exposed to the motion.

The recordings from single cortical cells fulfil the requirements for retinocentric stimulation because the experimental animals are anaesthetised and the eye is immobilised. Therefore any stimulus motion will have a geometrically corresponding retinal image motion. This rarely occurs with natural vision because of the eye movements that will be described in the next section. However, stroboscopic motion does come close to meeting the requirements for retinocentric stimulation: apparent motion can be seen between two brief, stationary and spatially distinct pulses of light, if the temporal and spatial separations are appropriate. Two different types of stroboscopic or apparent motion have been described. One is called the short-range process because it is confined to spatial separations between the stimuli of less than 15 min of visual angle, and temporal intervals of about 100 msec. The short range process can only be activated if both stimuli are presented to the same eye.

Relational motion

Waterfalls are not seen in isolation; they occur in a wide variety of terrains. Accordingly, waterfall illusions in the natural environment involve relational motion. The water descends with respect to the 'age-worn rocks immediately contiguous', and so there is available an alternative visible frame of reference – a patterncentric one. The motion after-effect examined in the confines of the laboratory is similarly dependent upon relational motion. Rotating sectored discs and spirals present relational motions between their individual parts, but after-effects based on linear motion require a patterned background relative to which the motion can be allocated. Therefore, even one of the phenomena that was thought to be dependent on uniform motion is in fact using patterncentric signals, too. It might be expected that a large uniformly moving display, like a vertically striped cylinder rotating around an observer, would be the ideal stimulus for generating a movement after-effect. In fact it is not; rather than producing a visual motion after-effect it results in the observer's apparent self motion. It is an example of vection, similar to the situation in the train mentioned earlier in the chapter.

Patterncentric signals register the relational motions between stimuli, rather than the retinocentric motions. One of the targets is adopted as a frame of reference relative to which the motion of the other target can be registered, and vice versa. Thus, patterncentric frames of reference are confined to interactions within the pattern projected onto the retina. The patterncentric signal remains the same even if the eyes move, because this does not alter the object separation. Eye movement simply adds a constant amount to the displacement of all retinal images, leaving differences in displacement unchanged. There are as many patterncentric frames of reference available as there are independently moving objects. Although this might sound a dauntingly complex process for the visual system to undertake, it is not so in practice because many of the patterncentric frames of reference are equivalent. Consider the eye fixed in space and viewing the waterfall. The patterncentric frame of reference could be taken as the descending water or as the rocks. In the former case the water would be taken as stationary and the rocks would be registered as moving upwards, or the rocks could be taken as stationary and the water descending. We do not need to use knowledge of the world to adopt the latter frame of reference, because there is much more correlated patterncentric information for the stability of the rocks rather than the water. Many other objects projected onto the retina, like trees, grass, or the river bed, yield the same outcome as that for the rocks, namely that the water is descending and the other features remain in the same relation to one another. Under normal circumstances, the environment provides a stable patterncentric frame of reference relative to which object motions can be allocated.

The night sky is somewhat unusual in this regard, and the induced movement of the moon provides us with a phenomenon that can be used to emphasise the points made above. Induced movement can be studied in the laboratory with displays like those shown in Figure 5.6, which allow us to study the uniform and relational components in retinocentric motion. One of the simplest displays consists of three points of light in an otherwise dark room; the central point remains stationary and the outer two move in the same direction at the same speed. Under these circumstances observers report that the central point appears to move in the opposite direction: motion is induced in it. The two moving points provide a more powerful patterncentric frame of reference than the single stationary one. On the one hand, if the patterncentric frame was the only factor operating then the two outer points would not appear to move at all; on the other, if uniform process operated alone the central point would appear stationary and the outer points would appear to move. However, what typically happens is that motion is seen in both components of the display. This outcome indicates that both uniform and patterncentric processes are implicated in induced movement. The same outcome applies to the other displays shown in Figure 5.6.

Up to this stage we have considered motion with respect to a single eye. Relational motion can also be considered to operate between the eyes. That is, different patterns of retinocentric stimulation can occur with respect to each eye. This can be illustrated in terms of the second type of stroboscopic motion, which is called the long-range process because it can occur with longer temporal intervals and greater angular separations between the stimuli. It is possible to present the first stimulus to one eye and the second to the other and apparent motion still occurs. This technique of splitting the stimulation between the eyes is widespread in vision research. It is called dichoptic stimulation, and it can be used to indicate whether a particular phenomenon is based upon neural processes at or before the stage of binocular combination or at or beyond it. The signals from the two eyes are first combined at the level of the visual cortex (see pp. 84–6). Therefore, if a phenomenon (like short-range apparent motion) cannot be elicited when the components are presented dichoptically, it is likely that it is due to neural processes occurring before the visual cortex. Alternatively, when the phenomenon (like long-range apparent motion) does occur with dichoptic stimulation, it is suggestive of a more central site for its occurrence, beyond the level of binocular combination.

Induced motion has also been examined dichoptically. That is, the inducing stimulus can be presented to one eye and the stationary stimulus to the other. The results from such experiments are not easy to interpret because some have shown dichoptic effects and others have not. The situation is difficult to examine experimentally because there is no common stimulus to keep the eyes in alignment. When induced motion has been produced under dichoptic conditions it is likely that the eyes moved with respect to one another, and so the motion seen could have been due to uniform motion alone. We consider that the evidence supports the view that the patterncentric processes are monocular, and occur before the level of binocular integration.

Another popular technique that addresses a similar question is interocular transfer. The movement after-effect can be elicited if one eye is used for observation and if both eyes are used. What would be the outcome if one eye observed the moving display and the other eye viewed the stationary test? The after-effect still occurs, but it does not last as long as when the same eye is used for both inspection and test. If the effect was confined to monocular processes alone it would not show interocular transfer; since it does, this suggests that binocular processes are also implicated in the motion after-effect. Typically, the magnitude of interocular transfer in after-effects is around 60 per cent; the value is about the same for the tilt after-effect as it is for the motion after-effect, which suggests that it might represent a fairly general feature of the way spatial information is coded in the visual system. The involvement of binocular processes in spatial after-effects is supported by the finding that individuals lacking stereopsis (usually as a consequence of an uncorrected squint in childhood) also fail to experience any interocular transfer of after-effects.

EGOCENTRIC MOTION

Human eyes are only stationary when they are paralysed or damaged. As a result, by far the most common cause of retinal image motion is the movements of the eyes themselves. Retinocentric motion information is therefore ambiguous, since it could arise from any combination of object movement and eye movement. In order for the visual system to allocate the retinal image displacement between object movement and eye movement correctly, there must be a source of information about eye movement. Only when both image displacement and eye movements are considered together is it possible to recover changes in the egocentric direction of an object in the environment. The outcome is a representation of object movement with respect to the self; that is, egocentric motion, which is independent of the motions of the eyes in the head.

Types of eye movement

Eye movements and their control have been studied intensively, because they offer the possibility of understanding in detail the link between a visual stimulus and a behavioural response, and of relating these to neurophysiological processes. Various methods have been devised for measuring eye movements, which vary in complexity and precision. The simplest procedure is observation of someone else's eye movements as they read, carry on a conversation, or look around the environment. The most common type of movement is called a saccade, which consists of a rapid displacement of the gaze to a new location. Saccades can reach very high velocities, approaching 800 deg/s at their peak. The size of a saccade is typically around 12–15 deg, but with significant numbers of both larger and smaller amplitudes. When a stimulus appears away from the fovea, there is delay of between 150–250 msec before a saccade starts. Therefore, stimuli can be presented for such short intervals (less than 150 msec) that saccades cannot take place while the stimulus is exposed. This technique of brief stimulus presentation enables experimenters to control the locus of stimulation on the retina, and perceptual phenomena can be examined without interference from retinal displacement due to eye movements. Most people maintain their gaze in one direction for a second or two at most, so saccadic movements are constantly producing image motion over the retina. A good way to elicit saccades is to ask someone to read a passage of text.

Figure 5.10 will allow you to observe your own saccades, through the effect they have on the apparent position of an after-image. After fixating on the white dot for about 30 s, move your gaze to the black dot. You will find that the after-image appears to jump about at irregular intervals, or to drift slowly in one direction. Each jump reflects the occurrence of a saccade. When the slow drift has led to a significant fixation error, it is corrected by a saccade back to the target. These movements are easier to see because the after-image is seen against the contrasting squares of the original figure. While saccades can be readily observed, there are also much smaller movements that are harder to detect. Microsaccades with an amplitude of around 5 min occur constantly, as does a high frequency oscillation of the eyes, known as tremor. The latter two types of movement probably reflect instability or noise in the nerves and muscles which control the positions of the eyes.

Pursuit eye movements occur when a moving target is followed with the eyes. They serve to stabilise the image of the tracked target on the retina. While a pursuit eye movement is taking place, the image of the rest of the visual scene is displaced over the retina in the opposite direction to the eye movement. Pursuit eye movements vary in velocity according to that of the target, although there is an upper limit to target velocity of around 30 deg/s

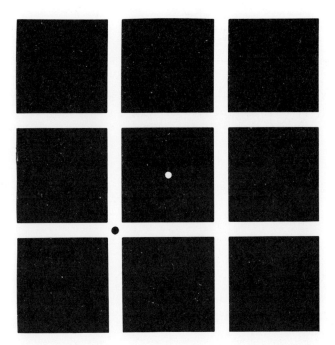

Figure 5.10 A pattern suitable for producing after-images. Fixate the central white dot for about 30 s, under good illumination, then look at a blank surface. The after-image will appear to be opposite in contrast to the pattern. Note how after-images of the squares appear to be different sizes when seen against surfaces at different distances. As you move your eyes, the after-images appear to move also. If you fixate the black dot after the white one, you will be able to see the effects of small involuntary eye movements, in the form of rapid displacements of the after-image squares. You will need to generate after-images several times in order to see all these effects.

if the eyes are to keep up with it. A characteristic pattern of eye movement known as opto-kinetic nystagmus (OKN) occurs when the whole visual scene moves. This happens when looking out of a window in a moving vehicle, and OKN was once known as 'railway nystagmus' for this reason. OKN has two components, called the fast and slow phases. In the slow phase there is smooth pursuit of the moving field, which stabilises the retinal image. If the velocity of field movement increases above around 30 deg/s, the eyes lag progressively behind, and the stabilisation is less effective. The slow pursuit phase alternates with fast, saccadic eye movements that return the eyes to the straight ahead position. OKN seems to be a primitive form of eye movement control, designed to prevent displacements of the retinal image during locomotion.

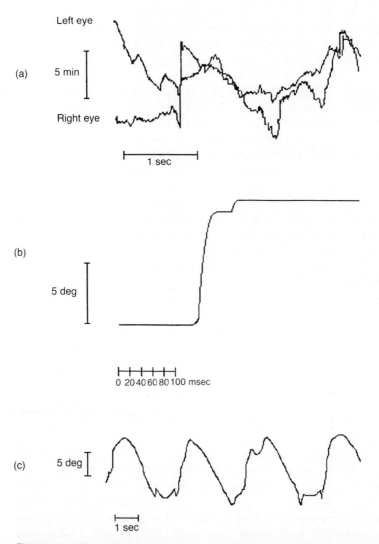

Figure 5.11 Typical examples of eye movement recordings. (a) Slow drift and tremor, during attempted binocular fixation on a point. As fixation error builds up, a corrective saccade brings fixation back on target. Note the absence of strong correlation between the drift in the two eyes, which is essentially random. (b) A refixation saccade. The trace shows an initial undershoot of the target, followed by a second saccade to correct the error. (c) Pursuit of a moving target. The target has a pendulum motion, which is followed by the eyes. Errors give rise to saccades which return the eyes to the target.

Detailed information about eye movements requires some means of recording and measuring the movements, with as much accuracy as possible. Film or video recordings of the eyes can be made under magnification, and a human or a computer program can analyse the movements. This is relatively insensitive, but does not require attachments to the observers' eyes or head. Electrical potentials can be recorded from electrodes placed around the orbit, which alter as the eyes move; this technique is known as electro-oculography. Another technique involves small infrared emitters and detectors which can be mounted on spectacle frames, and aligned so as to pick up the change in infra-red reflected from the boundary between the iris and the sclera, as the eyes move. Other methods make use of contact lenses. A small mirror mounted on a contact lens can reflect a narrow beam of light whose displacements follow those of the eye, and can be recorded with suitable detectors. Recently, contact lenses have been made with a coil of fine wire implanted in them. If the observer sits inside a strong magnetic field, any movement of the eye causes an induced current in the wire, which can be picked up. These procedures require trained observers, and usually interfere to some extent with natural viewing. They require very careful calibration if the measurements are to be accurate, but in principle eye position can be resolved to within less than one degree of angular rotation. Figure 5.11 shows typical recordings of the main types of movement that can occur.

The same methods can be used to interfere with the normal relationship between eye movements and image displacements. For example, the image can be made to remain on the same part of the retina no matter how the eyes move. The earliest attempts to do this in the 1950s used miniature projectors mounted on a thin stalk attached to a contact lens, to produce an optically stabilised image. Provided the lens was firmly attached, observers reported some striking perceptual effects. Most notably, after a few seconds, any pattern would fade completely from view. Before this, complex patterns typically fragmented into a number of components, which sometimes appeared to be related to the meaning of the pattern. For example, a figure consisting of the two letters 'H' and 'B' joined together might be reported to fragment into one or other letter, rather than a random selection of the component lines. It is now thought that reports of meaningfulness in the fragmentation of stabilised images probably reflected the verbal categories available to observers to describe what they saw, and not a perceptual mechanism as such. Similar effects can be observed with after-images, which are also a form of stabilised image, in that the locus of retinal stimulation remains the same regardless of eye movements.

After-images undergo complex patterns of fading and reappearance, until they finally cease to be visible. Coloured after-images in particular produce striking changes, since the colours alter as fading proceeds. Even voluntary fixation of a low-contrast pattern will suffice to produce disappearance; although the eyes still continue to move, this may not be enough to maintain the visibility of poorly defined contours. The effects of stabilisation demonstrate the importance of continual shifts in the pattern of stimulation on the retina. Prolonged and unchanging stimulation causes fatigue and loss of sensitivity at various levels in the visual system, and this leads to subjective disappearance and fading.

Compensation for eye movements

Eye movements are an inevitable counterpart of normal visual perception, whether to fixate on a different part of the visual field, to keep a moving target on the fovea, or to maintain visibility. Recovery of egocentric movement therefore requires information about both image movements over the retina and the movements of the eyes. In practice, it is only pursuit movements that create a significant problem. Saccadic movements are so fast that retinal stimulation is smeared out, during which there is little possibility of detecting any information. In addition, there may be a suppression of visual signals during a saccade. Image displacements during pursuit are, by contrast, similar in extent and velocity to those which occur with object movement. This process of compensation of the retinocentric signal for eye movements was described by Helmholtz, and has since been examined experimentally. In principle, to derive egocentric motion, the requirement is for addition of the retinocentric and eye movement signals, appropriately signed. Suppose that an object moves to the right through 5 deg while the eyes are stationary. The retinocentric motion signal will be proportional to this, and if for the moment we assume that the change in direction is correctly detected, the retinocentric signal can also be represented by a value corresponding to 5 deg. We are able to discriminate between opposite directions of movement, and this can be expressed by giving an algebraic sign to the motion signal. For purposes of discussion, leftward motion of an object will be signed negative, and rightward motion positive. (Rightward object motion corresponds to leftward image motion on the retina, and vice versa, due to the action of the lens.) Added to a zero value for eye movement, a retinocentric motion signal of +5 deg would yield a representation of egocentric motion which corresponds to the actual event. However, if the eyes move to track the object, and assuming that this is successful in maintaining the image on the fovea, then the retinocentric signal will have a value of zero. The eye movement signal will be +5 deg, and again addition of the two yields the correct egocentric motion. This example makes clear that if an object is perceived to be stationary, then this is a particular state of motion perception. A zero value for eye movements or image motion is informative, in that it determines the perception of location over time in the same way as positive or negative values.

What sources of information are available to the visual system regarding pursuit eye movements? There has been much discussion of this issue, generally focusing on the role of feedback from the extra-ocular muscles. Muscle groups, such as those that move the limbs, have sensors that respond to being stretched, and can signal the state of contraction of the muscle. This information provides feedback as to whether a movement is taking place as planned. The eye muscles might work in a similar way, and signal their state of contraction, and thus the movements of the eyes to which they are attached. In fact this does not seem to occur, at least as far as movement perception is concerned. A demonstration of this is that when an eye is moved passively, for example by gentle pushing, stationary objects in the environment appear to move. If there was information available from the muscles themselves, this would not happen. The major source of eye movement information is referred to as the efferent copy, which means that the signals sent to the eye muscles are stored and also used to represent how the eyes will in fact move. Evidently this can only work if the eyes actually move as they are commanded to do, and it may be faster than an afferent feedback loop. The role of efference in motion perception can be seen with after-images; when the eyes are moved voluntarily, the after-image appears to do so also. In this case the absence of retinal motion together with the efferent copy corresponds to an object moving at the same speed and in the same direction as the eyes. However, if the eye is moved passively, the after-image does not appear to move, since there is no voluntary command, and the efferent copy therefore specifies that the eyes are stationary. You can confirm this with an after-image obtained from Figure 5.10. Eye movements can, in principle, also be signalled by optical cues, as was pointed out earlier. When there is a pursuit eye movement, the whole retinal image displaces with equal velocity and by the same extent. This pattern of change could not normally occur for any other reason, and could provide reliable information about eye movements. To be used, there would have to be some means of detecting and comparing image motion across the whole visual field. At present, we have little information as to whether there is such a system, and how it might work.

The account of egocentric motion so far has been based on the assumption that image motions and eye movements are represented correctly in the visual system. Clearly, there might be many reasons why this would not be so. Detection of image motion, like any other sensory process, will depend on the stimulus exceeding a threshold value, and this may vary across the retina. Sensitivity to motion is better in the fovea than in the periphery, although motion is more likely to attract attention in the latter case. Similarly, the signal representing eye movements may not correspond to the actual value. When such mismatches occur, then there should be predictable errors of motion perception. Some examples were given above for active and passive eye movements, but these represent extreme cases. In general, if the extent of eye movements is under-represented, a visible

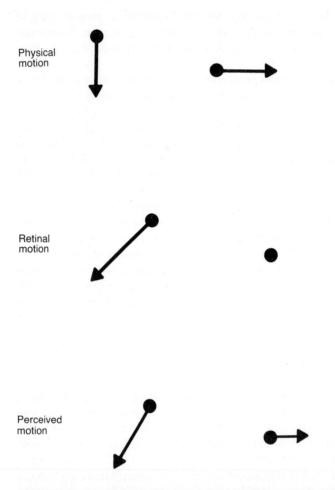

Figure 5.12 Physical, retinal and perceived motion during pursuit. The right hand target moves horizontally, and is followed by eye movements or by head movements. At the same time the left hand target moves downwards. As a result it has an oblique path on the retina. The perceived motion indicates a partial compensation for the retinal displacement due to pursuit, since it lies between the physical and retinal paths. The compensation is better with eye pursuit than with head pursuit. (After Wade and Swanston, 1988)

object will appear to move by more than it actually does, and the converse applies to image motion. Illusions like this can be observed. If a moving object, like a pencil, is pursued by eye movements across a patterned background, the background appears to move in the opposite direction. This can be explained if the internal value for eye movement is too small, so that subtracting it from the image motion of the background gives a non-zero result. If so, it would be predicted that people should underestimate the velocity of the pursued target. This underestimation does occur, and is known as the Aubert-Fleischl effect after its first investigators.

Also, compensation may not be as effective for image displacements in a different direction to the eye movement. If one object is pursued back and forth along a horizontal path while another undergoes vertical motion, the retinal path of the latter will be displaced considerably from its physical orientation. If the horizontal and vertical paths are equal in length, the orientation on the retina of the physically vertical path will be 45 deg. Observers report that the perceived orientation is displaced towards the retinal path (Figure 5.12), indicating that compensation for eye movements is limited. However, the extent of the pursued horizontal motion is not reduced as this would predict. Thus, while egocentric motion in principle represents object displacements independently of the effects of eye movements on retinal image motion, the human visual system does not always achieve a complete compensation. As a result, the motion information available for further analysis is subject to various distortions which may be described as illusions of motion perception. Further analysis is required, because egocentric motion is itself ambiguous whenever an observer is able to move freely in the environment.

GEOCENTRIC MOTION

The discussion of egocentric motion was concerned with displacements of the retinal image due to movements of the eyes in the head. Such eye movements are rotations, and can therefore be directly related to the angular extent of image motion. Compensation for the effects of eye movements can be based on simple representations of the extent of rotation of the eyes, and the extent of image displacement on the retina. However, retinal images may move as the result of head movements, which also change the location of the eyes in space. Eye movements occur with respect to a frame of reference provided by the head, but movements of the head occur in three-dimensional space. The head may turn with respect to the shoulders, but the centre of rotation is not the same as that of the eyes. A more common situation is that the head, and the eyes, move to different spatial locations as the result of movements of the whole body. These may be active, as in locomotion, or passive, as in travelling in a vehicle. These sorts of movement take place with respect to the physical environment, which therefore provides the frame of reference. Movement expressed with respect to the environmental frame of reference is geocentric. A change in egocentric direction as the result of a head movement cannot be interpreted unambiguously unless the extent of both the head movement and of object motion in three dimensions are known. A further stage of analysis, incorporating information for both self movement and perceived object distance, is therefore required. The geocentric representation which results is the basis for motion perception.

Perceived distance and motion

As an example of a phenomenon which demonstrates the interrelation of distance and movement perception, try folding a strip of paper into the shape illustrated in Figure 5.13. Note that the illustration is not the basis for the effect; it is necessary to observe the folded paper itself. Once it is prepared, place it on a table top in front of you under even illumination, and look at it with one eye, by covering the other eye with your hand. After a minute or so you should find that a striking perceptual change occurs, and that there is an inversion of the shape of the folded paper. The peaks become troughs, and vice versa, which means that their perceived distances no longer correspond to their physical distances. Once you have seen this configuration it will be easier to obtain in future, so it is worth persevering.

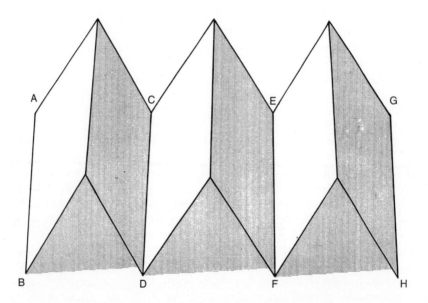

Figure 5.13 How to fold the paper strip for the demonstration described in the text. The paper should be placed on a flat surface so that all the labelled points are touching it. Observe with one eye, and a stationary head. After a time you should see a change in the apparent orientation of the strip. Points A, C, E and G will appear to be in the air, and B, D, F and H on the surface. AB, CD, EF and GH will appear vertical and nearest to you. Small movements of your head will create striking deformations of the shape of the strip.

You may notice changes in the apparent brightness of the illuminated and shaded surfaces, indicating that the interpretation of surface luminance is also dependent on distance information. More obviously, if you move your head slightly from side to side (large movements will destroy the inversion) you will see large shifts in the position of the folds. They will probably seem to move as if the paper is elastic, and being flexed from side to side, with the apparently nearer edges moving in the same direction as your head, and the apparently further ones in the opposite direction.

Similar effects can be observed with stereograms, since they also appear to move when the observer does. Points which are seen with crossed disparity, nearer than the image plane, will move with the head, while points with uncrossed disparity, that appear further away, seem to move against the head. These examples show that perceived distance directly influences the perception of motion. The explanation lies in the processes required to recover geocentric motion from egocentric motion. Consider a stationary object located at a constant egocentric distance. For a stationary observer, the egocentric motion will be zero, if changes in retinal stimulation due to eye movements are fully compensated for. But if the observer moves his head, there will be a shift in egocentric direction, whose extent depends on the distance of the object. Thus, a given head movement produces different retinal motions, and therefore egocentric motions, depending on how far away the observed object is. If the object is to be correctly seen as geocentrically stationary, despite head movements, then a representation is needed of its position in three-dimensional space. This can be obtained from the egocentric motion by scaling it according to perceived distance. If the perceived distance matches the physical distance, the scaled change in egocentric direction will match the extent of the head movement. However, if perceived distance is in error, errors of geocentric motion perception will result. Figure 5.14 shows the effects of underestimation and overestimation of perceived distance on the apparent motion of a physically stationary object. The object may appear to move either left or right, and by varying amounts, depending on the error in perceived distance. Clearly, stimulation on the retina is wholly inadequate to predict what will be seen.

The same analysis can be applied if an object is also moving during observer movement. As with a stationary object, its geocentric motion can only be obtained if its egocentric angular motion is scaled by its perceived distance. Errors in perceived distance could cause an object which is moving to the left being seen to move to the right, and vice versa. The various cues to perceived distance have been discussed in Chapter 4, and there are many situations where errors can occur. A good example is provided by looking out of a window that has marks or dirt on the glass. These are nearby, and there are good cues to their distance. Because of the equidistance tendency, objects seen through the window will appear to be

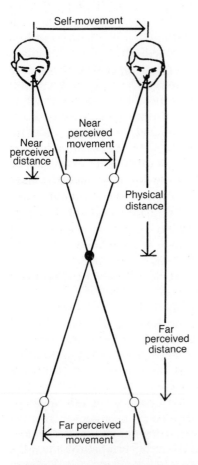

Figure 5.14 The relationship between the perceived position of an object, perceived distance and self movement. An observer moves his head through a distance towards the right, while observing a stationary object, represented by the filled circle. If the object is seen at its physical distance, it will not appear to move. However, if there is an error of perceived distance (open circles), then the object will be perceived as moving. If it is seen as nearer than it really is, it will appear to move in the same direction as the head; if it is seen as further away, the perceived movement will be opposite to the head movement. The extent and direction of apparent movement during self movement can therefore be used as an indirect measure of perceived distance. The same relationships apply if the object is physically moving; it will only be seen correctly during self movement if it is seen at the correct distance. (After Gogel, 1982)

in the same plane as the marks, and therefore to be nearer than they are. Consequently, if the head is moved laterally, objects beyond the window appear to move in the same direction as the head.

Perceived self motion

Our discussion of perceived distance in motion perception makes clear that information is also required about self movement. The egocentric motion signal with respect to a subordinate frame of reference (the head) needs to be compensated for the effects of head movements if geocentric object motion is to be obtained. Since head movements are three-dimensional, egocentric object movement must be expressed as a displacement in three-dimensional space before the two can be combined. An internal value for the extent of self movement plays the same role at the geocentric level as does the value for eye movement at the egocentric level. As might be anticipated, if perceived self motion differs from that which actually takes place, errors in perceived object motion will result. There are a number of sources of information which contribute to the sense of self motion, or proprioception. The vestibular system in the inner ear detects acceleration in each of the three spatial axes. The three semi-circular canals are fluid-filled tubes oriented at right angles to one another, so that a change in velocity of the head results in a movement of the fluid within the canals most nearly aligned with the direction of motion. Fluid movement is detected by the displacement of hairs embedded in cells lining the canals. This system detects only angular accelerations, and does not respond to a constant velocity of movement. Associated structures called the otolith organs detect the static orientation of the head with respect to gravity, as well as other linear accelerations. Sensory systems in the muscles, tendons and joints provide information about posture and limb movement. It is also likely that there is an efferent copy of motor commands to the limbs which functions similarly to the efferent copy of eye movements.

The function of the vestibular system, and its role in motion perception, is shown by the effects of prolonged stimulation. If you spin round on the spot, or are spun round on a rotating chair, there is strong stimulation of the vestibular system from the rotary motion. As is well known, there are marked after-effects of rotation. These may include nausea, and you should only try to experience the effects yourself with care. The fluid in the semi-circular canals continues to circulate for a time after rotation has ceased, giving rise to a stimulus which corresponds to continuing rotation in the opposite direction. This causes the observer to feel as if he is continuing to rotate, even though stationary. This illusory self motion is associated with an illusion of object motion called the oculo-gyral illusion. Stationary objects seen in isolation appear to be moving in the same direction and at the same speed as the observer's body. In addition, there is a characteristic pattern of eye movements, referred to as post-rotary nystagmus. This is similar to OKN, and consists of alternating fast and slow phases of eye movement, as if the visual scene were actually continuing to move.

Vision itself also contributes to the perception of self motion. Visual proprioception depends on the detection of characteristic transformations in the optic flow, such as the radial expansion associated with approaching a stationary surface. If the whole visual field, or a large part of it, changes in a defined manner, then this can be used to derive changes in posture. The process evidently depends on an assumption that it is the observer who is moving, and not the visual scene. This is most likely to be true if the transformation affects most of the visual field. We, and many animals, seem to make this assumption automatically, as is shown by the witch's swing example mentioned earlier. The advantage of visual proprioception is that it can signal constant velocities within the range of biological motion, which the vestibular system is unable to do. In laboratory studies of vection, the sense of self movement takes some time to build up. The initial rotation of the surrounding drum involves an acceleration from rest, and the visual signal conflicts with the vestibular signal. The latter takes precedence, and the drum is seen as moving. However, when the drum has reached a constant velocity, there is no sensory conflict. The signal from the vestibular system will be that there is no acceleration of the self, and this is compatible with moving at a constant velocity. Hence the observer experiences moving at a velocity determined by the visual motion. This is an illusion, in that the observer is actually stationary. As a result, if a stationary image is superimposed on the rotating drum, it is seen to move in the opposite direction. The geocentric motion of the stationary image is obtained by compensating the egocentric motion signal (zero) for perceived self motion (positive but incorrect).

When we travel in moving vehicles, the landscape outside often appears to be in motion. The cause of this is probably the lack of sufficient kinaesthetic information for self movement. Most vehicles have some form of cushioning or suspension, so vestibular stimulation is limited except when there is marked acceleration or deceleration. The optic flow may contribute some sense of motion, but perhaps because the velocity is higher than could occur from self-produced motion, this is not sufficient to override the vestibular signal for being stationary. Consequently, the egocentric motion of the landscape is mostly perceived as geocentric motion, and the world appears to be moving. The fact that we know that this is not the case may allow us to act appropriately, but does not change the perceptual experience.

REFERENCE NOTES

Gibson argued that almost all perception is motion perception, and so it is not surprising that this topic is covered in all his books (see Reference Notes for Chapter 1). He emphasised that motion over the retina is often a consequence of our own eye, head and body movements. Gibson's approach has been extended in Cutting's (1986) excellent book *Perception with an Eye for Motion*, in which object and observer motions are analysed in terms of optic flows and invariants that can be extracted from them. Johansson (to whom Cutting's book is dedicated) has studied many simplified situations in which structure is extracted from motion, such as in the case of the light points attached to an observer; these are clearly described in Held and Richards' (1976) collection of *Scientific American* readings, and in Epstein (1977). Howard's (1982) book has an extensive treatment of vection, the impression of self motion when the visible surround is actually moving, as well as a detailed treatment of eye movements and the factors that influence them.

Several nineteenth century accounts of motion phenomena, like Addams' description of the waterfall illusion and Silvanus Thompson's list of 'Optical illusions of motion', are reprinted in Dember (1964). Boring (1942) outlines the early experiments on visual persistence and apparent motion using instruments like the phenakistoscope and stroboscope, as does Wade (1983). Many of the motion phenomena mentioned are also described in *Scientific American* readings: there are articles on 'The Perception of Movement', and 'The Illusion of Movement', as well as on 'Stabilized Images on the Retina', 'Eye Movements and Visual Perception' and the 'Plasticity of Sensory-Motor Systems' in Held and Richards (1972). More recent reviews of apparent motion and induced motion can be found in Petersik (1989) and Reinhardt-Rutland (1988), respectively. The relationship between neurophysiology and apparent motion in the frontal plane is analysed in Spillman and Werner (1990); this book also has a chapter on motion in depth. Motion after-effects have received a great deal of experimental attention and Frisby (1979) gives a clear account of their interpretation in terms of physiological motion detectors. Several chapters in Spillmann and Wooten (1984) are concerned with a variety of motion after-effects and interpretations of them. Bruce and Green (1990) provide an introduction to the analysis of visual motion in terms of Marr's computational theory, as well as addressing issues of motion perception in active observers from the level of insects to humans. The textbooks by Goldstein (1989) and Sekuler and Blake (1990) have comprehensive chapters on motion and event perception.

The analysis of motion perception in terms of nested frames of reference, as presented in this chapter, is described in greater detail in Swanston, Wade and Day (1987), Wade and Swanston (1987) and Swanston, Wade and Ono (1990).

Chapter 6

Recognition

An object must first be perceived before it can be recognised. In the preceding chapters we have described how geocentric perception of the environment is obtained from the patterns of stimulation reaching the eyes. An important feature of this approach has been the emphasis on a moving, active observer. By moving our eyes and our heads we gain information about new aspects of the world that would otherwise not be available. This information has to be extracted from the complex changes in stimulation that are caused by our own movements. As a result we obtain a representation of the direction, distance and movement of objects with respect to the environment. Without this, we, and other animals, would be unable to carry out the coordinated activities necessary for survival. In addition, such a representation provides the basis for recognition, because it can be used to recover the defining characteristics of objects, like their size, shape and orientation.

In Chapter 1 we introduced the example of the dog guiding a blind human across the road. The guide dog must perceive its environment geocentrically in order to behave in the manner it does; it must respond to the edge of the pavement, the width of the road, and to the approaching vehicles in much the same way as a sighted human would. Both guide dogs and sighted humans respond to objects in terms of their locations and dimensions in three-dimensional space, rather than the projective aspects of these (the locations and dimensions on the retina). That is, objects are seen as having constant dimensions despite changes in their projected sizes and shapes. This is called perceptual constancy, and it is the prerequisite of any more complex perception like recognition, and it will be discussed in the first section of this chapter.

All animals need to respond to aspects of their environment that are important for their survival – for their sustenance, shelter and mating. All these aspects will be three-dimensional, and so the general rule is that perception is geocentric. This applies to guide dogs before their specialised training. They can avoid objects, bite them, paw them or climb onto them without any training by humans. Guide dogs require extensive training before they are assigned to a blind owner because they need to behave unnaturally. They are trained to stop at small steps that they could easily negotiate and to avoid projecting objects that they could easily run under. In short, they are trained to respond as if the space they occupied was equivalent to the dimensions of a human. It is rather like starting to drive, when we gradually learn to control a vehicle that occupies a greater volume of space than we do. Guide dogs are trained to discriminate features of their environment that are not intrinsically important to their behaviour. For example, a dog can be trained to discriminate between steps that are a few millimetres high (thereby not interfering with the blind person's gait) and steps that are higher (which might be tripped over). The dog is trained to respond differentially to two different states of the world (not to two different retinal projections), and so there will be some stored internal representation of these against which any present state can be compared. That is, the dog can recognise the distinction between the heights of steps. This behaviour is not restricted to the particular steps for which training occurred, but will be elicited by other, previously unexperienced, instances of these states. Therefore, recognition involves two seemingly incompatible aspects – discrimination and generalisation. Discrimination concerns assigning different behaviours to specific objects or object properties and these behaviours can be generalised to instances of these properties in other objects.

The points about discrimination and generalisation mentioned above can be illustrated further with an example more readily to hand. If the copy of this book that you are reading were to be placed with a number of different books, you could no doubt recognise it correctly. You could do this on the basis of the text on the cover, but even if any words were hidden you would probably still be successful. The information you would use would relate to the size, shape and possibly colour of the book. Evidently we must have this sort of information available in order to discriminate. If another copy were put in the place of this one, the task would become much more difficult. You might well suppose that the replacement copy was the original, and incorrectly recognise it. This would be an instance of generalisation, in which there is sufficient similarity between the characteristics of two objects for the response to both to be the same. In order to pick out this particular copy, it would be necessary to store some information about it that was sufficiently specific to allow discrimination between copies, like marks or damage to the cover. Generalisation gives an indication of the nature of the representation that has been stored, by comparing the characteristics of objects that are confused. It demonstrates the occurrence of recognition and shows the basis on which this has taken place. For instance, you would probably recognise this book if it were upside down; your response would generalise to different orientations of the same object, which means that the stored representation does not include the particular orientation in which the book was first seen. None the less, you would also recognise that its orientation had changed.

Would you mistake a picture of this book for the book itself? Would you expect a guide dog to do so? Much research on recognition seems to have been based on supposing that this would be the case. Since pictorial images are so widespread in both research and everyday life, it is important to know how the recognition processes that apply to real objects may generalise to them. Many animals, besides humans, have well developed capacities for discrimination and generalisation, which have been the subject of extensive investigations, usually in the context of studying the mechanisms of learning. While a full understanding of recognition would involve consideration of the processes responsible for learning, the initial step is to show how the perceptual information necessary for our ability to recognise can be acquired. The relationship between pictures and objects will be examined in the second section of the chapter.

OBJECT CONSTANCY AND IDENTITY

A fundamental requirement for perception is that both the changing and constant characteristics of the environment should be accurately represented. This has to be accomplished despite changes in the pattern of stimulation reaching the eye due to an observer's own activities. We need to be able to perceive that objects with a constant physical size are not changing in size when we move towards or away from them, and we must perceive an object's shape correctly even if it is seen from different directions. Without such abilities, recognition and identification would be impossible, as there would be no consistent description of an object to remember and make use of on subsequent occasions. It is equally necessary to perceive changes when they occur. An object may move between locations in the environment, or undergo changes in orientation, but it must still be possible to recognise it correctly. Perhaps the most characteristic property of living things is that they can change both their shape and their location. A tree may be blown by the wind and alter its shape considerably. Animals can move about in the environment, and adopt a wide variety of postures. Biological shapes are highly variable, but our capacity for recognition is most striking for just these sorts of patterns, like those which define an individual's identity. In this section we will examine the phenomena known as the perceptual constancies, which demonstrate our ability to perceive the intrinsic characteristics of objects, together with some of the explanations that have been proposed to account for this, and how theories of pattern recognition have been derived from the detection of such stable object features.

Perceptual constancies

The term perceptual constancy refers to the fact that we perceive objects as having constant characteristics, even when there are changes in the information about them that reaches the eye. In order to see this for yourself, hold up one hand with your palm facing you about 25 cm from your face, and the other with your arm extended. Separate your arms by an angle of about 30 deg, so that you need to turn your head to look from one hand to the other. When you do this, do your hands appear different in size? It is likely that they do not, in which case you are correctly perceiving their constant size despite large differences in the angles they subtend at your eyes. How can size constancy be explained? One possibility is that you see your hands as a constant size because they are familiar objects, and you already know from experience what size they are. This view, which might be the explanation suggested by common sense, cannot be correct. It would mean that size constancy would only apply to objects which we recognise, and whose size we know about from past experience. Clearly it would also mean that recognition of objects preceeds perception of their characteristics, and this presents logical problems. There is considerable controversy about the extent to which knowledge, in the form of past experience, influences current perception, but at least some perceptual information must be available if recognition is to be possible. An alternative approach would be to argue that we are mistaken in supposing that there really is a problem to be solved by the visual system. This view was strongly argued by Gibson, who pointed out that size constancy may simply be given by invariant features of the optic array. Suppose that an object like a car is seen at various distances. If only the optical projection of the car is considered, then our ability to see it as a constant size appears in need of explanation. The angle subtended at the eye by the car is apparently ambiguous, since the same angular subtense could represent a wide range of different sized vehicles, at different distances. However in practice we would not rely only on the visual angle of an object in order to determine its size. Other sources of information may be available in the retinal image which remove the ambiguity, and determine the perceived size. One suggestion made by Gibson was that the amount of adjacent background texture obscured by an object remains constant, despite changes in its distance and angular size. This would then constitute an invariant property of the optic array, which directly specifies size. While there is relatively little information available about which optical invariants are significant, and how they may be detected, the general point made by Gibson about the lack of real ambiguity in the retinal projection is a very important one.

There are other sources of information that determine an object's apparent size, as well as purely optical invariants, and the most important of these is perceived egocentric distance. Cues to egocentric distance were discussed in Chapter 4, and there is good evidence that perceived size is linked to perceived distance.

The relationship is known as size–distance invariance, and it can be expressed by the statement that perceived size is proportional to the product of visual angle and perceived distance; or, equivalently, that the ratio of perceived size to perceived distance is proportional to the visual angle (see Figure 6.1). Since visual angle is the ratio of physical size to physical distance, another form of the equation is that perceived size is proportional to the product of physical size and the ratio of perceived distance to physical distance. Therefore, if perceived and physical distance are the same, their ratio is one, and perceived size will be constant if physical size is constant, even though distance varies. For an object of constant physical size, the product of visual angle and perceived distance is a constant (invariant) characteristic, despite changes in distance. If angular size increases and perceived distance decreases, as would happen with an approaching object, then perceived size will remain constant. Size constancy is really a special case of size–distance invariance, which can also account for situations where errors in perceived size occur. Suppose that

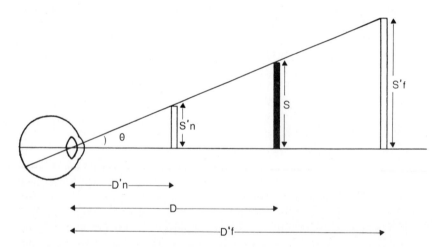

Figure 6.1 The relationship between perceived size, perceived distance and visual angle, as expressed by size–distance invariance. An object of a given physical size (S), at a given physical distance (D), subtends an angle of θ deg at the eye. Such a visual angle could correspond to an infinite number of different sized objects at different distances, all of which have the same ratio of size to distance, and therefore the same visual angle. By size–distance invariance, the perceived size of an object (S') depends on its visual angle and its perceived distance (D'). Thus, if the object is incorrectly seen as nearer than D (D'n), then it will appear to have a size of S'n; similarly with too large a perceived distance (D'f), the perceived size is S'f, so that the ratio of S' to D' is constant. In general, S' = (D'. S) /D, or S' = D'. tan θ, since tan θ = S/D.

the perceived distance of an object is increased by a decrease in convergence. Its visual angle remains the same, because its physical distance has not altered, so the product of visual angle and perceived distance will be larger. That is, the perceived size of an object with a constant visual angle should increase if its perceived distance increases, and decrease if perceived distance decreases. This outcome can readily be observed. An after-image can be produced by fixating on the black dot in Figure 5.10 for a minute or so. The after-image of the grid pattern can then be observed against a close surface like your hand, or a further one, such as the ceiling. You should find that the apparent size of the after-image changes, so as to appear larger when seen against the further surface. Clearly, there must be good cues to the distance of the surfaces. The retinal area stimulated necessarily remains a constant size, and is seen at the apparent distance of the background as a result of the equidistance tendency.

The Ames room (named after the American ophthalmologist Adelbert Ames who devised it) demonstrates size-distance invariance very clearly. Figure 6.2 illustrates the geometry of an Ames room. Although the far wall is at an oblique angle to the observer, all the internal features, such as the skirting boards and window frames, have been shaped to appear as if on a fronto-parallel surface. With monocular observation, the effective cues to distance (principally linear perspective) therefore correspond to a rectangular room, and the perceived distance of the far wall differs from its physical distance. As a result there are remarkable effects on the perceived size of objects placed within the room. Two identical objects placed in each corner look to be very different in size. If the objects change places, they seem to grow and shrink. It is not necessary to suppose that this has anything to do with knowing that rooms are generally rectangular, because the effects are exactly as would be predicted on the basis of size–distance invariance, given the available cues to distance. The apparent sizes of objects in the room are appropriate to the product of their visual angles (which depend on the physical size and the physical distance) and the perceived distance. Perhaps the most striking aspect of the Ames room is that knowledge about the true sizes of objects within it has no effect on perception. Even if people are observed moving around in the room, they still appear to shrink and expand.

The account of geocentric motion perception given in the previous chapter was based on a similar principle to size–distance invariance. The scaling of changes in egocentric direction by perceived distance is equivalent to the scaling of visual angle by perceived distance in size–distance invariance. The equivalence is apparent if you think of a difference in egocentric direction between the edges of an object as defining visual angle, and a difference in egocentric direction of a single point over time as defining movement. Our account of geocentric perception predicts both size constancy and location constancy. The latter

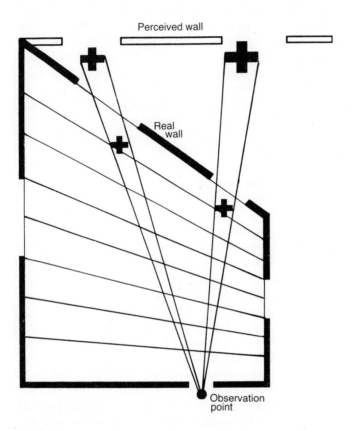

Figure 6.2 The layout of an Ames room. The actual shape of the room is trapezoidal, with the far wall sloping at an angle towards the observer. However all the available cues from linear perspective, texture gradients, etc. are adjusted to indicate that the far wall is at right angles to the observer. For example, the window frames are trapezoidal, but give rectangular projections at the eye due to the slope of the wall in which they are set. The far wall is therefore seen in the position shown, and as a result objects placed in the room appear to be distorted in size. Equal sized objects appear much larger when seen on the right than on the left. These perceived sizes are what would be expected from size–distance invariance, given the errors in perceived distance.

term refers to our ability to see stationary objects as stationary despite observer movement. Location constancy is a special case of a more general process of geocentric motion perception. An adequate explanation of spatial perception must account for both location and size constancies, as well as the systematic ways in which they break down.

The same principles can be extended to explain shape constancy. Consider a rectangular object like this book. When closed and face-on, the retinal projection of the book is rectangular, and corresponds to the physical shape. If the book is rotated about a vertical axis, the retinal projection of the cover is altered to a trapezoid, because the far edge now subtends a smaller visual angle than the near edge. The principle of size–distance invariance is sufficient to account for our ability to continue to see the cover as rectangular even when it has been rotated. If there are adequate cues to distance, the perceived size of each edge will correspond to its physical size, and thus the overall perceived shape will correspond to the physical shape.

In orientation constancy we compensate for changes in our orientation with respect to gravity so that objects appear to retain the same orientation despite their changing retinal orientation. This can be demonstrated under the reduced conditions of the laboratory. When only a single line of light is visible we can judge its orientation quite accurately even when the head or the whole body is tilted. This is possible because of information provided by the otolith organs in the vestibular system; they signal the orientation of the head with respect to gravity and these signals are used to modify the information for orientation relative to the retina. Outside the laboratory there is ample visual information to specify the vertical: our environment has been constructed to comply with the demands of gravity, and so buildings and their constituent parts tend to be vertical and horizontal. These conditions can be contravened in the laboratory. If an observer is placed in a rectangular room that is artificially inclined, then their judgements of orientation will be biased by the tilted room. Objects will appear vertical when they are tilted in the same orientation as the room, and the observer will feel tilted: if they remain vertical with respect to gravity they will feel to be tilted in the opposite direction to the room. Similar situations do occasionally occur in the natural environment. Some years ago there was an earthquake in Japan which resulted in the buildings in one district being inclined by a few degrees. Thus there was conflicting information from the visual and vestibular systems. One of the consequences of this was a dramatic increase in the number of people who consulted their doctors with postural problems like dizziness and nausea.

An alternative view of how we achieve perceptual constancy suggests that it is based on assumptions about the structure of physical objects. The best known is called the rigidity assumption, because it consists of interpreting retinal changes in terms of the rotation and translation of rigid three-dimensional objects. For example, the changes in the contours of a book as it rotates about a vertical axis could be produced by a large set of environmental events, in which the book itself undergoes changes in physical size and shape. If it is assumed in advance that objects are rigid and unable to change shape, then the retinal transformations allow only one interpretation. The difficulty with the rigidity assumption, and other sorts of a priori principles in perception, is that it constrains what can be seen. Objects can in fact change shape, since some are elastic. We can evidently see non-rigid transformations when they occur. A rigidity assumption may not be necessary if sufficient information is available about an object, in addition to its retinal transformations.

Underlying much discussion of perceptual constancy is the conception of a retinal image which is intrinsically ambiguous. This point of view has led to the development of explanations of how we resolve the ambiguity, and see a particular object which normally corresponds to its physical characteristics. It is unarguable that the retinal image of a given object considered in isolation provides ambiguous information for size, location and shape. Like any ambiguity, this can be resolved if other information is available. The major theoretical approaches to this have been to incorporate past knowledge, prior assumptions, other concurrent sources of visual information such as distance, or other information in the retinal image like texture and perspective. However, objects are seldom seen in isolation outside the laboratory, and if they are, they may well be perceived incorrectly. The appearance of an object can be changed by the visual background in which it is set, and there is little doubt that the visual system interprets the retinal image of an object in the context of other retinal patterns, although we know little about how this comes about. As has been demonstrated, information about egocentric distance is critical in determining perceived size, motion and shape. These perceptual character-istics can best be understood as aspects of spatial perception, which must be geocentric if behaviour is to be appropriately directed. In addition, a geocentric representation provides a description of objects in terms which would permit subsequent recognition.

Two further perceptual constancies may be less closely related to the processes of spatial perception. Colour constancy refers to the fact that we see objects as being a constant colour even when the wavelength of ambient illumination changes. Under white light, an object will reflect a part of the total spectrum, which determines its colour. If the ambient illumination is restricted to, say, the longer wavelengths (so as to appear red), the object will continue to appear the same colour as before, even though it now reflects a quite different range of wavelengths. In effect we are able to compensate an object's apparent colour for any bias in the colour of the prevailing illumination. In order for this to happen, there must be sufficient information about ambient illumination. Thus, if an object is illuminated by a narrowly focused source of coloured light, which does not impinge on the rest of the scene, then colour constancy will fail, and the object will seem to be a colour determined by the fraction of the incident wavelengths which it reflects. A similar process, known as lightness con-stancy, occurs with changes in the intensity of ambient illumination. A piece of coal will appear black and a sheet of white paper will appear white, even when the intensity of the light they reflect is changed over a wide range. Even more strikingly, if the paper is in shadow, it may reflect less light than the coal, but the coal will still appear darker than the paper. Again, this is dependent on being able to perceive the intensity of the ambient illumination. If the paper and the coal are placed side by side and the coal is illuminated by a hidden spotlight, it can be made to appear whiter than the paper. Colour and lightness constancy are not well understood, and at present we do not know how they are produced, or how to integrate them with other perceptual constancies.

Features and patterns

The processes responsible for perceptual constancies provide a geocentric description of objects which captures their unchanging, intrinsic characteristics. This description also conveys information about changes in objects that do not alter their identity, such as their location and orientation, and it is therefore a suitable basis for recognition. To recognise an object it is necessary to have access to information which is independent of particular conditions of observation; that is, an object-centered description which is the same whenever a given object is encountered. The investigation of recognition and identification has a very long history. Both Greek and Chinese philosophers confronted the issue of how we can recognise an object as a member of a general class, and also as an individual instance of that class. While philosophers concentrated their thoughts on the problems of knowing about real objects, psychologists, at least in this century, have tended to study recognition in terms of very simplified laboratory tasks, generally involving two-dimensional patterns. This issue, and its consequences for the misinterpretation of picture perception, will be taken up in the next section.

Two contrasting theoretical approaches to pattern recognition can be identified, reflecting a dichotomy that runs widely throughout psychology. On the one hand, a pattern can be thought of as a collection of characteristics, or features, which can be independently detected. This represents an analytical approach, which requires the reduction of a complex process into a set of simpler elements that can be studied in isolation. It necessarily raises important questions as to how measures of elementary properties can be recombined to give an integrated perception. By contrast, a holistic approach would deny that complex stimuli are perceived as a collection of responses to elementary components, and would stress the importance of the overall pattern of stimulation. The statement that the whole is more than the sum of its parts, which is often used to summarise Gestalt psychology, exemplifies this viewpoint. The difficulties here are concerned with explaining how a complex pattern of stimulation is

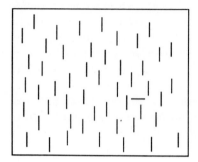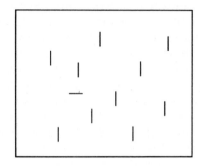

Figure 6.3 Objects defined by simple features are immediately discriminable from their background. Both the horizontal lines are detected easily, without a delay for searching, despite the larger number of distracting objects in the frame on the left. The same effect would be found if the target was identified by colour; e. g. a red vertical line in a background of green vertical lines. However if the target is defined by a conjunction of features (such as a red horizontal line in a background of red verticals, green verticals and green horizontals), the time to find it increases with the number of distractors, and it does not stand out on first inspection. These findings may reflect the operation of parallel processing of simple features to give rapid detection, and a slower serial search to find a target which differs from the background because of two or more characteristics.

detected as a whole, and how similarities can be identified between members of a class that are the same in some respects and different in others.

In recent years the analytical, feature-based approach has been the most influential. In part this has been due to neurophysiological studies of the organisation and response specificity of single cells in the visual pathway and visual cortex. As described in Chapter 3, cells display properties which can be described as feature detection. That is, they are organised in groups, or maps, which respond to one particular characteristic of visual stimulation, such as direction of movement, retinal disparity, colour or orientation. This sort of organisation could be interpreted as a mechanism for identifying and measuring elementary properties of any arbitrary pattern. Such a pattern would produce simultaneous activity in those maps which are able to detect its particular features. Colour, movement and orientation would be determined at the same time, in parallel. There is psychophysical evidence to support the existence of a process like this. For example there are circumstances under which a target is immediately discriminable from other patterns presented with it. The target seems to 'pop-out' from the rest, provided it differs in respect of a simple feature. A single horizontal black line in a background field of vertical black lines is detected very quickly (Figure 6.3), as is a red horizontal line amongst green horizontal lines. This rapid segregation of visual information is not affected by the number of background patterns, which suggests that the process is based on simultaneous evaluation of all visible patterns. It is not necessary to examine each one successively to see if it is the desired target. However if the target is defined by a conjunction of two features, then it takes much longer to find, and the time needed increases with the number of background patterns. A red horizontal line in a background of red verticals, green horizontals and green verticals is not readily visible, and can be found only by a successive, serial examination of each pattern. These experimental results may shed light on camouflage strategies found in nature, because the purpose of camouflage is to prevent immediate visibility in the natural environment.

If there is an initial stage of feature detection in pattern recognition, how might a unified perception be achieved? One approach to this, from which computer-based pattern recognition schemes have been derived, is to apply a decision process to the outputs of the feature detecting stages. Suppose that the letter E is to be identified. A number of features in this pattern could be found, such as the presence of three horizontal lines and one vertical line. The decision process would examine this set of features, and compare it to a stored description of letters of the alphabet expressed in the same terms. Various other letters, like F or B would partially fit the input, while others, like O or W would not fit at all. A decision as to which letter has been presented would be based on the best fit between the input and the stored descriptions. A system like this can work reasonably well for a small well-defined set of patterns, like letters or numbers, and it can even be used to recognise single spoken words. However it has little success when the patterns to be recognised are subject to distortions and ambiguity. In this case, the recognition system needs to be provided with extensive information in advance about the patterns that are likely to occur; in effect, a database of world knowledge that gives a context for events. It seems unlikely that perception in animals with nervous sytems less developed than a human's could operate in this way. An alternative, which also draws on neurophysiology, is to postulate hierarchies of feature detectors. For example the output of detectors for vertical and horizontal lines could be fed to a cell which responds to the joint activation of both, that is, to a cross. A traditional objection to this is that the numbers of special purpose high-level units would have to be enormous. There would need to be distinct units for every possible pattern that could be recognised, from yellow Volkswagens to your grandmother, to use the examples that are normally cited. The problem is known as the combinatorial explosion, and it is hard to see how it could be solved. Nevertheless, it is possible that hierarchical feature detection plays a part in recognition of some biologically important patterns, like faces. Single cells have been reported in monkey infero-temporal cortex which are selectively responsive to particular individuals, such as the monkey's keeper. Some cells may be even more selective than this, and respond only to certain types of action by an individual, like approach.

A recent development in the field of pattern recognition makes use of analogies with interconnected nets of nerve cells, which are not initially selective in their responses. Inputs can be fed into the net, which spread through it by means of the interconnections between the elements. These interconnections can be weighted, that is, they can be set to transmit more or less activity to the next element. If the weights are altered as the result of the output of the system, a form of pattern recognition can be achieved. The net is 'taught' the connection between a particular pattern of input activity, and a particular response. The study of neural nets in biological and computational systems is in its early stages, but it may provide an indication of how a holistic pattern recognition system could operate.

It has to be borne in mind that there has been very little investigation of the recognition of real, three-dimensional objects, rather than arbitrary two-dimensional patterns. Such patterns play an important role in human activity, in the form of alphanumeric symbols and pictures of all sorts, but are not encountered in the natural environment. The next section considers pictorial representations and their relationship to reality in more detail.

PICTURES AND OBJECTS

Most experiments on object recognition use pictures of objects rather than the objects themselves. Accordingly, we know quite a lot about picture recognition. In order for this knowledge to be of use in furthering our understanding of object recognition we need to appreciate the relationship between pictures and objects. The artist René Magritte painted a picture in the late 1920s which epitomised the problem of pictorial representation: it was called 'The perfidy of images' and a variant of it is shown in Figure 6.4. The caption beneath the pictured pipe reads 'This is not a pipe'! If it is not a pipe, what is it? The simple answer is that it is a picture of a pipe; the pictured pipe cannot be held or smoked, and it is not even supported by anything, as the object would need to be. The title Magritte chose for the work indicates that he was acutely aware of the problems associated with equating the pictures of objects with the objects themselves.

Magritte was able to make this point forcefully because we can recognise the pictured pipe as representing a curved briar pipe. The orientation he chose for its representation was not arbitrary; had he painted it from other orientations its recognition would not have been as rapid. For example, the four pictures shown in Figure 6.5 are photographs of the same pipe as was used for producing Figure 6.4, but they were in different orientations with respect to the camera. Some might not even be recognised as representing a pipe if they are presented in isolation and without any context. You could

Ceci n'est pas une pipe.

Figure 6.4 This is not a pipe. (After Magritte)

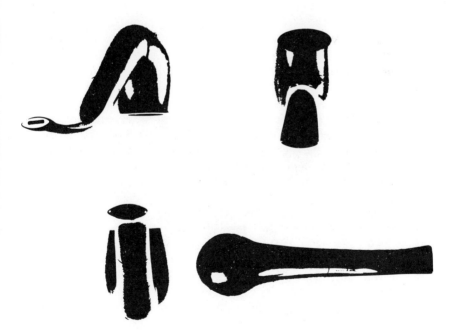

Figure 6.5 Four photographs of the same pipe from different viewpoints.

(b)

(a)

Figure 6.6 Photographs of a cube (a) with its sides vertical and (b) with its sides inclined by 45 deg.

try this out by showing someone the picture in the lower left quadrant on its own, by covering up the others, and asking them to say what object it would correspond to. We would not have the same difficulty in recognising an actual pipe in a number of orientations, because we would have information for its orientation in space and its dimensions. Therefore, if we are dealing with pictures of objects we need to consider the viewpoint from which the pictures are taken, and the orientation in which the picture itself is presented.

Orientation and bearing

It is clear from this example that some pictures of the same object can be recognised more easily than others, according to the viewpoint from which they are imaged. Clearly this only applies to asymmetrical objects: different views of a sphere would be equivalent, but almost all objects in our environment are asymmetrical. Even a symmetrical object like a cube can be pictured in many different ways, depending upon the orientation of the faces with respect to the viewpoint. With a camera mounted on a tripod, imagine photographing a cube with its near face in the frontal plane and the centre aligned with the optical axis of the camera. The outline of the photographic image would be a square (see Figure 6.6a), and the same configuration would result from any rotation of the cube around the optical axis of the camera. Figure 6.6b shows another view, with the face of the cube rotated by 45 deg with respect to the camera. The only difference between these two pictures is their orientation, but this is a critical one for our perception. We can discriminate differences based upon orientation alone, so that even though we can recognise that the configuration is a square in both instances, we can also discriminate the difference between them. In fact in this example we are likely to give different names to the same configuration, based solely on orientation: a would be called a square whereas b would be described as a diamond.

Changes in the orientation of pictorial images can be achieved in two ways: the cube could be rotated with respect to the stationary camera, or the camera could be rotated with respect to the stationary cube. The resulting photographs would be indistinguishable, if the rotations had been equivalent. This projective equivalence would also apply to an observer but the two states would not be perceptually equivalent. If a square is presented vertically and at 45 deg we can discriminate the difference with ease. On the other hand, if we view a square with the head vertical and then with the head rotated so that the square is at 45 deg with respect to the retina, the two will not be easy to discriminate because of orientation constancy.

The photographs of a cube we have considered so far have shown only one of its faces, and its rotations have been around the optical axis of the camera. In order to picture two faces of the cube it is necessary to rotate it around a vertical or horizontal axis, and three faces are imaged with rotation about both (see Figure 6.7). When all three faces are pictured there is a wide range of viewpoints that can be adopted to display varying proportions of each. Only when a diagonal axis of the cube is in the optical axis of the camera will the area and configuration of the three imaged faces be equal.

Parallel sides on a face of a cube converge in the photographs shown in Figure 6.7. The degree of convergence depends upon the characteristics of the lens used in the camera, the size of the cube and the distance from the camera. The photographs of the same cube shown in Figure 6.8 were taken with different lenses, and they have been enlarged to the same pictorial dimensions. The focal length of the lens in a conventional 35 mm camera is about 50 mm; Figure 6.8a shows a photograph taken with such a lens; the parallel sides converge by a moderate amount, and much more than in the case of a long focal length (200 mm) telephoto lens (Figure 6.8b). The convergence is considerable with the wide angle lens used to produce Figure 6.8c. If the eye is to be likened to a camera, then we should try to compare like with like. The focal length of the eye varies from 14–17 mm, according to the state of accommodation. A lens with these characteristics in a camera would produce an image with massive distortions – straight lines would appear curved and the convergence of parallel lines would be considerable. Clearly, what we see does not correspond to the image formed in a camera with similar optical properties to the eye.

Stereotypical viewpoints

No photograph of a cube can be said to represent adequately a cube as an object, because they can, at best, only show three of the cube's six faces. The object pictured can only be a cube if it is assumed that the unseen faces correspond to those that are imaged. Exactly the same set of photographs to those shown above could have been produced with an object having only three connected faces rather than six – it could have been an empty shell. Despite this shortcoming we are remarkably good at recognising pictures of objects as representations of the objects. However, as was hinted above, not all pictures of the same object are treated equivalently. Returning to Magritte's pictured pipe, some viewpoints are more readily recognised than others. These have been called canonical, typical or stereotypical views of an object, and they apply principally to asymmetrical objects like pipes and people. What are the features that the stereotypical view has, that render it more readily recognisable? Magritte's pipe provides a good vehicle for considering this issue. All the photographs of pipes shown in Figure 6.5 are in accurate central perspective, as is that in Figure 6.4. Therefore, accurate representation is not the feature that distinguishes

(a)

(b)

Figure 6.7 Two photographs of a cube (a) with two faces imaged, and (b) with three faces imaged.

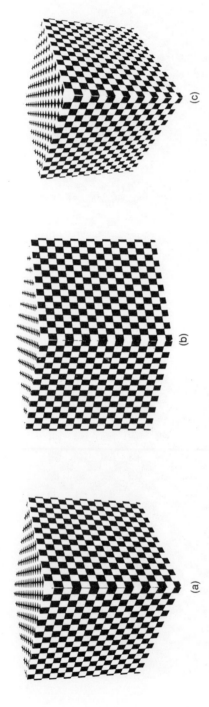

Figure 6.8 Three photographs of the same cube taken with (a) a 50 mm lens, (b) a 200 mm lens, and (c) a 20 mm lens.

the stereotypical view from others. Many objects have a fixed polarity; they have a defined orientation with respect to the surface of the earth. This applies to people, who maintain a fixed posture with respect to gravity, and it applies to pipes, because tobacco will be retained in the bowl more readily in a particular orientation. Therefore, the stereotypical view needs to retain the normal orientation of the object. The normal orientation is retained in several of the photographs in Figure 6.5, but they are not stereotypical views because they foreshorten a critical dimension of the pipe – that along the stem.

The structure of any object can be described in terms of a set of three-dimensional coordinates of all points on its surface. This would enable its surface structure to be reproduced. Another way of achieving such a structural description would be to take three projections of the object from three orthogonal directions. This is rather like taking a silhouette of an object from three viewpoints at right angles to one another, and this has been done for a pipe in Figure 6.9. One silhouette corresponds to a view from the side, another from the front, and a third from above. (Note that this is treating the pipe as though it has a clearly defined side, front and top.) Each silhouette maximally foreshortens one of the dimensions of the pipe. Of the three silhouettes one is more readily recognisable than the other two as representing a pipe, and that is the side view. The most difficult silhouette to recognise is that from the front, and that from above does not distinguish between a curved and a straight stemmed pipe. Accordingly, the stereotypical view corresponds to the most recognisable silhouette of an object. It also corresponds to the viewpoint that minimally foreshortens the most asymmetrical dimension of the object. It will be noted that in Figure 6.4, as in Magritte's painting, the viewpoint was shifted slightly from the side view, so that the circularity of the bowl could be represented as an ellipse. Thus the three dimensions of the pipe are present in the picture, but the most asymmetrical dimension is least foreshortened.

This analysis is easier with pipes than with people, because the surfaces are smoother with pipes. There is a great deal of significance attached to the

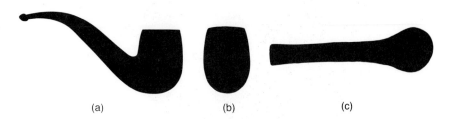

(a)   (b)   (c)

Figure 6.9 Silhouettes of a curved briar pipe viewed from (a) the side, (b) the front, and (c) the top.

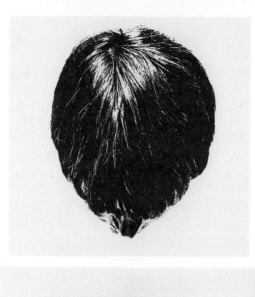

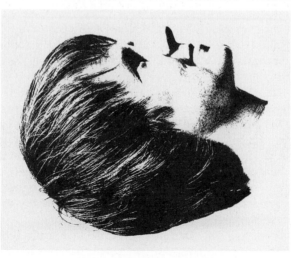

Figure 6.10 Three photographs of a head viewed from (a) the side, (b) the front, and (c) the top.

patterning of features on people's heads, and so rather than take silhouettes we could take normal photographs from three orthogonal viewpoints.
If we consider only the head, then it could be photographed from the front,
the side and from above, as is shown in Figure 6.10. Here it is not so obvious
from which viewpoint the face can be recognised most easily. It is clear
which is the poorest – the view from above, but the other two seem equally
informative. Thus, it seems as though there are two stereotypical views for
the human head. It is not coincidental that criminal 'mug shots' are taken
from profile and fullface views, and that most portraits are in three-quarter
profile, so that dimensions of the protruding facial features are not lost.

Photographs and drawings

Cameras are designed to produce pictures that are in central perspective;
most of the pictures that we see in newspapers and magazines have been
derived from a camera and so are in perspective. The situation is somewhat
different when we consider drawing and other graphic arts. Perspective
arrived rather late on the scene in Western art, and cannot be considered in
any way as universal. Paintings were made in caves about 20,000 years ago,
and we can recognise the objects (usually animals) that are depicted. They
are nearly all represented in the stereotypical view – outline profiles of
bison, deer and horses. Thus, from the earliest examples of art outlines have
been used to describe and delineate representations of objects. When we
draw objects we initially define their boundaries with lines, and often do
not proceed any further. Outlines or contours are very informative, and
they can be sufficient to establish the relationship between a drawing and
the object it is intended to represent.

Drawings or outlines are used extensively in perceptual research, far
more so than photographs. Outline drawings are used so widely because,
in large measure, are so easy to produce and manipulate. The situation
has been compounded by the onset of interactive computer systems which
enable an observer to manipulate characteristics of the outline display. This
is one of the factors that has led to the burgeoning of research on visual
illusions – they can readily be drawn and manipulated. Indeed, simple
outline drawings have even been used to determine complex perceptual
dimensions, like the facial expressions, as in the experiments illustrated in
Figure 6.11. There are consistencies in the emotions observers attach to
these simple outlines, but it is difficult to know how to interpret them. In
order to do so, we would need to know how the outlines relate to static
views that are more representative of actual faces (e.g., photographs), and
then how photographs relate to actual faces. Neither of these steps is
understood at present.

Contours in drawings are abrupt changes in the amount of light
reflected from a surface; they correspond to the boundaries of an object, but

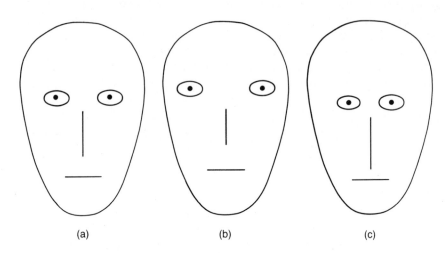

Figure 6.11 Examples of schematic faces. Brunswik and Reiter produced nearly 200 schematic faces, all within the same oval outline, by manipulating: the height and separation of the eyes, the height and length of the nose, and the height of the mouth. Of the three examples shown here (a) corresponds to the neutral standard, (b) was rated by observers as young, good, likeable and beautiful, whereas (c) was rated as sad, old, ugly and unlikeable. (After Brunswik, 1956)

there are rarely such well-defined transitions between light and dark in the original scene. One of the problems that has beset workers in the area of computational vision is to define the boundaries of an object in a well-structured scene. Therefore, an outline drawing of an object is an abstraction that does not correspond readily to any features of the pattern of light projected from a scene. We are exposed to such simplified representations from a very early age, and so we learn how to interpret them. Experiments have established that we extract information not only from contours but also from the regions of a drawing where contours change direction or intersect.

It is clear that humans have produced pictures for as long as recorded history, and a variety of styles can be discerned. Linear perspective is amongst the most contrived because it requires picture-makers to forego their perception of space and to record visual angles. Unlike the art forms that preceded it, linear perspective set out specific rules for representing the sizes of objects on the picture plane and, more importantly, the dimensions of texture on the receding ground plane. These were determined by the distance of the station point from the picture plane and the height of the station point from the ground plane (see Figure 2.3). Thus, all the 'painter's cues' to distance, described on pp. 126–7, can be enlisted to increase the allusion to distance on the flat surface of the picture. Artists have to learn to draw in linear perspective and similarly observers have to learn to interpret pictures so produced. The drawing can be assisted by all manner of aids, the simplest of which were suggested by Alberti and Leonardo in the fifteenth century. If the picture plane is replaced by a pane of glass then, with a single eye at a fixed position (the station point) the contours in the scene can be traced on the glass surface: the tracing will be in accurate linear perspective.

The rules of linear perspective provide a consistent way of treating the dimension that the picture itself lacks – depth or distance. When three dimensions are reduced to two it is possible to play tricks with the transition, and to create worlds on paper that could not exist in three-dimensional space. Figure 6.12 illustrates two 'impossible figures' that employ perspective capriciously. The impossible triangle is in accurate perspective at all the corners, but the connecting lines create the impossibility. The devil's pitchfork is another example that is based upon the minimum requirements for representing a cylinder and a rectangular bar: the twelve horizontal lines are connected to six ellipses on the left, representing six cylinders, but they constitute only four rectangular bars on the right. Impossible figures like this have been manipulated with great graphical skill by the Dutch artist Maurits Escher.

Allied to these impossible figures are others that are not sufficiently specified to be perceived unambiguously. Perhaps the most famous of these is called the Necker cube, after the Swiss crystallographer Louis Necker who first described it in 1832. He was observing a crystal under the microscope and noted that its structure appeared to alternate in depth. Necker actually observed a rhomboid rather than a cube, but subsequent

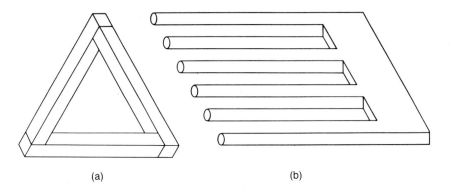

(a)   (b)

Figure 6.12 Impossible figures: (a) an impossible triangle, and (b) the devil's pitchfork.

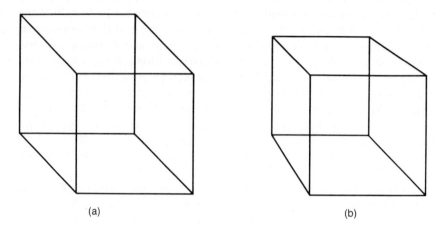

Figure 6.13 Necker cubes drawn with (a) parallel and (b) converging sides.

illustrations used a cube, and that is the structure with which he is epony-mously linked. The Necker cube is an outline figure that is equivalent to a skeleton cube imaged with a telephoto lens so that the sides remain parallel (see Figure 6.13a). The figure appears to fluctuate in orientation, at one moment it seems to be pointing down and to the left, then it flips to appear pointing up and to the right. Note how the fluctuation is less pronounced for a representation of a skeleton cube which has converging sides (Figure 6.13b). Some artists have manipulated a related form of perceptual ambi-guity in which the same outline can be seen as representing two different objects, only one of which is visible at once.

Perceiving pictures

We perceive pictures in the same way that we perceive other objects in the environment: they are flat, mostly on paper, but occasionally in frames. There is nothing peculiar about pictures as objects. However, this is not what is usually meant by picture perception. The term refers to the interpretation of the marks on the surface of the picture – to the recognition of the marks as referring to objects that are not actually there. Thus, pictures have a dual reality: they exist as objects and, in addition, the marks signify other objects and spaces than those they occupy. In the first sense, pictures pose the same problems as pipes and people; they have locations and dimensions that need to be resolved by the perceiver. In the second sense, they are paradoxical because they allude to another space or to other objects.

It is possible to arrange conditions such that a picture is not seen on the surface it occupies. Such works are called *trompe l'oeil* because they 'fool the eye'. Successful *trompe l'oeil* paintings are very rare, and they are exceedingly contrived. One example can be found in the National Gallery, London; it is a perspective cabinet painted by the seventeenth century Dutch artist, Samuel van Hoogstraten. The scene represented is an interior of a house with many interconnecting rooms, which can be seen through open doors. The interior of the cabinet can only be viewed through a peephole. What is of interest is that the surfaces upon which the various parts are painted are complex and do not correspond to those in the scene: a chair, for instance, is painted on three surfaces at right angles to one another! The painting achieves its aim (i.e., not to appear distorted) because of the constraints placed on the observer: it can only be viewed from the fixed station point with one eye, and the viewing angle is such that the extreme edges of the painted surfaces cannot be seen. Neither of these conditions apply to the pictures we normally see: we use both eyes, look at them from many different positions, and we can see the borders that separate the picture from its surroundings.

It would seem, from this discussion, that pictures are very complex stimuli. Because we can recognise the objects represented from such a wide range of viewpoints we cannot be processing a pattern of stimulation like that from the original scene. It is more likely that we apply shape constancy to the border of the picture before processing the contents and interpreting the cues to depth. If this is the case then processes involved in picture perception must occur after those for object recognition. One consequence of this conclusion is to question whether the insights derived from picture recognition can be of any utility in furthering our understanding of object recognition.

REFERENCE NOTES

The subject of perceptual constancies is treated in virtually every book on visual perception, and in most general psychology textbooks. However, it is not generally considered as a precursor to object recognition, as we do here. The frequency with which constancy is discussed is unfortunately not correlated with the clarity or accuracy of the discussion. Several of the sources cited for earlier chapters contain good general discussions of constancy, for example, Gregory (1977), Kaufman (1974), Haber and Hershenson (1980) and Rock (1984). Gibson's argument that the problem of constancy is easily understood when perception occurs in normal environments is expressed in most of his writings and those of his followers (see Gibson (1966), and Michaels and Carello (1981)). Also, many of the references for Chapter 4 are appropriate here, especially Epstein (1977). There is a close connection between the perception of distance and the perception of object constancies, as we have attempted to make clear. Gogel and DaSilva (1987) develop a two-process theory of distance and size perception, incorporating the effects of past experience of familiar objects, and distinguishing between perceptual and cognitive factors. The Ames room, and the principles for its construction, are described by Ittelson (1968) in *The Ames Demonstrations in Perception*. This is a fascinating account of the ingenious perceptual demonstrations devised by Ames, and includes practical details for setting up and using them. Howard (1982) provides a wealth of information on orientation constancy. Theories of pattern recognition based on feature detection have developed in tandem with neurophysiological studies of the visual cortex, as was described in Chapter 3. The best, and probably most influential account of this interaction is Neisser's (1967) *Cognitive Psychology*. Although now mainly of historical interest, this book conveys much of the enthusiasm and excitement aroused by the prospect of linking cognitive and neurophysiological discoveries. Triesman (1988) reviews much of her work on the detection of object features, and the experimental method devised to distinguish between serial and parallel feature detection. Gordon (1989) gives a brief but very clear introduction to the principles of parallel distributed processing and neural networks.

Pictures and their perception have often proved a fascination for visual scientists. One of the most lucid introductions to this topic can be found in Pirenne's (1970) book mentioned earlier. Rock (1984) examines perception and art from a cognitive viewpoint, as does Gregory (1977). Gibson (1966, 1979) has been especially critical of experiments based solely on two-dimensional representations of objects and has argued that the relation between such indirect perception and the direct perception of objects is a complex one. Gibson's essays on this topic have been collected by Reed and Jones (1982), and his ideas are evaluated by Gordon (1989). Wade's (1990) *Visual Allusions: Pictures of Perception* presents a model of the imaging stages in vision and relates these both to the development of styles of representational art and to the allusory perception of depth in pictures.

Chapter 7

Summary and conclusions

The study of perception has a long history, as long as the history of science itself. The framework for science and for the study of perception was outlined by Greek philosophers, but we have concentrated upon the advances made in the modern era, following the scientific revolution in the seventeenth century. Our current theories of perception have been shaped by ideas in physics, art, physiology, biology, philosophy and psychology. Physics contributed an understanding of the nature of light and of the laws of optical transmission in air and in the eye. The former led to a recognition that vision is not due to the emission of energy from the eye, and the latter made it possible to understand how objects in the external world were represented as images on the retinal surface. The laws of optics were also employed in artistic representation: the formation of an image on a transparent screen at a fixed distance in front of the eye will produce a picture in linear perspective; if the screen is considered to lie at the back of the eye then a similar pattern will be produced (though inverted and reversed with respect to the external picture). When this similarity between image formation in the eye, in cameras and in art was appreciated the problem of perception was thought of in terms of extracting information from a two-dimensional image. The retinal image was conceived in terms of a static picture, which has had profound effects upon both theory and experiment. It has meant that pictorial representations of objects could be considered as adequate experimental substitutes for the objects themselves, and that the dynamic aspects of vision could be too readily ignored. Because our eyes are in constant motion, the retinal image is an abstraction, not actually present in the eye unless a scene is viewed for a very brief interval, too short for the eyes to move. Anatomists examined the structure of the retina and of the optic nerves. Physiologists conjectured how the brain could distinguish between neural signals arising from different sense organs.

Towards the end of the nineteenth century specific cortical regions were found which received neural signals from the different sense organs. The biological perspective, following Darwin's theory, placed humans in a closer relationship to other animals and so added to the relevance of experiments on animal perception to interpretations of human perception. It emphasised developmental processes in both behaviour and perception; and it also examined instinctive and learned behaviours in more detail. Issues of innate and learned processes in perception have provided constant conflict within philosophy. On the one hand the nativists argued that certain aspects of perception (like space and time) were inborn, on the other the empiricists proposed that we derive our knowledge of the world through the senses and we learn to perceive spatial attributes by a process of association. These distinctions remain with us and have permeated psychological theories generally. Psychology has provided the study of perception with its basic experimental methodologies. It was the harnessing of psychophysical methods and the invention of a novel one for studying consciousness (analytic introspection) that led to the formation of psychology as an independent discipline. The psychophysical methods have stood the test of time (with constant improvements), but analytic introspection has fared less well: its demise saw the emergence of Gestalt and Behaviourist psychologies in the early part of the twentieth century, with the former showing more concern with perceptual matters than the latter.

Gestalt theory drew upon facts of magnetic and electrical fields in physics and speculated about similar field influences in the brain. That is, it considered that both perception and its underlying physiology were modelled on organising principles that could not be reduced to the operations of simplified elements. The Gestalt psychologists emphasised the holistic aspects of perception rather than the analytic: they did not believe that perception could be explained by reducing either stimuli or responses to their simplest levels. This contrast between holistic and analytic approaches to perception is one that remains in theories of perception. Ironically, the subsequent advances in the neurophysiology of vision have been based on precisely the reductionist ideas that the Gestalt psychologists rejected. The detailed study of the structure and function of nerve cells has suggested the ways in which complex patterns of light striking the retina are analysed in terms of simplified features that they contain. Thus, features like the retinal location, contour orientation, direction of motion and colour are extracted by single cells in the visual cortex of higher mammals. The presence of such feature detectors has been related to certain simple phenomena like visual after-effects. Not only can their occurrence be plausibly accounted for but details, such as interocular transfer, can also be encompassed within a feature detector model. However, the range of phenomena that has been successfully interpreted in neurophysiological terms remains limited. The more recent developments in modelling the behaviour of neural nets may provide a basis for returning to a more holistic approach to perception. Such networks have capacities for learning which are not localised in particular units, but which are a property of the net as a whole.

We know much more about the visual neurophysiology of cats and monkeys when presented with simple patterns than we do of humans. On the other hand, we have a great body of knowledge about human perception under similar simplified circumstances. In recent years this has been extended by the use of patterns of parallel lines called gratings. It seems as though such patterns are processed at early stages in vision, and there is evidence that spatial frequency is another stimulus dimension that is extracted by some single cortical cells. This has been a case of psychophysical experiments with human subjects leading to the neurophysiological search for a specific class of detectors in monkey visual cortex.

We still do not know how these feature detectors are involved in perception generally. This is largely because in almost all the neurophysiological experiments that are conducted with experimental animals the eye muscles are paralysed to avoid any eye movements during the presentation of stimuli. In our terms these studies are concerned with stimulus processing at the retinocentric level. That is, the representation of features like contour orientation, spatial frequency, direction of motion and colour is with respect to the retinal coordinate system alone. Such a representation is unlikely to be adequate for vision in an animal with moving eyes, because retinocentric displacements could be a consequence of object movement or eye movement.

Perception of objects in the world involves seeing where they are, when they occur and what they are. That is, we need to determine their location, whether they are moving, and to recognise them. These characteristics are defined relative to a frame of reference, so that statements about an object's motion, for example, are typically made with respect to the surface of the earth. Perception of object characteristics needs to conform to the frame of reference within which behaviour takes place, which will also normally be the surface of the earth. Such perceptions can be termed geocentric. An active perceiver, whether human or animal, must recover the geocentric properties of objects, despite self motion. We have described the frames of reference relative to which information can be represented, and from which geocentric information can be derived. The first, retinocentric level is the one that is studied by neurophysiologists: information is coded in terms of the coordinate system of the retina. Retinocentric information describes image characteristics with respect to retinal coordinates, but it is not necessarily localised in the retina. The fact that a response occurs in the visual cortex, or elsewhere, need not preclude it from being retinocentric in character. The term retinocentric expresses the nature of the information, and not its anatomical site.

This level is essential for vision but it cannot serve as a basis for object perception because we have two eyes and both of them move. The next frame of reference uses an integrated binocular signal from the two eyes together with their movements to provide an egocentric frame of reference, the origin of which lies between the eyes. We perceive the directions of objects with respect to the egocentre. Visual direction alone would not enable us to locate objects in space; in order to do this we also need to determine the distance objects are away from us. There are many sources of information for the relative distances between objects – which is nearer or further – but these need to be anchored by information for egocentric distance before objects can be adequately located in space. If information for the observer's own movements is incorporated, then objects will be represented in the geocentric frame of reference. When we have derived a geocentric representation of objects, we are in a position to behave appropriately with respect to them. The operation of these frames of reference can be more fully illustrated in the context of motion perception.

Perceiving whether, and to what extent, an object is moving depends on many factors. Consideration of retinal stimulation alone cannot account for geocentric visual perception. Many other sensory systems are involved in

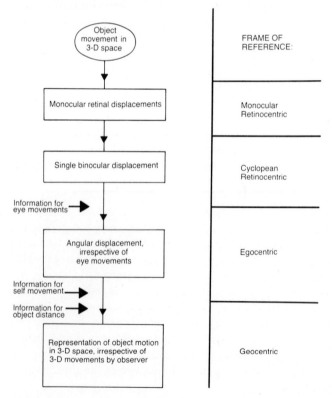

Figure 7.1 Levels of representation in motion perception, see text for details.

the recovery of the location and movement of objects in space. For example, information from the vestibular system is used to determine accelerations of the head in three dimensions, and this is essential if the pattern of retinal change arising from a head movement is to be interpreted unambiguously. The integration of these sensory systems constitutes visual perception, and it would be wrong to suppose that visual perception can be understood solely in terms of light reaching the eye. Figure 7.1 summarises the process of recovering geocentric movement. Initial registration of retinocentric motion in each eye gives rise to a single binocular (cyclopean) retinocentric signal. This expresses motion with respect to a point located between the eyes. Since the two eyes move by equal amounts when version occurs, a single signal for eye movement can be combined with the binocular retinocentric signal to give an egocentric representation. This carries information for changes in angular direction with respect to the observer, despite movements of the eyes. It will correctly express changes in object direction, but will only represent the position of objects in the environment if the observer is stationary. If the observer's head moves (either with or independently of the rest of the body), then the eyes necessarily move too. This causes displacement of the retinal image in a way which cannot be interpreted unless the extent of self motion and the distance of the object are known. Scaling the egocentric information by perceived distance gives the three-dimensional location of objects with respect to the observer. This can be corrected for the effects of self movement, since both are expressed in terms of three-dimensional displacements, to produce a geocentric representation of the movement of objects in the environment. Information for eye movement, self movement and distance may be derived from a number of sources, including visual ones. For example, when there are several objects at various distances, their relative displacement during self movement may provide information for their relative distance. At this level of analysis, the nature of the information required is defined, rather than its sources. The concern is with the rules and relationships that permit a geocentric representation of the external world by an observer who can move in the environment, and whose sense organs can move with respect to the body. A geocentric representation is required for effective action in the environment, since it conveys information which is independent of the observer's movements. A geocentric representation has the properties required for perceptual constancies, such as size, shape and location. It will not change despite changes in viewing distance or angle of regard. It will therefore provide a basis for object recognition, since objects are represented in a manner which is consistent even when the conditions of observation change. If a geocentric representation is stored in memory, it can be matched to the same object when encountered on a subsequent occasion, because it is independent of the observer and the circumstances of observation. There may of course be errors in the process of recovering a geocentric description. Eye movements, self movements or distance may not be accurately detected, and image displacements on the retina may be more or less than the signal to which they give rise. If so, then there will be misperceptions of shape, size or movement, and object recognition may fail. The model shown in Figure 7.1 is a description of the steps needed to achieve geocentric perception; in practice these may be carried out more or less successfully. In terms of Marr's levels of analysis described on pp. 5–6, Figure 7.1 describes the computational theory of geocentric perception. Questions about the performance of the visual system in relation to this model are concerned with the algorithms that actually carry out the computations, as are the details of how information for eye movements or distance is acquired.

Geocentric representations may be employed to carry out tasks that are expressed in terms of other coordinate systems. For example, someone may be asked to state the direction of an object with respect to their head, or some other part of their body. Alternatively, it may be necessary to judge the location of one object with respect to another. These tasks can be accomplished on the basis of geocentric information. Although the required frame of reference is no longer explicit, it can be recovered when needed if information about the articulation of the eyes, head and body is preserved. It is important to distinguish the frame of reference used to describe an activity, from that which determines an observer's spatial perception.

All perception is necessarily geocentric, but it may not seem so under restricted laboratory conditions. Stimuli may be exposed for intervals too short for the eyes to move during their presentation. If very briefly exposed stimuli are used, eye movements will not take place, and perception will correspond to the egocentric level. It might be thought that in this case perception would be retinocentric, but binocular combination is unavoidable, even when one eye is covered or non-functional. Egocentric directions and movements are always based upon binocular signals, at least in humans and other species with overlapping monocular visual fields. If the observer remains stationary, then the importance of perceived distance and perceived self motion in spatial vision will not be appreciated. A high proportion of studies of human spatial perception incorporate restrictions that eliminate one or more of these factors.

Although this discussion has been expressed in terms of the fundamental requirements for human perception, it is interesting to consider the similarities, and differences, that may apply to other species. Few animals have large overlapping binocular fields of view, and some have more than two eyes. In some crustaceans and insects, eyes are mounted on the end of flexible stalks which can move in three dimensions independently of the rest of the body. Despite these complications, it is still necessary to obtain a geocentric representation of the world. Even a cursory examination of animal behaviour shows that most actions require information about the location in space of salient objects like predators, prey, mates or offspring. Although we have considerable knowledge about the physiology of vision in many species, we know much less about the logic of the perceptual processes which they serve. One point at any rate is clear: geocentric perception is not necessarily based on knowledge of the world expressed in linguistic symbols. If this were so, only humans and perhaps the higher primates would be able to act effectively in the natural environment. Of course, a geocentric representation may be achieved in quite different ways by different species, just as a given arithmetical problem may have a number of equally valid routes to the correct answer. Nevertheless, the underlying requirements are the same; to obtain from the senses information which is capable of guiding the activities required for survival.

It is arguable that the widespread use of two-dimensional stimuli in perceptual experiments has led to a neglect of the geocentric frame of reference for spatial perception, and to the development of theories that are of little value in accounting for normal everyday perceptions. Object recognition has been examined almost exclusively with pictorial stimuli, too. Even many researchers who have adopted the theoretical views of Gibson use pictorial stimuli for their experiments, rather than three-dimensional objects. This trend has reached its nadir in studies of perceptual development: photographs, schematic drawings and in some cases jumbled faces (somewhat like those in Figure 6.11 with the elements randomly rearranged) have been presented to infants in order to determine whether they can recognise the objects which they represent. Studies employing two-dimensional stimuli can be useful in determining the limits of perception, like visual acuity, or colour discrimination, but they are not likely to further our understanding of object perception and its development. Pictures are obviously of great importance to us, because we acquire information about the world through them. Pictures can be still, as with photographs, paintings and writing, or in sequences to appear moving, as in film and television. We can even recognise gross distortions, like caricatures and cartoons. However, we need to learn how to achieve these remarkable feats of recognition. Recognising pictures is a process that will follow after object recognition not precede it.

The role of cognitive processes in perception has been exceptionally difficult to establish. To an extent, this has become a matter of theoretical dispute. Those who have followed Gibson's approach have regarded perception as wholly independent of cognition, and determined entirely by a direct response to patterns of stimulation without any intervening process. By contrast, others have claimed that perception is akin to high-level cognitive processes like problem-solving and hypothesis formation. What we see would then be determined at least as much by what we know as by what is there to be seen. It is in the context of arbitrary stimuli, like pictures and written script, that the cognitive approaches to perception are at their strongest. We learn to attach significance to certain shapes that formerly were of no importance to us. However such learning processes are not confined to humans. Pigeons can discriminate between letters of the alphabet, and many artificial seeing machines can carry out industrial inspection tasks. Our metaphorical guide dog is also able to learn the significance of initially arbitrary objects and act on them, like stopping in front of overhanging barriers that it, but not a human, could walk under.

The goal of this book has been to concentrate on the functions which a perceptual system must perform, and to show how the understanding of these has developed in the modern era. It is very clear that many of the theoretical issues defined in the eighteenth and nineteenth centuries are still not resolved, and they persist despite great advances in techniques for manipulating visual stimulation. Nevertheless, vision is an endlessly fascinating object of study, drawing as it does on such diverse disciplines for insight and advance. Even if the final goal is not in sight, the journey is worth the effort.

Bibliography

Addams, R. (1834) 'An account of a peculiar optical phenomenon seen after having looked at a moving body', *London and Edinburgh Philosophical Magazine and Journal of Science*, 5, 373–374.

Aubert, H. (1865) *Physiologie der Netzhaut*, Breslau: Morgenstern.

Barlow, H.B. and Mollon, J.D. (eds) (1982) *The Senses*, Cambridge: Cambridge University Press.

Berkeley, G. (1709) *An Essay towards a New Theory of Vision*, Dublin: Pepyat.

Blakemore, C. (1973) 'The baffled brain', in R. L. Gregory and E. H. Gombrich (eds) *Illusion in Nature and Art*, London: Duckworth.

Bloom, F.E. and Lazerson, A. (1988) *Brain, Mind, and Behavior*, 2nd edn, New York: Freeman.

Boring, E.G. (1942) *Sensation and Perception in the History of Experimental Psychology*, New York: Appleton-Century-Crofts.

Bruce, V. and Green, P.R. (1990) *Visual Perception. Physiology, Psychology and Ecology*, 2nd edn, London: Erlbaum.

Brunswik, E. (1956) *Perception and the Representative Design of Psychological Experiments*, Berkeley: University of California Press.

Burton, H.E. (1945) 'The optics of Euclid', *Journal of the Optical Society of America*, 35, 357–372.

Cornsweet, T.N. (1970) *Visual Perception*, New York: Academic Press.

Crombie, A.C. (1972) 'Early concepts of the senses and the mind', in R. Held and W. Richards (eds) *Perception: Mechanisms and Models*, San Francisco: Freeman.

Cutting, J.E. (1986) *Perception with an Eye for Motion*, Cambridge, Mass. : MIT Press.

Darwin, C. (1859) *On the Origin of Species by Natural Selection*, London: Murray.

Darwin, C. (1872) *The Expression of the Emotions in Man and Animals*, London: Murray.

Dember, W.N. (1964) *Visual Perception; The Nineteenth Century*, New York: Wiley.

Descartes, R. (1637/1902) *La Dioptrique*, in C. Adam and P. Tannery (eds) *Oeuvres de Descartes*, volume VI, Paris: Cerf.

Descartes, R. (1664/1909) *Traité de l'Homme*, in C. Adam and P. Tannery (eds) *Oeuvres de Descartes*, volume XI, Paris: Cerf.

Descartes, R. (1965) *Discourse on Method, Optics, Geometry, and Meteorology*, trans. P. J. Olscamp, New York: Bobbs-Merrill.

Descartes, R. (1972) *Treatise of Man*, trans. T. S. Hall, Cambridge, Mass. : Harvard University Press.

Edgerton, S.Y. (1975) *The Renaissance Rediscovery of Linear Perspective*, New York: Basic Books.

Ellis, W.D. (ed.) (1938) *A Source Book of Gestalt Psychology*, London: Routledge & Kegan Paul.

Epstein, W. (ed.) (1977) *Stability and Constancy in Visual Perception: Mechanisms and Processes*, New York: Wiley.

Fancher, R.E. (1990) *Pioneers of Psychology*, 2nd edn, New York: Norton.

Favreau, O.E. (1977) 'Psychology in action: disillusioned', *American Psychologist*, 32, 568–571.

Frisby, J.P. (1979) *Seeing. Illusion, Brain and Mind*, London: Oxford University Press.

Gardner, H. (1987) *The Mind's New Science. A History of the Cognitive Revolution*, New York: Basic Books.

Gibson, J.J. (1950) *Perception of the Visual World*, Boston: Houghton Mifflin.

Gibson, J.J. (1966) *The Senses Considered as Perceptual Systems*, Boston: Houghton Mifflin.

Gibson, J.J. (1979) *The Ecological Approach to Visual Perception*, Boston: Houghton Mifflin.

Gogel, W.C. (1982) 'Analysis of the perception of motion concomitant with lateral motion of the head', *Perception and Psychophysics*, 32, 241–250.

Gogel, W.C. and DaSilva, J. (1987) 'A two-process theory of the response to size and distance', *Perception and Psychophysics*, 41, 220–238.

Goldstein, E.B. (1989) *Sensation and Perception*, 3rd edn, Belmont, California: Wadsworth.

Gordon, I. (1989) *Theories of Visual Perception*, London: Wiley.

Gregory, R.L. (1977) *Eye and Brain*, 3rd edn, London: Weidenfeld and Nicolson.

Haber, R.N. and Hershenson M. (1980) *The Psychology of Visual Perception*, New York: Holt, Reinhardt & Winston.

Harris, J. (1775) *A Treatise of Optics: Containing Elements of the Science: In Two Books*, London: White.

Hearnshaw, L. (1987) *The Shaping of Modern Psychology*, London: Routledge.

Held, R. and Richards, W. (eds) (1972) *Perception: Mechanisms and Models*, San Francisco: Freeman.

Held, R. and Richards, W. (eds) (1976) *Recent Progress in Perception*, San Francisco: Freeman.

Helmholtz, H. von (1924/1925) *Treatise on Physiological Optics*, Volumes I-III trans. J.P.C. Southall, Menasha, Wis. : Optical Society of America.

Hering, E. (1868/1942) *Spatial Sense and Movement of the Eye*, trans. A. Radde, Baltimore: American Academy of Science.

Herrnstein, R.J. and Boring, E.G. (1965) *A Source Book in the History of Psychology*, Cambridge, Mass. : Harvard University Press.

Hershenson, M. (ed.) (1989) *The Moon Illusion*, New Jersey: Erlbaum.

Howard, I.P. (1982) *Human Visual Orientation*, London: Wiley.

Howard, I.P. and Templeton, W.B. (1966) *Human Spatial Orientation*, London: Wiley.

Hubel, D.H. (1979) *The Brain. A Scientific American Book*, San Francisco: Freeman.

Hubel, D.H. and Wiesel, T.N. (1979) 'Brain mechanisms of vision', in D.H. Hubel (ed.) *The Brain. A Scientific American Book*, San Francisco: Freeman.

Ittelson, W.H. (1968) *The Ames Demonstrations in Perception*, New York: Hafner.

Kandel, E.R. and Schwartz, J.H. (1985) *Principles of Neural Science*, 2nd edn, New York: Elsevier. .

Kaufman, L. (1974) *Sight and Mind*, Oxford: Oxford University Press.

Kemp, M. (1990) *The Science of Art*, Hartford, Conn. : Yale University Press.

Kirby, J. (1755) *Dr. Brook Taylor's Method of Perspective Made Easy, Both in Theory and Practice. In Two Books*, 2nd edn, Ipswich: published by the author.

Köhler, W. and Wallach, H. (1944) 'Figural after-effects: an investigation of visual processes', *Proceedings of the American Philosophical Society*, 88, 269–357.

Leonardo da Vinci (1721) *A Treatise of Painting*, trans. from Italian, London: Senex and Taylor.

Livingstone, M.S. (1988) 'Art, illusion and the visual system', *Scientific American*, 258 (1), 68–75.

Locke, J. (1690/1975) *An Essay Concerning Human Understanding*, Oxford: Clarendon.

Lopez, B. (1986) *Arctic Dreams*, London: Macmillan.

Marr, D. (1982) *Vision*, San Francisco: Freeman.

Michaels, C.F. and Carello, C. (1981) *Direct Perception*, Englewood Cliffs, N.J. : Prentice-Hall.

Miller, G.A. (1962) *Psychology. The Science of Mental Life*, London: Penguin.

Morgan, M.J. (1977) *Molyneux's Question. Vision, Touch and the Philosophy of Perception*, Cambridge: Cambridge University Press.

Müller, J. (1839/1842) *Elements of Physiology*, Volumes I and II, trans. W. Baly, London: Taylor and Walton.

Neisser, U. (1967) *Cognitive Psychology*, New York: Appleton-Century-Crofts.

Newton, I. (1704) *Opticks: or, a Treatise of the Reflections, Refractions, Inflections and Colours of Light*, London: Innys.

Ono, H. (1981) 'On Wells's (1792) law of visual direction', *Perception and Psychophysics*, 32, 201–210.

Ono, H. (1990) 'Binocular visual directions of an object when seen as single or double', in D. Regan (ed.) *Vision and Visual Dysfunction, Volume 9: Binocular Vision*, New York: Macmillan.

Petersik, J.T. (1989) 'The two-process distinction in apparent motion', *Psychological Bulletin*, 106, 107–127.

Pirenne, M.H. (1967) *Vision and the Eye*, London: Chapman and Hall.

Pirenne, M.H. (1970) *Optics, Painting and Photography*, Cambridge: Cambridge University Press.

Reed, E. and Jones, R. (eds) (1982) *Reasons for Realism. Selected Essays of James J. Gibson*, Hillsdale, N.J. : Erlbaum.

Regan, D. (ed.) (1990) *Vision and Visual Dysfunction, Volume 9: Binocular Vision*, New York: Macmillan.

Reid, T. (1764) *An Inquiry into the Human Mind. On the principles of common sense*, Edinburgh: Millar Kinnaird & Bell.

Reinhardt-Rutland, A.H. (1988) 'Induced movement in the visual modality: an overview', *Psychological Bulletin*, 103, 57–71.

Rock, I. (1984) *Perception*, San Francisco: Freeman.

Roth, I. and Frisby, J.P. (1986) *Perception and Representation: A Cognitive Approach*, Milton Keynes: Open University Press.

Rubin, E. (1915) *Synsoplevede Figurer*, Copenhagen: Gyldendalske.

Schnapf, J.L. and Baylor, D.A. (1987) 'How photoreceptor cells respond to light', *Scientific American*, 256 (4), 32–39.

Sekuler, R., and Blake, R. (1990) *Perception*, New York: McGraw-Hill.

Spillmann, L.S. and Werner, J.S. (eds) (1990) *Visual Perception. The Neurophysiological Foundations*, London: Academic Press.

Spillmann, L.S. and Wooten, B.R. (eds) (1984) *Sensory Experience, Adaptation, and Perception. Festschrift for Ivo Kohler*, London: Erlbaum.

Swanston, M.T. and Wade, N.J. (1988) 'The perception of visual motion during movements of the eyes and of the head', *Perception and Psychophysics*, 43, 559–566.

Swanston, M.T., Wade, N.J. and Day, R.H. (1987) 'The representation of uniform motion in vision', *Perception*, 16, 143–159.

Swanston, M.T., Wade, N.J. and Ono, H. (1990) 'The binocular representation of uniform motion', *Perception*, 19, 29–34.

Triesman, A. (1988) 'Features and objects: The fourteenth Bartlett Memorial Lecture', *Quarterly Journal of Experimental Psychology*, 40A, 201–237.

Wade, N. (1982) *The Art and Science of Visual Illusions*, London: Routledge & Kegan Paul.

Wade, N.J. (1983) *Brewster and Wheatstone on Vision*, London: Academic Press.

Wade, N.J. (1987) 'On the late invention of the stereoscope', *Perception*, 16, 785–818.

Wade, N. (1990) *Visual Allusions: Pictures of Perception*, London: Erlbaum.

Wade, N.J. and Swanston, M.T. (1987) 'The representation of non-uniform motion: induced movement', *Perception*, 16, 555–571.

Watson, R.I. (1968) *The Great Psychologists. From Aristotle to Freud*, 2nd edn, Philadelphia: J. B. Lippincott.

Watson, R.I. (1979) *Basic Writings in the History of Psychology*, New York: Oxford University Press.

Werblin, F.S. (1976) 'The control of sensitivity in the retina', in R. Held and W. Richards (eds) *Recent Progress in Perception*, San Francisco: Freeman.

Author index

Subject index

abducens nucleus 88
aberrations of the eye 40, 49–51
absolute distance 110
accommodation 22, 45–52, 94, 109, 123;
    ageing and 48; and convergence
    106; as cue to distance 112; far point
    45, 47; mechanism of 45; near point
    46, 48
action potential 60, 74
acuity 52–5, 87, 94, 101, 106, 197;
    grating 54–5; patterns for
    measuring 54; vernier 54
adequate stimulus 74
aerial perspective 126
afferent feedback 155
after-effects 28, 36–7, 94, 161;
    dissipation 92, 138; motion 28, 91,
    124, 138–40, 145–7, 149, 163; tilt 90,
    138, 149
after-image 28, 90, 150–1, 153, 155, 169;
    coloured 153; fragmentation 153–4
algorithms 6, 196
allusion to depth 19–20, 187–8, 190
alphanumeric symbols 175–6
amacrine cell 62, 69, 71, 74
ambient illumination 172
ambiguity 5, 34, 149, 167, 172, 175,
    187–8; motion 129
amblyopia 51–2
Ames room 169–70, 190
anaglyphs 121
analytic approach to perception 173–6,
    192
analytic introspection 31–3, 192
angular accelerations 161
animal perception 1, 10, 192, 196–8
aniseikonia 48
apparent distance 111

apparent motion 140, 146–7, 163;
    long-range 147–8; short-range 147–8
apparent self movement 159–61
apparent size 12, 20–1, 167–8; of
    after-image 169
aqueous humour 44
art 16, 19–21, 185, 190–1
artificial intelligence 14
associationism 29, 32, 192
astigmatism 49–50
Aubert-Fleischl effect 156–7
auditory cortex 26
autokinetic phenomenon 138
automata 7

balance 2
Bartlett's schema 38
bearing 134, 179–80
Behaviourism 32–3, 192
binocular cells 85, 91
binocular combination 194–5; site of
    148–9
binocular disparity 85–6, 93, 118–25,
    127–8, 174
binocular eye movement signals 103,
    110
binocular fusion 116, 121
binocular interaction 91, 149
binocular overlap 71
binocular pathways 23–4
binocular rivalry 103, 106, 109
binocular single vision 91, 93, 103,
    106–10, 119, 123
binocular vision 23–4, 48, 53, 91, 101,
    106–10, 116, 121, 123–5, 194–5
biological computation 6–7
biological motion 130, 135–6, 162
bioluminescence 41